REMAKING COLLEGE

REMAKING COLLEGE

∎ THE CHANGING ECOLOGY

OF HIGHER EDUCATION ∎

EDITED BY
MICHAEL W. KIRST AND
MITCHELL L. STEVENS

Yours Mitchell

STANFORD UNIVERSITY PRESS ∎ STANFORD, CALIFORNIA

Stanford University Press
Stanford, California

©2015 by the Board of Trustees of the Leland Stanford Junior University. All rights reserved.

Printed in the United States of America on acid-free, archival-quality paper

Library of Congress Cataloging-in-Publication Data

Remaking college : the changing ecology of higher education / edited by Michael W. Kirst and Mitchell L. Stevens.
     pages cm
  Includes bibliographical references and index.
  ISBN 978-0-8047-9167-0 (cloth : alk. paper) — ISBN 978-0-8047-9329-2 (pbk. : alk. paper)
 1. Education, Higher—United States.   2. Universities and colleges—United States.   I. Kirst, Michael W., editor of compilation.   II. Stevens, Mitchell L., editor of compilation.
  LA226.R475 2015
  378.73—dc23

                                                                          2014010119

ISBN 978-0-8047-9355-1 (electronic)

Typeset by Newgen in 10/14 Minion

CONTENTS

TABLES AND FIGURES

Tables

Figures

ACKNOWLEDGMENTS

Many people and organizations contributed to the work assembled here. First, thanks go to Hilary Pennington, Ann Person, and Daniela Pineda, our program officers at the Bill & Melinda Gates Foundation, who saw promise in our nascent thinking and found ways to fund this project flexibly. Colleagues throughout Stanford's Graduate School of Education and the Center for Education Policy Analysis devised canny solutions to myriad puzzles of administration. Gratitude goes to Lauren Ellison, Hiep Ho, Irene Lam, Michelle Lin, Phoenix Liu, Justin Nguyen, and Jennifer Yu in this regard. The Scandinavian Consortium for Organizational Research supplied bottomless coffee cups and a comfortable table for the scores of discussions that composed our teamwork at Stanford. In an exceptional act of scholarly hospitality, the Steinhardt Institute for Higher Education Policy at New York University hosted a working session for all of the authors in November 2012. For this we owe a debt to Ann Marcus and to Tu-Lien Nguyen, who expertly followed through on details.

Scholars and practitioners from throughout the United States participated in a series of convenings in Palo Alto, California, and at a special session at the meeting of the American Educational Research Association in San Francisco in 2013, in which earlier versions of these essays were developed. Elizabeth Armstrong, Tom Bailey, Eric Bettinger, Amy Binder, Pat Callan, Teri Cannon, Kevin Dougherty, Sue Dynarski, Joni Finney, Bernardine Fong, Sara Goldrick-Rab, Laura Hamilton, Kevin Henson, Caroline Hoxby, David Labaree, Bridget Terry Long, Ann Marcus, Laura Perna, Jim Rosenbaum, Doug Shapiro, Nancy Shulock, Fran Stage, Scott Thomas, Sarah Turner, Jane Wellman, and Ralph Wolff provided insight at critical stages of development. Our Stanford colleague, Tom Ehrlich, joined the project in its early days and has lent good wisdom ever since. Liza Dayton came on as a postdoctoral fellow in 2012 and quickly had us wondering how we had ever managed before.

At Stanford University Press, Kate Wahl encouraged the project very early in its gestation and later introduced us to editor Frances Malcolm, who brought the book to full maturity with meticulousness, intelligence, and good humor. She also secured two anonymous reviewers for the manuscript whose insightful comments helped us focus and improve the book as a whole.

We reserve special thanks for Linda Thor, who reminded us of how easily academic researchers can float naïvely above the real world and who patiently did the favor of tethering us back down.

REMAKING COLLEGE

INTRODUCTION

The Changing Ecology of U.S. Higher Education

Mitchell L. Stevens

Between 1945 and 1990 the United States built the largest and most productive higher education system in world history. The scale of this accomplishment has only recently been fully appreciated. There were few problems for which higher education was not deployed in remedy during the decades immediately following World War II. Investments in science would ensure the technological supremacy of the United States and enable it to improve the lives of people worldwide. New college and university campuses would make parochial places more cosmopolitan. Expanded access to college educations would facilitate individual mobility and help remediate injustices of socioeconomic inequality. Such ambitions were pursued through a complicated compact between businesspeople, politicians, and academic leaders who viewed higher education expansion as reciprocally beneficial to their interests (Brint & Karabel, 1989; Kerr, 2001; Loss, 2012; Lowen, 1997). The enterprise was resourced by the longest-lasting and most broadly distributed economic prosperity in American history.

There can be little doubt that this golden era is over. Steadily eroding state government support for higher education has made college completion harder to attain, as public systems cut budgets for academic and student-support services ever closer to bone. Tuition and fees have long been rising faster than the rate of inflation with virtually no regulatory constraint, while greater proportions of college costs are borne by students and their families in the form of government-subsidized loans. The accountability revolution that transformed K–12 schools has come to higher education, bringing new expectations for colleges and universities to demonstrate efficiency and productivity—however these terms may be defined. At the same time a host of new businesses offering an array of educational services has emerged offering new alternatives to academic business as usual.

As with any epochal transition, it is tempting to feel a sense of loss about the fading past. Yet this transition has many positive features as well: agreement that attending college has become too expensive, canny entrepreneurial activity in the higher education sector, and productive ferment in national discussions about how college might be more effectively and humanely delivered.

This is the spirit in which the work assembled here was written. Supported with funding from the Bill & Melinda Gates Foundation, Mike Kirst and I convened a series of national discussions on the fate and future of U.S. higher education at this moment in history. Our focus was on *broad-access schools*: the community colleges, comprehensive public universities, and for-profit institutions that offer admission to most of those who seek to enroll in them. Our goals were straightforward: (1) assemble some of the most provocative writers on higher education irrespective of field and put them into conversation; (2) focus their collective attention on broad-access schools, rather than the academically selective ones that receive the lion's share of academic and media attention; and (3) give writers as much freedom as possible to reimagine how the study of college might be pursued in light of the seismic changes taking place in U.S. higher education. The result is a collection rich with new tools for helping people make more informed and humane decisions about college—for themselves, for their children, and for American society as a whole.

Just as there is little doubt that a golden era has passed, there is little uncertainty that Americans' desire for more higher education will only grow in the coming years. Our country already has invested so much in the promise of higher education that it could hardly be otherwise. Ever more intense and global competition for highly educated workers means that demand for college-level academic services will only grow in the future (Goldin & Katz, 2008). Yet whether those services will come bundled in a package called the *traditional college experience*—on physical campuses, with dormitories, full-time enrollment requirements, and spectator sports—is an open question.

Forward discussions about the future of U.S. higher education will be constrained if we continue to use terms, priorities, and conceptual models developed by education researchers in the twentieth century. First, inherited academic and policy wisdom assumes a proper and relatively bounded stage of the life course for college: a period just after high school but before career initiation, childbearing, and cohabitation. It imagines a student who enrolls in college full time, ideally resides on a physical campus, remains unmarried and childless while in school, engages in minimal paid work, and completes a degree within four to six years. But in contemporary America, students fitting this description are a shrinking minority of the overall college-going population. Academic research and policy discourse organized on the presumption of such students misrepresents reality.

Second, most inherited academic and policy research is organized as analyses of students *moving through* school. This movement usually is described by linear regression models applied to aggregated individual-level data. Most of what is known about attendance, persistence, completion, and returns to college is a product of this mode of inquiry. Yet this way of doing research systematically obscures schools themselves as units of analysis. When they do appear, schools are independent (not dependent) variables, assemblages of easily measurable characteristics (not complex wholes), and presumed to be vehicles for students' pursuit of their own interests (not actors with interests of their own). While invaluable for twentieth-century education science and policy, such models by themselves are incapable of capturing the organizational fertility, variety, and turbulence of the current historical moment.

Third, educational social science tends to privilege four-year residential education at research universities and liberal arts colleges as the ideal expressions of higher education. This was problematic in the twentieth century— albeit optimistic, as these forms long have held special prestige in the national academic status system. It is simply untenable now. Community colleges are the workhorses of U.S. higher education, serving most of those who attend college and coalescing the academic activity of countless towns and regions. For-profit schools, long important for human-capital development in many skilled trades, now provide the gamut of educational services. They are the fastest-growing component of the national postsecondary sector and are fed by a remarkably large proportion of federal tuition aid.

Fourth, educational social science has long presumed that college requires physical copresence. Researchers have taken for granted that the activities that constitute college necessarily occur on physical campuses through face-to-face interaction among students and instructors. In light of the recent explosion of online instructional opportunities available to learners world-wide, this presumption can no longer be sustained.

The writers in this collection offer new ways of understanding higher education unconstrained by these limitations. In the next few pages I provide an overview of the intellectual tools many of us have found especially useful for remaking the study of college.

The Ecology Idea

When the authors in this volume describe a higher education ecology, they refer to a specific way of thinking about how organizations work in relation to one another and to their social context. An ecological approach can free analysts of the conceptual limitations imposed by traditional students, linear models of individual academic progression, narrow idealizations of form, and the presumption that college happens through copresence.

For over fifty years the primary analytic strategy that social scientists have used to appraise, understand, and measure higher education has been to model students moving through schools in cohorts. The paradigmatic expressions of this approach are statistical analyses of large aggregations of individual-level data. In narrative form most of them go something like this: those finishing high school are functional adults who make decisions (whether conscious or unconscious, well informed or not) about whether, when, and where to pursue college educations. As these functional adults move through college, they accumulate different amounts and kinds of academic credits. They variably persist at a particular college, transfer or "swirl" between multiple schools, or drop out altogether. Persistence at a single college whose academic profile appropriately matches the academic aptitude of the student is the default ideal. The entire process is presumed to have a proper timetable. College attendance directly after high school, undiluted by paid work, and completed within some specified time window is widely understood to be the optimal way through college.

This way of narrating and modeling higher education fit tidily with an enduring interest across the social sciences in mobility processes in industrial societies and was reinforced by the mathematical apparatus of linear regression analysis. It has been methodologically convenient to model U.S. higher education as the sum of individual students making individual choices about where, when, and under what statistically described conditions they attend college. This analytic strategy continues to define normal social science approaches to the study of postsecondary education and remains intellectually profitable. Indeed much of the work assembled here is predicated on the huge stock of findings generated by this way of making knowledge. Yet by themselves, linear models of students moving through college profoundly limit our ability to think about colleges themselves as active players in the production of education. Economists describe the problem succinctly: social scientists focus primarily on the demand side and are weak on the supply side of higher education.

Attending more carefully to the supply side is important because of varied changes that together make for the end of an epoch. Table I.1 provides a schematic depiction of these changes: chronic declines in state funding for public colleges and universities; unabated tuition price escalation and an ongoing shift of college costs from governments to students and their families; an accountability revolution obliging schools to measure learning and other kinds of productivity as never before; rapid growth of for-profit education businesses; the expansion and normalization of digitally mediated instruction; and an overall shift in the cultural meaning of higher education, from a collective project of nation-building to an individual project of income growth and career enhancement.

TABLE I.1   Recent epochs of U.S. higher education

	Cold War (1945–1990)	Contemporary (1990–present)
Funding	Massive state and federal investment supplemented by individual/household investment	Diminished state and federal investment supplementing growing individual/household investment
Governance	Highly legitimate peer accreditation based on symbolic review	Peer accreditation facing legitimacy challenge; calls for certification based on precise measurement
Student learning	Rarely measured directly	Increasingly measured directly
Business model	Public and private nonprofits; small for-profit sector	Public and private nonprofits; growing for-profit sector
Mode of delivery	Copresence presumed; minimal options for distance learning	Declining presumption of copresence; rapid proliferation of digitally mediated delivery
Dominant logic	Education for strong and prosperous nation; reward for national service/citizenship	Education for job security and earnings over life course

The ecology idea provides a strong tool for comprehending these changes. We borrow it directly from a vital stream of organizational social science (Aldrich, 1979; Baum & Shipilov, 2006; Hannan & Freeman, 1989). An ecological approach asks analysts to conceive of higher education as comprising myriad service providers, instructional and administrative labor, funders, and regulators interacting in a messy system of educational production. These entities simultaneously cooperate and compete for scarce resources. Resources include students (of varying academic preparation and ability to pay), academic labor, tuition, government and philanthropic financial support, visibility, evaluative authority, legitimacy, and prestige. Ecological approaches ask us to consider how components of the ecology are interdependent. Schools do compete. Higher education is indeed a market. But schools also cooperate: through accreditation and credit transfer systems, tuition exchange agreements, and athletic league affiliations, for example. They routinely exchange ideas, information, and personnel and enter alliances to protect privileged niches.

On this view, student trajectories into and through college are necessary but not sufficient means for understanding how higher education works. We need also to know how schools seek to survive and flourish in a competitive and changing market, how faculty and administrators pursue careers, how accrediting agencies and government education agencies try to maintain their legitimacy, and how philanthropies seek influence and entrepreneurs seek market share.

A big advantage of the ecology idea is that it enables a comprehensive view of the entire higher education sector and so can accommodate the possibility of systemic change. As the resource flows feeding the ecology shift—for example, by the chronic contraction of state-level funding for public colleges—we can expect repercussions throughout the entire ecology. Parties with unmet needs, such as students unable to find seats in desired courses at their local community colleges, may seek comparable services from other kinds of educational providers. New categories of players, such as for-profit academic service purveyors and the venture capital firms funding them, may see opportunity in the dynamic and act entrepreneurially to exploit it. The ecology idea also enables us to see tendencies toward inertia. For members of the organizational population that have flourished under a fading resource arrangement, for example, change may be resisted—especially when change advocates are "outsiders" attempting to direct resource flows in new directions.

As W. Richard Scott explains in Chapter 1, in organizational ecologies change is rarely merely instrumental and its course is never preordained. This is true for several reasons. First, ecologies are culturally thick. They are infused with multiple and sometimes contradictory meanings that matter to those who hold them. Any change will be mediated by the cultural commitments and blind spots of powerful players. Second, individuals and organizations are constantly strategizing for their own relative advantage. Change does not just happen to them. Individuals and organizations can opt to work with or against larger change processes, and with or against one another, to further their own particular interests. In the process they shape the course of history in ways that are hard to map in advance. Third, the higher education ecology is extraordinarily complex, with many different kinds of players and resource streams. As in any complex system, apparently small or isolated changes can sometimes have large consequences.

Disruptive Innovation

Colleges and universities with essentially open admissions enroll most U.S. students, yet until very recently they received a small proportion of the scholarly attention given to higher education. Academic researchers, policy makers, journalists, and the general public are often seduced by the glamour of academically selective schools—the handful of elite institutions to which admission is a coveted prize. This attention bias in favor of elites is a generic feature of collective life. But as Harvard Business School professor Clayton Christensen and his colleagues have now famously explained, it systematically diverts attention from where the most fateful innovation takes place.

In a wide variety of industries, from automobile and steel manufacturing to consumer electronics, the pattern of disruptive innovation is similar. While a given moment's blue-chip firms serve the most coveted clients, canny upstarts outside the limelight of the elite market are figuring out how to profit from the clients that blue-chip providers ignore. Clients who cannot afford today's top products are opportunities for suppliers flexible enough to devise different ways of getting a job done. Unconstrained by the costly performance standards that define tasks in the elite market, upstarts experiment with alternate versions of the product and seek new niches among clients with lesser demands. In the process they lay the groundwork for becoming the next generation's leaders (Christensen & Eyring, 2011).

We concur with Christensen and his colleagues that this is precisely what is happening in U.S. higher education. By the end of the twentieth century, four-year residential higher education had become a mature industry. The bachelor's degree, ideally obtained on the residential campus of a public or private nonprofit school with selective admissions, had become the "real" college education. Schools providing these diplomas were the most prestigious players in the ecology. In Washington, at state capitols, and on accreditation boards, leaders of these schools spoke confidently on behalf of the whole of U.S. higher education. Faculty with tenure-line appointments at these schools enjoyed higher prestige than their colleagues at community colleges and for-profit schools—if indeed these others were regarded as colleagues at all. Higher education social science abetted this prestige hierarchy by consistently emphasizing the greater net returns to timely completion of four-year bachelor's degrees.

Yet by the beginning of the twenty-first century, a great deal of creative activity was taking place in the larger academic world beyond the blue-chip colleges and universities. The diffusion of Internet access, coupled with rapid developments in computer technology and digital media, encouraged an explosion of new online curriculum products and academic services. A long tradition of correspondence schooling developed into a profusion of online college offerings. In Chapter 2, Anya Kamenetz explains how digital media have made possible the development of an extraordinarily diverse array of vehicles for learning. She also points out how venture capital has discovered the great potential of an ever more digital higher education. Washington, D.C., and Silicon Valley calendars are now dotted with annual higher education "summit" meetings where edtech people and money people meet and mingle. The Obama administration's Department of Education now officially speaks in the vernacular innovation.

Having long been a lively but small portion of the higher education ecology, for-profit providers have mushroomed in number and variety in recent years. They offer new versions of college that fit more comfortably into people's lives: delivering courses online, in geographically convenient physical locations, and at a wide variety of hours and start dates. Their occasionally stunning profitability, usually fed by government-subsidized grants and loans, has generated suspicion among the academic establishment in the public and private/nonprofit parts of the ecology. But as Paul Fain and Doug Lederman explain in Chapter 3, for-profits survive and flourish precisely because they do not play by the rules of the establishment schools. Instead they meet students where they are in their lives and fit services into those lives, all the while doing the ideological work of convincing regulators and the general public that these new educational services are legitimate, "real" college experiences.

With its built-in presumption about college as a physically copresent activity and its normative preoccupation with full-time college enrollment in the years after high school, much higher education social science is poorly fitted to comprehend these phenomena. Yet some forward-thinking scholars had been doing some disruption of their own in recent years by lending sustained attention to adult learners and to community colleges, comprehensive universities, and for-profit schools. The work of scholars such as Paul Attewell, Thomas Bailey, Steven Brint, Patrick Callan, Kevin Dougherty, Jeremy Karabel, David Lavin, and Nancy Shulock provide a solid foundation for a more comprehensive higher education social science. Much of the thinking represented in this book is indebted to that pioneering work.

Nevertheless, describing the whole of U.S. higher education is a formidable intellectual and methodological challenge. Sociologists Martin Ruef and Manish Nag make a large contribution here in Chapter 4, providing a novel means for describing the organizational variety of U.S. higher education quantitatively. They call for an analytic alternative to the Carnegie Classification, a taxonomy developed during the Cold War era of massification and still widely in use despite radically changed ecological conditions. Ruef and Nag draw from recent developments in organizational theory to develop a technique for modeling organizational variety in a manner that accommodates plural, fuzzy, and dynamic organizational characteristics of the ecology. Using the familiar Integrated Postsecondary Education Data System (IPEDS) to brilliantly novel effect, they demonstrate how schools can be empirically described in many different ways simultaneously: as collections of official identities, or of functions, or as serving particular demographic groups. We believe their approach is a major advance for scholarship in higher education.

College and the Life Course

Higher education has been the primary vehicle for upward mobility in American society for several generations. Guided by social scientists and ambitious philanthropies, the U.S. state and federal governments funded an array of programs that made college attendance an attainable dream for millions of

Americans in the decades following World War II. This historically unprecedented expansion changed the character of U.S. higher education and the composition of the college-going population. The experience of college became much more diverse. Some students lived on residential campuses while others commuted to college, often attending school part time while working and raising families. Some students enrolled in college directly after high school, while others entered or reentered college after years of parenting or paid employment. Yet despite this great variety, the notions of traditional-age students on traditional campuses have retained powerful ideological force.

Traditional is not an empirical description but a normative standard against which other kinds of students and colleges are easily viewed as lesser approximations. Higher education researchers' use of this term has not been ill intended. Enabling one's children to attend college full time, right after high school, has long been a mark of adult prosperity, and the lifelong benefits that accrue to young people who complete four-year college degrees early in life are indisputable. Calling this version of college "traditional" has often gone hand in hand with advocating for its provision to as many Americans as possible. Yet however well intended, the dream of providing four full-time years on residential college campuses to every young person is not a realizable one at present, if ever it was.

It may not even be a good idea. Thoughtful observers are becoming newly suspicious of the purported benefits of full-time residential colleges for all young people. They point to the pervasive party culture on college campuses, huge investments in intercollegiate sports, modest or nonexistent yearly learning gains, majors catering to teenage tastes rather than labor market realities, high and rising rates of school leaving, and sometimes crushing debt from student loans (Armstrong & Hamilton, 2013; Arum & Roksa, 2011; Seaman, 2005; Selingo, 2013). The chronic fiscal crises in public higher education provide additional and probably inarguable incentive for a redefinition of the ideal college experience.

Sociologists Richard Settersten and Regina Deil-Amen provide succinct rationales for such a redefinition in Chapters 5 and 6. For young people coming of age in relatively affluent middle- and upper-middle-class families, college has become a pivotal rite of passage. It marks a special period of increasing independence from parents and an incremental transition to adulthood. While this model of college may remain in place for the most privileged young people, it will not define the experience of the demographic majority of young adults who experience the transition to adulthood more variably. For them other rites of passage come before, alongside, or instead of college: household formation, marriage, parenthood, first job. There is a profound disconnect between what continues to be called an ideal college experience and the more complicated ways in which most people experience college and early adulthood.

Echoing the basic tenets of the "traditional" college ideal, education researchers have long argued that a variety of paths through college is risky for students. For evidence they point to the inverse relationship between school transitions and college completion. In general, the more frequent the moves into, out of, and across colleges, the less likely students are to finish their degrees. While this empirical association is certainly robust, citing it as evidence to condemn deviance from a full-time pathway discounts how most people attempt to integrate college into complicated lives. This is the problem that an increasingly confident for-profit higher education sector seeks to help people solve. College itself is changing to accommodate real lives. Scholarly models of college must change as well.

The massification of college access in the twentieth century changed the character of the whole of American life. It extended the period of adolescence and brought about a new life stage—early adulthood—with its own challenges and experts (Settersten, 2010). It changed employers' expectations for what counted as adequate educational preparation for work (Labaree, 1988). It reorganized marital selection (Schwartz & Mare, 2005), transformed the way affluent families raise their children (Stevens, 2007), and in general recalibrated the nature of stratification and inequality (Fischer & Hout, 2006). So we should not be surprised if the remaking of college in the contemporary epoch has repercussions across the society. The increasingly lively national conversations about just what "college" is, how much it should cost, who should pay for it, and when and where it should occur are very telling in this regard. College and the life course are reciprocally evolving.

Assessment and Governance in a Changing Ecology

As this coevolution continues, the assessment and governance of higher education will change as well. There already has been a great deal of national discussion on how academic productivity should be measured as the logic of fiscal scarcity continues to define policy discourse on higher education. Whether educators like it or not, the government largesse that fed the postwar expansion of the postsecondary sector is unlikely to return anytime soon. This is especially true at the state level, where several decades of antitax politics have structurally constrained the capacity of legislatures to raise more public resources even presuming public will (I. W. Martin, 2008). Providing more education at higher quality and lower cost has become the policy mantra among higher education philanthropies, in state capitols, and in Washington.

U.S. higher education has long enjoyed the privilege of self-governance, in the form of officially voluntary institutional accreditation. I say "officially" voluntary because government tuition grants and subsidized loans are contingent on accreditation, as is the transfer of credit between institutions. Avoiding the accreditation system entirely is impossible for all but the most iconoclastic schools. Yet accreditation is a weak coercive instrument. Accreditation agencies are financially supported by associated schools, which also contribute the faculty and administrative labor to carry out accreditation appraisals. The system is focused heavily on inputs: attributes such as campus facilities, faculty credentials, and academic programs, for example. The signal output measures have historically been graduation rate and average time to degree. More muscular productivity and output measures, such as cost/price per student, measured learning or civic participation, and earnings returns have only recently received anything more than conjectural consideration.

The legitimacy of this inherited regulatory system is now in question. Spiraling college costs and the transfer of ever more of those costs to students and families are key drivers of the new skepticism. A growing and rapidly diversifying for-profit sector is another. Providers whose services and organizational forms bear little resemblance to those expected by accreditation guidelines are eager to see the rules changed, especially when it comes to access to government subsidy. Yet another challenge came in 2011 with the publication of Richard Arum and Josipa Roksa's *Academically Adrift: Limited Learning on College Campuses*. This study deployed a highly regarded test of critical-thinking skills to measure student learning in college among a national sample of students on four-year residential campuses. The results were sobering. Nearly half of the students failed to demonstrate any measured learning in their first three college semesters. *Academically Adrift* surfaced the uncomfortable fact that for many undergraduates, and perhaps also for many faculty, student learning is not a priority.

In their contribution in Chapter 7, Arum and Roksa call for a serious national conversation about what the purposes of college educations should be. Only once we know those purposes can we specify appropriate performance measures. Arum and Roksa make a frank distinction between technical and normative aspects of educational assessment. The technical aspects are the "how" of measurement and are properly the purview of social scientists and psychometricians. But the normative aspects of assessment must not be consigned to measurement experts alone. What features of college performance we choose to measure is a reflection of what we choose to value about higher education. "Deciding what to measure is a political decision," they write, and thus appropriately the responsibility of citizens and taxpayers, students and their families.

Given the deep implication of higher education in the national political economy, it is remarkable just how little attention political analysts have given to colleges and universities. As William Doyle and Mike Kirst explain in Chapter 8, the preponderance of academic scrutiny given to education has long been directed to K–12 schools. Just why this is the case is a large question that still awaits a sufficient intellectual history, but several pieces of the answer are clear: the much deeper embeddedness of K–12 schools in local politics, the complex intertwining of K–12 school policy with the unfinished project of racial equality in the United States, and the fact that access to elementary and high school educations has been universally required by law. Additionally, as Doyle and Kirst point out, national opinion about higher education has until recently been decidedly favorable. Americans have a respect for higher education in general and may even "love" particular schools in ways that give academic professionals a great deal of political cover. Savvy higher education leaders have long understood this (Thelin, 2004). Yet national sentiment is becoming more critical, feeding conditions for further turbulence in the ecology.

A New Research Agenda

With its dedicated focus on students, twentieth-century educational social science often elided the variety, complexity, and agency of schools as organizations.

The ecology idea enables us to correct this elision. Schools are revealed as *actors*, with their own histories and ambitions. Additionally the women and men who produce higher education come into view as equally analytically important to those consume it. Not just students but also teachers and administrators have careers in the higher education ecology. As the ecology changes, so too do academics' professional lives. Understanding these dynamics is essential for anyone interested in the quality and efficiency of higher education delivery.

As simple as this insight might be, investigating it empirically is difficult. Economists Susannah Loeb, Agustina Paglayan, and Eric Taylor explain why in Chapter 9. First, the production function of colleges and universities is complex. Compared with K–12 schools, colleges and universities have a wide variety of expected outputs. Broad-access colleges must be many things to many people, providing instruction on a broad range of academic knowledge. At comprehensive universities, faculty research outputs may be valued at parity with instruction or given priority. Athletic programs may consume a great deal of administrative and student attention. Second, student learning in college has rarely been systematically measured, making it hard to compare instructional productivity across classrooms, faculty, organizational divisions, and schools. Third, there are no national-level data describing the population of postsecondary instructors and administrators. The study of human resources in higher education remains a frontier, but there is much to learn from the now-mature scholarship on teacher and administrator labor markets in K–12 schools. Loeb, Paglayan, and Taylor extract these lessons here.

There also is much to learn from researchers in broad-access schools themselves. During the course of this project we were humbled to learn just how much quantitative data and research wisdom exists at the level of particular colleges and universities. Academic researchers too rarely recognize these organization-level assets. We have been convinced that better bridging academic and institutional research is a necessary task of any purposeful higher education social science. In Chapter 10, economists Michal Kurlaender, Jessica Howell, and Jacob Jackson provide a vivid case for how this kind of research cooperation can be productively pursued.

We seek to encourage a radical expansion of the research landscape of U.S. higher education. We want to incorporate the essential insights of prior scholarly generations without being limited by outdated assumptions. We want to recognize the coevolution of the higher education ecology and the character of the life course. We want to figure out how instructional and administrative performance can be transparently and humanely assessed, how occupational excellence can be encouraged and rewarded over the arc of entire careers, how meaningful learning and personal development can be nurtured among the widest possible range of learners. In Chapter 11, Daniel Klasik, Kristopher Proctor, and Rachel Baker serve the corpus of this book by providing a concise map of the expanded terrain.

Our work is not merely academic. Good scholarship never by itself engenders good change, but it properly clarifies the terms of debate. What is college for? What kinds of purposes and students get priority? Which species of life in the higher education ecosystem are essential to preserve, which are best lost to history, and what new kinds should be seeded and encouraged? We hope that these essays surface such questions and usefully inform their discussion.

PART I

UNDERSTANDING THE CHANGING ECOLOGY

1

HIGHER EDUCATION IN AMERICA

Multiple Field Perspectives

W. Richard Scott

Many informed observers believe that the field of higher education is on the cusp of a major change if not a full-fledged revolution. The increased costs of attending college combined with steady reductions in public support have helped undermine confidence in and support for the status quo. Concerns for low completion rates and limited learning have grown (see Chapter 7). These developments have been accompanied by the rapid onset of the digital revolution, which commenced in scattered ways among peripheral players in the 1970s but has now invaded the major colleges and universities and spawned entirely new types of organizational providers (see Chapter 2). I attempt to place these developments in context—historical, structural, and cultural—by employing the concept of organization field. The field approach reminds us to take account of the full range of educational organizations, to realize the extent to which these organizations are supported and constrained by other types of actors, and to attend to sources of change, reactive mobilization by incumbents, and unanticipated effects following from these contending forces.

More importantly, viewing higher education as an organization field allows (forces?) us to recognize the extent to which existing structures and beliefs shape present and future developments. While we describe new initiatives intended to disrupt and renew, we also consider the inertial properties and interests vested in the current systems, emphasizing both their resilience and their capacity to resist and co-opt challenging groups. As DiMaggio (1991) reminds us, examining the origins of fields as well as periods of contestation and struggle reveal much about the underlying and often concealed power processes embedded within every field.

The field concept can be fruitfully employed at the local, regional, national, and even international level. This chapter concentrates on the national level, specifically, the case of the United States. During the forty or so years since the concept first emerged in organization studies, it has been elaborated and challenged by alternative formulations, each of which offers important, and different, insights. I organize this chapter around three competing field models: (1) higher education as an institutional field, (2) higher education as an arena of strategic action, and (3) higher education as a demand-generated outcome. I devote more attention to describing the first, foundational model because it is more fully developed and more widely employed as a guide to understanding our current system. However, the two later-developing models may provide more purchase in understanding recent developments and have more to teach us about the future of higher education.

Higher Education as an Institutional Field

This conception of the field of higher education seeks to explain why there exists a limited number of types of colleges, depict their origin and salient characteristics, and describe the diverse, complex collection of other types or organizations that has arisen to control and support them.

In their foundational formulation, DiMaggio and Powell define an *organizational field* as consisting of

> those organizations that, in the aggregate, constitute a recognized area of institutional life: key suppliers, resource and product consumers, regulatory agencies, and other organizations that produce similar services or products. (DiMaggio & Powell, 1983, p. 148)

Like the concept of "industry," an organization field is constructed around a focal population of similar organizations—in our case, colleges and universities—but expanded to include other types of organizations that interact with this population, including exchange partners, clients, funding, and regulatory organizations. Fields incorporate both relational systems, as organizations and their participants create networks to exchange information and resources and enter into status and power relations, and symbolic systems, as these relations are grounded in and infused with shared cultural-cognitive and normative frameworks. In this view, organizations within a field "share a common meaning system and interact more frequently and fatefully with one another than with actors outside of the field" (Scott, 1994, p. 208). Because these fields are defined by a set of commonly shared institutions, they are here termed *institutional fields*. Such "local social orders" are the building blocks around which modern societal systems are constructed (Fligstein, 2001, p. 107).

Diverse Providers

According to current accounts, higher education is among the most successful "industries" in the United States. A recent survey of the top universities in the world by the Institute of Higher Education at Shanghai's Jiao Tong University reported that the top one hundred universities included fifty-three U.S. universities, while the top twenty included seventeen U.S. universities (Institute of Higher Education, 2011). While this view is heartening (if you are an American), it is fundamentally misleading. The top-tier universities are hardly representative of the thousands of colleges and universities in America—some forty-two hundred—that have emerged during the past half century and now account for most of the providers and enrollments in higher education. The elite schools and universities serve less than 15 percent of college students. A field perspective urges attention to the full range of organizational forms—including those programs educating the vast majority of students.

A crude but instructive classification identifies six types or populations of colleges:

1. baccalaureate colleges (liberal arts colleges)

2. comprehensive colleges (baccalaureate and advanced degrees)

3. research universities (focused more on advanced degrees and knowledge creation)

4. associate degree programs (community colleges)

5. special-focus institutions (e.g., theology, medicine, law, art)

6. for-profit entities (special-focus, baccalaureate, and associate degrees)

Each of these types is associated with a distinctive structure strongly influenced by the circumstances present at the time of its emergence.

Baccalaureate colleges, the prototypical college form, carry features based on their medieval European counterparts and remain the oldest and most familiar form. Their defining features include relatively small size, high ratios of teachers to students, and emphasis on undergraduate, residential education. Until recently, these organizations provided the basic structural template for colleges following in their wake, being organized as either public or nonprofit systems and employing a model in which professional academic participants are given considerable autonomy, working within collegially controlled departments, while managers oversee support structures (e.g., buildings, residential systems, student services).

Comprehensive colleges emerged in the late nineteenth century, as a collection of more advanced vocational and professional training programs were added to existing undergraduate colleges. These forms are typically public systems, supported by states and large cities. This model was substantially advanced by the passage of the Morrill Land-Grant Act, in 1862 and 1890, when the federal government commenced its partnership with the states to "promote the liberal and practical education of the industrial classes in the several pursuits and professions in life" (see http://www.law.cornell.edu/us code/text/7/304). It was also fueled by the professionalizing efforts of many occupations during this period, who were attempting to elevate the status of their training programs by embedding them in colleges (Bledstein, 1976).

Research universities were modeled on late-nineteenth-century German programs that emphasized the role of knowledge creation and research training as central to the mission of higher education, although in the United States these programs typically also include more traditional undergraduate and professional training programs. Although these forms are the most visible and prestigious (e.g., Columbia, Harvard, Stanford, Yale), they are outliers and unrepresentative of U.S. educational providers.

Associate degree (community college) *programs* first emerged in the early twentieth century, but their most rapid growth occurred after the 1960s in response to a public sector political agenda to expand opportunity by increasing college capacity, allowing greater numbers of high school graduates to obtain access to college. In these forms, however, faculty autonomy is weakened and professional controls are subordinated to managerial and union-negotiated work arrangements. Community colleges serve a wide range of goals including preparation of transfer students, vocational, and adult education.

Special-focus institutions concentrate on specialized technical or professional training in multiple areas, but the bulk of these programs are concentrated in health, business, and the arts.

For-profit entities operated for many years on the margins of the field as special-focus institutions, but in the 1980s they began to provide generalized college training. They have grown rapidly. This subpopulation is not defined by its academic mission but by its distinctive form. Rather than the professional organization model embraced, in theory if not in practice, by other forms of college organizations, for-profits have adopted the corporate model of organization. Curricular decisions are highly centralized, and teaching staff are accorded much less autonomy than in traditional colleges.

Isomorphic Pressures

A core argument of the institutional field approach is that pressures—both competitive and symbolic—arise that foster structural and procedural *isomorphism* (similarity) (Meyer & Rowan, 1977). To be recognizable, acceptable, and legitimate, organizations performing the same functions within the field come, over time, to be strikingly similar in their ways of organizing and modes of acting. Consider the types of colleges just discussed. As noted, these colleges appear at differing times in history in response to changing circumstances, arising in "spurts" followed by periods of less rapid growth. The structural features adopted by the organizational population tend to be stable—the colleges are "imprinted" by features adopted at the time of their founding that are reproduced over time by succeeding organizations (Stinchcombe, 1965).

These tendencies toward isomorphism are enhanced by the development of category systems. The categories of colleges that we employed are informed by more detailed classification systems developed by organizations such as the Carnegie Foundation for the Advancement of Teaching. These systems both reflect reality—being based on observations of real differences in modes of organizing and ways of pursuing goals—and help reinforce and even reify these differences. If you find that you are in an organization considered to be a member of a class of other organizations, you begin to make comparisons and to seek models, both positive and negative, from this subpopulation. Such pressures have increased in recent decades with the widespread use of rating and ranking systems in the mass media. For example, *U.S. News and World Report* began to introduce rankings of colleges in the 1980s based on college characteristics, such as student selectivity, faculty-student ratios, and performance indicators, later including student and alumni surveys—data that have encouraged colleges to adopt the structures and practices of their more successful competitors (Bastedo & Bowman, 2009).

More broadly, isomorphic pressures, which do much to provide coherence and order in a field, stem from many sources, including regulatory and coercive pressures from oversight agencies, normative pressures stemming from professional and administrative associations, and mimetic pressures of the type just described, which encourage organizations to imitate those whom they believe to be more successful (DiMaggio & Powell, 1983; Scott, 2013).

Supporting Systems

Colleges are the focal organizational populations in a field, but they are surrounded and supported by many other types of actors, including associations of organizations whose members are organizations—and associations of individuals. Many associations of organizations link colleges of the same type (e.g., Catholic colleges, research universities) who, although competitors, come together to create mechanisms for advancing their common interests. In a parallel fashion, there are many associations whose members are individuals, including professional associations for both faculty and staff members; unions composed of teachers, staff, or graduate students; and alumni associations for former students. Of primary importance, however, are the disciplinary associations among faculty, because they serve as central components of the overarching governance structure of higher education.

As B. R. Clark reminds us, in addition to being a network of varying enterprises (colleges), "a national system of higher education is also a set of disciplines and professions" (1983, p. 29). Disciplinary associations are especially salient for schools in the upper tiers of the field: the elite colleges, comprehensive colleges, research universities, and special-focus institutions. For faculty members in these settings, discipline typically trumps enterprise. Abbott argues that the resilience of the academic disciplines within higher education rests on their "dual institutionalization":

> On the one hand, the disciplines constitute the macrostructure of the labor market for faculty. Careers remain within discipline much more than within university. On the other hand, the system constitutes the microstructure of each individual university. All arts and sciences faculties contain more or less the same list of departments. (Abbott, 2002, pp. 208–209)

In addition, these associations and their members help colleges oversee the quality of their faculty appointments as well as help assess the overall performance of their departmental programs. (These comments apply much less to broad-access institutions, including comprehensive and community colleges, in part because such a high proportion of the faculty in these colleges has adjunct status, as discussed shortly.) Professionals also staff accreditation agencies that provide certification for colleges. Whereas in most countries, these functions are carried out by public ministries of higher education, in the United States they are assigned to a collection of six regional accreditation agencies. A favorable assessment, while not required for a college to operate, is a significant marker of legitimacy and also a condition for students enrolled to be eligible for federal loans to finance their education. Accreditation programs for special-focus institutions and for professional schools in comprehensive colleges and universities are carried out by the relevant professional associations. It is hard to overstate the extent to which normative controls exercised by professional associations and their members provide structure for the field of higher education: meaning, coherence, standards, templates for organizing, and protocols for guiding the educational activities of college participants.

In addition to these professional oversight systems, important governance functions in higher education are carried out by local, regional, state, and federal governments (Hearn & McLendon, 2012). Throughout most of the past century, the vast bulk of colleges have been public institutions, heavily dependent on governmental sources of support. The states provide the lion's share of funding for comprehensive colleges and associate degree programs. While the federal government does not directly fund colleges, with the exception of military academies, from the 1940s it has served as the most important source of support for research and research training in universities as well as a major source of student grants and loans through the GI Bill in the 1940s and today's Federal Student Aid programs. With funding comes oversight, both legislative and administrative, although colleges have been less subject to governmental regulations than have elementary and secondary schools (see Chapter 8). The controls exercised over colleges involve primarily fiscal accounting rather than curriculum or academic performance.

Private colleges, both nonprofit and for-profit, are also subject to the regulation of public agencies but to a lesser degree. While some nonprofit private schools are independent, many are parts of larger systems—for example, colleges associated with religious orders. Some are members of loose confederations that provide support but also exercise modest control. Most private schools that are for-profit follow a different model. These colleges are operated more like branch offices under a central corporate office that provides uniform curricular materials to the individual programs, organizes marketing, oversees performance, and maintains financial control over all operations. Faculty members and local administrators are given much less discretion, and professional disciplinary bodies exercise little influence either within or external to the school.

The courts exercise a unique role in American society, providing an independent route for individuals or groups to claim the protection of constitutional rights and a distinctive forum for the resolution of disputes. Colleges can be called to account for their behavior in a number of areas, including those confronting any large employer or service provider, such as employee protections, but are also subject to a number of distinctive disputes arising in areas such as protection of free speech, student and faculty diversity, separation of church and state, freedom of information, and patenting of inventions and protection of intellectual property.

To an extraordinary degree, these oversight systems are both *federalized* (operating at multiple levels of governments) and *fragmented* (administered by relatively independent governmental and private organizations). Scott and Meyer (1983, 1991) argue and empirically demonstrate that fragmented and federalized control systems produce higher levels of administrative complexity within organizations subject to their control. During the past half century, the administrative structures of all college institutions have increased in size, diversity, and cost relative to the academic core.

In addition to these structural controls, the institutional field approach emphasizes the centrality of cultural frameworks. Much of the stability and resilience of the structure of higher education resides in the widely shared societal belief systems concerning the value of colleges and universities and mental models regarding what "real" colleges are, do, and look like (Meyer, Ramirez, Frank, & Schofer, 2007).

An Established Field

As a specialized sector of our society, higher education in America has become a sturdy institutional field. As emphasized, it has deep historical roots and strong traditions; its organizational forms and practices are familiar and largely taken for granted by participants and the wider public (Meyer, 1977). It is what economists refer to as "a mature industry." In the language of institutional theorists, the field is highly "structurated" (DiMaggio & Powell, 1983;

Giddens, 1979)—exhibiting dense interactions among the actors, multiple channels carrying massive flows of information, strong isomorphic pressures among organizations of the same type, clear structures of status and prestige, and stable patterns of coalition among participants. This system is created and maintained by the combined pressures of competitive and institutional mechanisms that induce shared assumptions and conceptions of educational work: who is to do it and how it is to be carried out.

Like all mature industries, higher education has supportive relations with the nation-state. Indeed, as with many specialized areas dominated by professionals in the United States, such as medicine, higher education operates somewhat as a "para-state" (Loss, 2012, p. 2). Since Americans strongly prefer a "noninvasive central state," the field of higher education enjoys substantial autonomy and exercises considerable authority over educational matters, collaborating with public officials to set and carry out important public activities, such as spurring innovation and development, expanding educational opportunities, and advancing the rights revolution. "Slowly during the interwar period, then rapidly after World War II, the state and higher education joined forces to fight economic depressions and poverty, to wage world wars hot and cold, and to secure the rights of previously marginalized Americans" (Loss, 2012, p. 1).

The major thrust of this founding perspective of institutional fields is to explain the extraordinary uniformity of organizational forms within established institutional fields—to answer the question "Why are there so *few* kinds of organizations within a given sector?" Given the huge variety of geographic, demographic, and economic conditions occurring throughout the United States, the system of higher education has been remarkably stable and has enjoyed wide acceptance and credibility. The framework privileges the overpowering effects of regulative, normative, and cultural isomorphic pressures creating uniform structures and procedures and lending legitimacy to actors that adopt and display them (Scott, 2013).

Higher Education as an Arena of Strategic Action

The founding conception emphasizes the development of a limited number of organization forms providing higher educational services and describes the field forces at work to reinforce and maintain this structured diversity.

In doing so, it highlights the constraining role of the external environment and the passive behavior of the colleges subject to these forces. During the early 1990s, an alternative conception of organization fields began to take shape that has challenged the foundational conception, both augmenting and attempting to replace it. It argues that the initial approach placed too much emphasis on structures, whether relational or symbolic, and not enough on actors and action; was too quick to assume that conformity to institutional pressures is the default response rather than to recognize that actors often exhibit challenging and strategic responses; and was based on the presumption that fields are organized around a consensual "taken for granted" reality rather than recognizing that most fields are highly contested—arenas in which actors compete for dominance. This more critical perspective has drawn primarily on the analysis of "social fields" by Bourdieu, on the work of management strategy theorists, on approaches to institutional logics, and on social movement theory.

Agency and Strategic Action

While all actors, both individual and collective, are partially shaped by and responsive to their institutional contexts, they all possess in varying degrees the capacity to exercise *agency*—the ability to act independently, to resist and sometimes to change the relational and symbolic contexts within which they are embedded (Emirbayer & Mische, 1998; Lawrence & Suddaby, 2006). In his early work on "social fields," Bourdieu argued that within modern societies, all action takes place within "a number of relatively autonomous social microcosms" exhibiting a complex of rules or "regularities" that are the "product of the competition between players" (Bourdieu & Wacquant, 1992, pp. 97–98). Each field is organized around competition for one or another kind of *capital*: some fields stress the importance of economic capital; others focus on social capital, based on access to networks of relationships; and still others stress cultural capital, emphasizing the importance of status, prestige, artistic, and scientific values (Bourdieu, 1986).

Rather than assuming, as the founding field conception does, that individuals and organizations routinely conform to the pressures exerted by the institutional environment, analysts such as Oliver (1991) pointed out that a range of more strategic responses is often observed, including compromise, avoidance, manipulation, and defiance in response to external demands. Actors are both constrained and enabled by institutional frameworks, and they are capable of using them to pursue their own interests as well as challenging and attempting to change frameworks if necessary. Moreover, while fields are made up of many established and institutionalized actors who have a vested interest in maintaining the status quo, they also include other types of players whose interests have been suppressed and who, given the opportunity, mobilize to promote change and reform. All fields contain both incumbents and challengers. Social movements involving the mobilization of excluded actors around divergent goals and interests provide a vital source of change in organizational fields (Davis, McAdam, Scott, & Zald, 2005). Far from being islands of tranquillity and harmony, fields are arenas of contestation for power among players with diverse interests and agendas (Fligstein & McAdam, 2012).

Evidence of strategic processes at work abounds at the field level, as organized associations each representing the interests of some type of college (e.g., research universities, community colleges) or professional groups (academic; specialized administration, such as college presidents; or financial officers) mobilize to represent, defend, and lobby for their interests at state, regional, and national levels (Cook, 1998). In mature industries, leading organizations shape governmental policies in ways favorable to their interests.

Strategic processes and the competition for capital of various kinds generate diversity in organizational fields. As noted, the founding conception of fields stressed the uniformity of organizational forms, and classification systems like the Carnegie system embrace a hierarchical imagery that overemphasizes the role of the top-tier institutions, ignoring both the contribution of broad-access colleges that educate more than 85 percent of all postsecondary students and their diversity. The structures and missions of these colleges exhibit wide variety and serve complex mixtures of "nontraditional" students—including larger numbers of minority students, a wider range of age groups, married as well as single students, and part-time as well as full-time enrollees. A focus on isomorphism masks this diversity in mission and clientele.

Competition among colleges has escalated in part because the continuing decline in public funding for higher education. From the 1970s into the first decade of the twenty-first century, public expenditures have plateaued, in the case of federal funding, or substantially decreased, in the case of state funding. With the end of the Cold War and the arrival of more conservative policies, federal support for research and training in universities has not kept pace with increases in enrollments or expenditures. At the state level, public funding of state colleges has declined, from covering 50 percent of higher education budgets in 1970 to under 30 percent in 2012. Community colleges have been particularly hard-hit by these cutbacks. While public revenues have declined, enrollments have continued to increase. Total undergraduate enrollment in degree-granting postsecondary institutions has nearly tripled, increasing from 7.4 million students in 1970 to 18.1 million in 2011. Postbaccalaureate enrollments have also grown but at a lower rate (Aud et al., 2012). It is against this background of declining support for public institutions and increased enrollment pressures that we have witnessed an intensification in competition among colleges for revenues, as well as the rise of a new type of provider: the for-profit college.

Relying in past decades primarily on public or philanthropic funding, colleges increasingly seek funds from tuition and fees, and some have developed lucrative financial ties to the corporate sector. Also, the reality of market forces has been made even more tangible by the emergence and growth of rating agencies, briefly described previously, who doggedly score and rank every facet of a college's makeup and programs, including student body, faculty, residential facilities, curriculum, athletic programs, social life, and ambiance. Colleges have become more aware of their direct competitors, and many if not most consciously work to improve their ratings (Toma, 2012).

Colleges compete with one another to secure resources, including the most desirable students and the most productive and/or promising faculty, but also revenue. The competition for students often involves balancing the academic qualifications of students and their ability to pay tuition. Although liberal arts colleges have long insisted on their adherence to admitting students who are best qualified academically, over time they have begun to accord more weight to the ability to pay. Kraatz, Ventresca, and Deng (2010) suggest that this transformation has been aided and abetted by "mundane" changes in administrative structure. Whereas admissions departments had long made their decisions "blind" of financial condition, the introduction of "enrollment management" departments, combining admissions and financial aid officers into a single department, raised the salience of financial considerations, increasing pressures on admissions personnel to take into account a student's ability to pay in their admissions decisions. These structural innovations were endorsed and heavily promoted by a professional association, the American Association of Collegiate Registrars and Admissions Officers, in part as a way of increasing the influence of these officials within their colleges. Another example of competition among colleges for students with financial resources is provided by the practice of many state colleges and universities to recruit out-of-state and international students. Declining state support has caused many colleges to seek to attract students from neighboring states, giving them priority over their own students, because out-of-state students can be charged higher tuition rates. Money is required, but it can also undermine mission (Weisbrod, Ballou, & Asch, 2008).

Within colleges, departments and administrative units compete for scarce resources. Academic disciplines have long jousted with one another over status and jurisdiction over intellectual turf (Abbott, 1988), and now recent accounting schemes have begun to treat departments as profit centers, shifting resources to those more able to contribute to the bottom line. "Faculty and degrees too are increasingly rewarded according to their market value, thereby creating enormous disparities in incomes between universities, but also between disciplines within universities, as well as within disciplines" (Burawoy, 2012, p. 147). Many faculty members have organized to protect their financial interests. By 1995, roughly 40 percent of full-time faculty in higher education were represented by labor unions (Julius & Gumport, 2003), and union membership has increased by about 24 percent between 1998 and 2006 (National Center for the Study of Collective Bargaining in Higher Education and the Professions, 2006). However, a sobering trend among college faculty is the large and growing number of part-time members employed on a contract basis: the adjunct faculty. Part-time and adjunct faculty constituted half of college faculty members in 2011, compared to about 25 percent in the 1970s (U.S. Department of Education, National Center for Education Statistics, 2013). Most adjuncts do not receive benefits, and their pay scale is low and has been declining in recent decades. Most are in, but not of, the university, lacking an office and having little to no contact with faculty colleagues. Adjunct faculty are neither supported by nor subject to the professional controls exercised by disciplinary associations. Even within elite institutions, the proportion of faculty covered by the tenure system has dropped from 55 percent in 1980 to 31 percent in 2007 (Clawson, 2009). Financial capital dominates cultural capital in a growing number of colleges.

During the 1950s through the 1980s, the capacity of the higher education system was expanded, almost entirely with increased public funding (Fischer & Hout, 2006). Since the 1980s, however, the system has undergone privatization, both in the sense that students bear a larger and larger share of funding their education through increased tuition rates and fees and because for-profit colleges have been the most rapidly growing segment of the sector. Although these colleges remain a minority of providers, they have grown vigorously in recent decades. Two-year for-profit colleges numbered only 140 in 1980 and increased fivefold to 636 by 2010. The rate of increase for four-year colleges has been even higher, from 18 in 1980 to 563 in 2010 (Aud et al., 2012). Their educational efforts are both fueled and enabled by the revolution in information and communication technologies (ICT), which support distance learning. Once curricular materials are created, they can be transmitted virtually costlessly to widely scattered consumers. While they operate in ways to reduce costs so as to increase profits, tuition at two-year for-profit colleges averages more than six times that of a community college (Gonzalez, 2009). For-profit entities constitute the most significant challenge ever posed to the traditional model of providing education.

Institutional Logics

Friedland and Alford (1991) introduced the concept of institutional logics, not simply to emphasize the principles around which a given field was organized but to point out that modern societal systems are composed of many diverse fields, each with its own dominant logic, and to note that these logics compete for attention and adherents. Fields such as higher education intersect and interact with other fields, such as political and economic systems, and actors must work to manage the conflicting logics at play. Indeed, as Stevens, Armstrong, and Arum (2008) have observed, higher education in modern society is an important "hub" interacting with the state, the economy, kinship and stratification systems, and the professions and sciences. The following are among the principal contested logics at play.

Liberal versus practical arts. For many years, the logic dominating colleges in the United States has been a belief in the value of liberal education. The core disciplines of the humanities, mathematics and the natural sciences, and, later, the social sciences have long held center stage. However, as we have noted, during the late nineteenth century with the establishment of the land-grant colleges, this model was not so much challenged as amended to include programs devoted to the cultivation of the mechanical and practical arts. For the next hundred years, these contrasting models coexisted and, to some extent, competed as liberal arts colleges continued to multiply alongside those devoted more specifically to vocational programs. (Programs devoted exclusively to vocational training have long existed in this country, but over time most of them have moved outside the traditional boundaries of the field of higher education to operate within companies that provide tailored training for their employees [Carnevale, 1987]).

Within the field of higher education, the relatively new population of community colleges—associate degree programs—has evolved in recent decades to offer more courses serving vocational (rather than transfer) objectives, offering certificates in a variety of semiprofessional and technical fields. Brint and Karabel (1989) use historical data to support their argument that, at least in the critical period of expansion during the 1960s, this vocational emphasis was supported by a number of foundations and the federal government and by the interests of administrators and college leaders who resented being treated as inferior by four-year colleges and sought to differentiate themselves. Rather than being on the bottom rung of the liberal arts hierarchy, they opted for being at the top of the occupational training hierarchy.

Meanwhile, even within mainstream colleges, since the 1970s, the practical programs, including business, engineering, health care, and computer science, have made substantial inroads on the liberal arts, so that by 2010 the most commonly selected majors were in the fields of business, management, marketing, personal and culinary areas, and health services (Brint, 2002). These changes reflect the increasing emphasis on economic values and goals—the incursion of economic logic into the core of higher education—as education is expected to justify its worth in terms of its contribution to economic development (e.g., the development of "human capital"). Gumport identifies three mechanisms that have converged to push public colleges and universities along a "utilitarian trajectory": the rise of academic management changing academic into corporate discourse and criteria for decision making, the rise of academic consumerism emphasizing economic-consumer interests, and the "re-stratification of academic subjects and academic personnel, based upon the increased use-value and exchange-value of particular knowledges in the wider society" (2000, pp. 68–69). Beginning in the 1970s, academic research and training programs have increasingly been viewed primarily if not exclusively as a vital engine of economic growth and development (Berman, 2012).

Elite versus mass education. Because the field of higher education intersects with the political arena, American democratic values of equality of opportunity have long pressured colleges to provide increased access to a college education for all. The convergence of social movements pressing for reform and the actions of Democratic administrations during the 1940s and 1960s expanded educational opportunities. Beginning with the GI Bill in 1944, which provided financial assistance to demobilized servicemen to pursue a college education, to the Higher Education Act of 1965, which promoted statewide plans and provisions for expanding higher education throughout the nation, to the Federal Student Aid programs that provide loans to college students, the federal government has worked to improve educational access (Cole, 2009).

An important vehicle of expanding opportunities for advanced education was the community college movement. Although the form had been available from the early 1900s, the most rapid period of expansion occurred during the 1960s. In 2012, over one quarter of full-time students and over 60 percent of part-time students were enrolled in public community colleges (Aud et al., 2012). State governments have increased access largely through enlarging the number of public institutions, both two- and four-year colleges. In combination with federal programs, these efforts greatly expanded the capacity of the system: "At the end of World War II, there was space enough in colleges and universities for only one-fifth of Americans age eighteen to twenty-two; by the early 1990s, there was space for about four-fifths of them. The expansion came about almost solely through the construction and subsidization of *public* higher education" (Fischer & Hout, 2006, p. 251; emphasis in original). However, as costs have escalated and public funding has decreased, low- and middle-income students are struggling to obtain access to the courses they need or even to remain in the system.

An important component of the effort to expand opportunities involves increasing academic diversity of both faculty and students, which critics argue pits the value of equality against that of merit and academic achievement. Major social movements mobilizing efforts to improve civil rights emerged during the 1960s in arenas outside higher education, but colleges quickly found themselves embroiled in controversies ranging from antiwar protests to affirmative action initiatives involving the full range of disadvantaged groups, including ethnic groups, women, and gay and lesbian groups (Loss, 2012). While substantial progress has been made in increasing equity of access for most citizens, the most important barriers still to be overcome are financial. With the rising costs of higher education, low-income populations remain at a disadvantage (Zemsky, 2009).

Education as a public versus private good. Related to the distinction between liberal and practical arts is the debate over the proper mission of higher education. From its founding period—a time of institutional "imprinting"—colleges have been set apart from the economic and political pressures of the societies that supported them: "ivory towers" providing sanctuaries for study and contemplation. Many academics see themselves as following a "calling"—a commitment to preserving cultural and intellectual treasures, enriching them, and passing them on to succeeding generations. Although, as we have described, the intrusion of the practical world occurred early in U.S. higher education, and educational missions began to be elaborated and programs differentiated, most public and nonprofit students—as their tax status suggests—have insisted that they were dedicated to scholarly values and serving the broader public good, not simply the demands of individual students.

However, as noted, new organizational forms have emerged during the last few decades that do not simply bend to the wider pressures of market logics but embrace them. Thus, for-profit colleges primarily seek to maximize profits and returns to their shareholders, by either growing as rapidly as possible or finding new ways to cut costs, or both. This has resulted in the exploration and exploitation of new technologies of teaching but also in the use of hard-sell, sometimes misleading marketing to prospective students; the de-skilling of faculty; and the ascendance of managerial and financial logics. These new types of organizations are closer in their DNA to the factory than the monastery.

Higher Education as a Demand-Generated Field

The institutional field and the strategic views of organization fields differ in important ways regarding the processes and mechanisms by which fields operate and undergo change. The former privileges the role of relational and symbolic structures as they provide meaning and order for multiple types of interdependent actors. The latter shifts attention to the work of actors, both organizations and individuals, who possess varying types of capital, are guided by diverse institutional logics, and compete to gain advantage within the field. However, both approaches share a common assumption: field analysis should focus on the activities, interactions, and structures of the *providers* of goods and services.

A third, emerging perspective departs from this fundamental assumption, suggesting instead that analysts attend to the motivation and actions of actors who *consume* educational services. Advocates of this view suggest that we should substitute a demand-side for a supply-side approach to higher education. As Illich (1971) argued more than fifty years ago, it is important not to confuse the supplier with the service: the school with education. Education—in the sense of learning and development—has long been available outside formal schooling to individuals in all walks of life. Lessons are there to be learned in everyday experiences, from friends and strangers, from the media and books, from travel and participating in the arts. Given advances in information technologies, these long-available and familiar resources have been vastly augmented by the reach of the Internet. Under such conditions, who needs colleges and universities? They have no monopoly on information and knowledge, and, in any case, many of these proprietary systems are increasingly making their courses available online. Education is being delivered to hundreds of thousands of students through a new vehicle known as MOOCs—massive open online courses. In one such course, offered in the fall of 2012 by Stanford faculty members, more than 160,000 students from 190 countries were enrolled (Lewin, 2012).

Kamenetz cogently reviews developing approaches to unleashing what has been termed the "edupunk": the liberated independent learner at the center of a web of intellectual resources, supported by "community- and practice-based learning" (2010, p. 109; see also Chapter 2). Using resources such as those developed by the Open University in the United Kingdom, the Massachusetts Institute of Technology (MIT) with its OpenCourseWare Project, or more recently, edX and Coursera, involving a consortia of elite-university providers, students can design their own curriculum. Freely available materials including lectures from highly regarded faculty members can be combined with self-organized groups of learners, both colocated and virtual. In short, students are encouraged to design their own university. This model offers a radical recipe for reforming higher education, suggesting that students simply ignore the existing system with its complex of requirements, gatekeepers, fifty-minute lectures offered at set hours, and end-of-term examinations—and instead be empowered to create their own customized program of education.

While such an approach presents an intriguing and heady vision of the future of learning, it appears to posit a heroic, and probably unrealistic, view of the agency, maturity, and perspicacity of individual learners and their capacity to effectively mobilize the intellectual and social resources scattered throughout their environment. Somewhat ironically, the skills and discipline needed to create one's own educational experience appear to be those that we commonly associate with a highly educated person (Rosenbaum, Deil-Amen, & Person, 2006)! Herbert Simon (1997) first taught us about the cognitive limits of individuals and suggested that the primary purpose of organization is to simplify work by subdividing it and to support decision making by creating formal channels to supply appropriate information to diverse participants as needed, authority figures to select goals and coordinate contributions, and rules to constrain choice. In sum, he argued that *organization* is required to support individual rationality.

Indeed, it appears that new types of organization are beginning to emerge to enable and support individual learners but also, perhaps, to exploit naïve customers and take advantage of new business models and income streams. New firms, some nonprofit, others for-profit, are emerging to select and package course offerings, serving as an intermediary between student and course and deciding whether and how to generate revenues from course offerings. This is a major concern of existing colleges and universities, many of whose faculty are beginning to participate in the development of MOOCs. In addition, a host of governance issues have begun to surface, including the following: How is the adequacy of a course to be determined? How is student performance to be evaluated? How are we to develop trustworthy alternative credentials to signal varying levels of accomplishment to employers and others? A variety of new, intermediary organizations is emerging, providing competing solutions to these challenges.

In short, it would appear that a new, alternative field of providers, intermediaries, and governance systems is beginning to surface, perhaps displacing or perhaps allying with earlier, traditional providers and associated organizations. Note, however, that *for these new players, their most salient environment is the existing field of higher education!* They develop not in an open and unstructured arena but in the middle of a highly developed institutional field, as well as in a highly contested arena. Given the familiarity, widespread acceptance, and credibility of these earlier forms, it would be surprising if the new educational entrepreneurs did not appropriate, adapt to, and repurpose many of them as they construct the new edifice. And, indeed, this is what we are observing. Current developers of online materials are contracting with existing colleges for the use of the courses, negotiating with them about providing college credit for this work, and working with educational associations such as the American Council of Education to have their courses approved for certification. The old order is under attack, but it is not likely to disappear anytime soon.

Conclusion

A fundamental insight stemming from institutional theory is that new practices, technologies, and organizational forms arise out of, build with, and rest on elements contained in existing institutional systems. Over time, institutions decline in force and decay in use, giving way to new modes of thinking and acting. However, the pace of institutional change is slow. Existing forms are highly inertial, protected by vested interests, sunk costs, and widely shared taken-for-granted beliefs, assumptions, and cognitive schemata. New practices are shaped and constrained by existing frameworks that, rather than being displaced by them, are combined with or coexist alongside them. Most of the institutional fields that surround us are layered and multiplex affairs, containing both dominant forms and challenging actors, shared and contested values. For this reason, I believe that all three perspectives will continue to be helpful to scholars and practitioners as they attempt to understand and control the field of higher education.

2

D I Y   U

Higher Education Goes Hybrid

Anya Kamenetz

The days in which the phrase *digital higher education* is meaningfully distinguishable from simply *higher education* are numbered. Few moments of our lives are free of the influence of electronic media. And the digital atmosphere we breathe reaches farther than we know: there are six billion mobile subscriptions for the world's seven billion people (International Telecommunication Union, 2012). The ability to hold a global conversation at the tap of a button and to find any bit of information in an instant cannot help but transform education. So while a third of the nation's postsecondary students were taking at least one online course in the United States in 2010, in a broader sense, nearly all education today is hybrid (Allen & Seaman, 2011). Whether designated "traditional," "online," or some combination of the two, it consists of live humans located in physical locations pursuing knowledge by whatever means available—digital, analog, and usually both.

That said, we have a legacy infrastructure, particularly for broad-access institutions, built before the digital mode existed. The further hybridization of higher education will not automatically result in better outcomes for the students these institutions serve. Until now, online education has been primarily associated with for-profit colleges, which have poor graduation rates and account for a disproportionate share of all student loan defaults (Senate Committee on Health, Education, Labor, and Pensions, 2012). More recently, a range of innovative nonprofit and public providers have joined them. Still, for-profit service providers (and certain venturesome nonprofit foundations) are heavily involved in bringing new technologies to higher education, with complex implications that will be noted later on.

I am interested in the ways that technology might serve the traditional mission of broad-access institutions. I discuss five in this chapter.

Meet the New Traditional Learner

"Nontraditional learners" have at least one of these characteristics: they have no high school diploma, enrolled more than one year after high school, are financially independent from parents, work full time, or are responsible for children or other dependents. Three fourths of all enrolled students are "non-traditional" by these measurements (Wirt et al., 2002). To these student groups of special concern we might add the overlapping populations from the bottom quartile of income, immigrants, and first-generation college students, who have trouble succeeding in college because of lack of comfort, lack of money, or both. Students facing economic pressure are more likely to be concerned, at least initially, with earning a credential that will connect them with better employment; having other demands on their time, they may also struggle with motivation. Faculty and administration at broad-access institutions have a challenge to engage the new traditional student more deeply with learning and the social, emotional, intellectual, and civic benefits of higher education. They must work with comparatively limited resources to help meet students where they are and bring them to a better place.

What does technology promise for nontraditional students and their institutions? Convenience. Cost. Customization. Completion. Connection. And more.

Convenience: Learning When and Where You Need It

Merely offering classes online, or posting recordings of lectures after the fact, does not necessarily meet the threshold for convenience for broad-access students today. Best-of-breed programs offer anytime, anywhere access to classes.

"They're not all studying at home," says Mark Milliron (personal communication, September 19, 2012), chancellor of Western Governors University–Texas (WGU), a nonprofit, low-cost, online, competency-based undergraduate institution integrated with the state's public university system.

With additional state branches in Indiana and Washington State, WGU nationally serves a largely adult working-class population of more than 40,000 students (see Western Governors University, n.d.). Milliron explains, "They're accessing materials during an hour break at work, or waiting to pick up their kids in the car for twenty minutes. That's why we're rolling out a BYOD—bring your own device—portal accessible through multiple platforms." As with a Netflix or Kindle account, whether WGU students sign in on their phones, tablets, or laptops, they will be able to see all their course materials and pick up where they left off.

Nontraditional students are more likely to experience bandwidth and connectivity issues. University of the People, a nonprofit and accredited online college, offers four-year undergraduate degrees in computer science and business administration for free. It has admitted 1,600 students from 142 countries and designed the course materials to be accessible for students who may be accessing the Internet on their mobile phones (see University of the People, n.d.).

Billy Sichone is a forty-year-old nonprofit worker from Zambia who studies business with University of the People. He explained, "Last year I was traveling abroad to Ghana on business. But my Nokia smartphone was very helpful for doing my assignments and sending them in on time. I can be at any point in the globe, traveling, as long as there's a network" (quoted in Kamenetz, 2011a).

Convenience may mean rolling starts: Rio Salado College in Arizona has forty-eight start dates a year (see Rio Salado College, n.d.). For online and hybrid programs it also means access to support and information when and where it is needed, by phone, Skype, e-mail, text, or whatever method the student chooses. "We have to pick up the phone, treat our students as customers, respect their opinions," says Yvonne Simon, director of online programs at Southern New Hampshire University (SNHU), a nonprofit brick-and-mortar campus whose Center for Online and Continuing Education (COCE) is the largest online-degree provider in New England (Kamenetz, 2012c). SNHU's president, Paul LeBlanc, hired Steve Hodownes, former CEO of an online customer-relationship company, to shape online operations in the style of award-winning online retailers like Amazon or Zappos.

Convenience is a word from the world of customer service, which may make it distasteful to some traditional educators. It is exactly that attitude that the innovators are challenging in the name of better reaching underserved students. While sticking with deadlines might be viewed traditionally as a sign of motivation and commitment to a program, giving students flexible timetables to reach mastery of a subject is an approach that meets the demand of instructional differentiation.

To be sure, there is a balance to be struck between student-centeredness and the rigor required for advanced learning. Convenience does not necessarily mean being fully disconnected from the calendar or refusing to put any demands of time and place on students. Most online programs have some synchronous elements, such as proctored exams. Even the massively open online course platforms, like Coursera and Udacity and edX, where courses have thousands of registrants, have start and end dates and weekly deadlines with penalties for lateness. Timeliness maintains course integrity, a sense of urgency, and the social benefits of a class cohort.

Cheaper Cost to Students

Meaningful innovation in any field requires improvement to come simultaneously with cost reduction. Moore's law is the famous observation by Gordon Moore, of the computer chip manufacturer Intel, that over the life of computing hardware the number of transistors on integrated circuits doubles approximately every two years. Economics actually "dictates" the law as originally stated: chips must not only get faster and smaller but get faster and smaller while also minimizing cost (Moore, 1965). An iPad would be far less useful not only if it were the size of a refrigerator but also if it cost millions of dollars.

The need to hold down college costs likewise offers a prime rationale for doing things differently. And broad-access institutions, serving lower-income students with fewer dollars per head, feel this impetus most keenly. Or at least they should.

Universities in the real world seem to conduct their accounting instead by Bowen's rule: they get all the money they can and spend all the money they can get. The large for-profit universities like Kaplan and Phoenix follow the same rule. Despite the lower costs of online delivery, they tend to set their tuition at the maximum rate allowable by student loan limits, getting close to 90 percent of their funding from federal student aid—essentially making them federal contractors (Senate Committee on Health, Education, Labor, and Pensions, 2012).

Over the past thirty years, public broad-access institutions have responded to cuts in state spending by raising tuition while putting less money into instruction and more into administration (Desrochers & Wellman, 2011). As tuition has risen at double the rate of inflation for four-year colleges, graduation rates have stagnated (Lewin, 2011).

Under this regime, new technologies—whiteboards and clickers in lecture halls, high-speed Internet in residence halls, massive enterprise-based software systems, audiovisual recordings of classes—have added costs without subtracting any to speak of (Desrochers & Wellman, 2011).

Cost and Technology: Three Bites of the Apple

A few programs are showing a different way forward. Technology offers paths to cost savings that maintain or improve teaching and learning. Originating at Stanford and MIT in early 2012, the massive open online course (MOOC) movement ushered in a new era of visibility and awareness—not to say a craze—for the transformative force of technology in higher education. Although the first era of hybrid higher education belonged to the corporate for-profits at the bottom of the prestige totem pole, the entry of most of the Ivy League into partnership with the for-profit MOOC platform Coursera during 2012 changed the game considerably. For the first time, higher education felt itself obliged to take technology seriously. But where to begin?

For many, the first bite of the apple is sharing and reuse of digital course content. The second bite is learning models that replace paid instructor, staff, and administrative time with a combination of digital tutors and social platforms that increase the role of peers in learning and assessment. The third, most radical bite challenges the very notion of "seat time," improving efficiency of the entire system while encouraging learners, with sufficient support, to take a more active role in identifying and pursuing their goals. Technology supports strategies such as centralized course planning, streamlining of degree programs, cutting administrative overhead, data-driven instruction, competency-based learning, credit by portfolio and credit by exam.

In March 2013, the U.S. Department of Education invited colleges to submit programs for consideration under Title IV aid that do not rely on the credit hour. The stated goal of President Obama is to encourage colleges to innovate in controlling costs while serving students admirably. The new competency-based programs are all online or hybrid. College for America, operated by the private nonprofit Southern New Hampshire University, and the for-profit Capella University's FlexPath were the first two programs to get permission from the federal government to award degrees based on tests, papers, and other assignments rather than class time. Other major competency-based efforts at public institutions include the UW Flexible Option, a project of the University of Wisconsin Extension, which launched in the fall of 2013, and Northern Arizona University, which is partnering with Pearson Education.

Most of these programs pattern themselves after WGU in important ways. WGU, as mentioned earlier, represents all three bites of the apple when it comes to cost cutting. Students work through self-paced material designed with input from subject matter experts and corporate board members such as AT&T and Oracle. They always have the option of earning credit by passing an assessment. There are no professors per se.

"Our goal is to increase productivity fast enough to give a better education without having to raise tuition," says chancellor Bob Mendenhall (personal communication, October 3, 2012). The institution pushes efficiency through new technologies—for example, they just moved from administering exams at test centers to virtual proctoring, verifying identities through webcam observation and biometrics. Meanwhile, they carefully track metrics on student engagement, performance, satisfaction, and success, including independent tools such as the National Survey of Student Engagement and the Collegiate Learning Assessment.

In the 2011–2012 academic year, the governors of Indiana, Washington, and Texas each invited WGU to integrate with their public university systems by opening virtual branch campuses. Not lost on these states, surely, is that WGU is completely self-sustaining on tuition of $6,000 a year with no outside funding—a figure that has remained flat for five years, during which time tuition at the average public university rose 4 to 6 percent each year (College Board, 2013).

Not every institution can or should be a WGU. The college focuses on older adults who already have a chosen career. More than three quarters are already working full time. They are a self-selecting group with the high self-motivation and sufficient technical skills to participate in online learning. The university offers programs in only four disciplines, with limited attention to the liberal arts or sciences, and no research. The state governments that have adopted WGU into their "family" of public institutions, as Indiana's governor Mitch Daniels puts it (WGU Indiana, 2010), as well as the new competency-based programs like those at the University of Wisconsin, see the model as filling a gap, not providing a comprehensive solution for broader access. "We have between 750,000 and a million people in Wisconsin who have some college but no degree," the Wisconsin system's president, Kevin P. Reilly, told me. "According to surveys by our extension department, about 60,000 of them would go back to school right now if they didn't have to quit their jobs, put their dog into a kennel and move into a dorm to do it" (quoted in Kamenetz, 2013).

Dropout rates are higher in online courses, and underprepared students are often especially disadvantaged by the format (Bell & Federman, 2013). Broad-access institutions that serve more traditional-age or remedial-level students may stop at one or two bites of the apple of technology: by adopting open content or accreditation policies for open learning, by including blended learning options in a face-to-face classroom, or by accepting online courses in an on-campus degree program.

Digital Content

Traditional college textbooks cost typical full-time students around $900 per semester (Allen, 2010). For community college students, that is similar to their tuition. Over the past decade there has been a growing international movement, headed by the OpenCourseWare Consortium, to create digital open educational resources (OER) that are licensed under a Creative Commons license, permitting free remixing, reuse, and redistribution digitally at a marginal cost of approximately $0.0007 per copy (Allen, 2010).

Since early 2012, there has been a new brand of free digital resource on the block: the MOOC. Offered first by professors at Stanford and MIT (building on earlier work at Brigham Young, Canada's Athabasca University, and elsewhere), a MOOC is a sequence of video lectures often broken up into five- to ten-minute chunks, interspersed with quick recall questions, longer assignments, and a final exam (Milliron, 2012). All of this material is free and accessible through a website with social features, such as a message board and wiki, that can accommodate tens of thousands, even 250,000 students, at once. Once such a course is created, it can be run infinite times, with additional costs limited to the cost of servers and live support.

Coursera, a for-profit venture started by two Stanford professors, has partnered with 107 leading international universities to enroll 5.2 million users as of October 2013, offering over five hundred courses (see Coursera, 2013); edX is a joint nonprofit venture of Harvard, MIT, Berkeley, and the University of Texas at Austin; and Udacity has an original curriculum created by professors at Stanford and elsewhere (Pappano, 2012). Each is offering its materials largely for free, without accreditation. (Only edX courses are technically "open," meaning the software platform on which they are published and the content therein remains open source and licensed by Creative Commons; rules for remixing and reuse of course content vary from platform to platform. The Saylor Foundation, Peer to Peer University, and Codecademy have offered an open "mechanical MOOC" that remixes material available around the web to construct a course in the programming language Python.)

MOOCs are currently causing a huge stir throughout the world of higher education (Pappano, 2012). The *New York Times* reported that Helen Dragas, the University of Virginia (UVA) board member responsible for the summary dismissal of President Teresa Sullivan, forwarded an article about Coursera to a board colleague with the subject line "Why we can't afford to wait" (Rice, 2012). The reinstated Sullivan announced that UVA would partner with Coursera.

For a small percentage of nontraditional students, MOOC platforms may constitute the first viable and radically cheap alternative for undergraduate and graduate study and professional development. Coursera founder Andrew Ng reports that more than 80 percent of users already hold a bachelor's degree or equivalent. The successful students I have talked to are remarkable for their intelligence, curiosity, and self-motivation. These are often working adults, often in other countries, who are supplementing or enhancing an existing university. Anuj Kumar, twenty-eight, of Bangalore, has an Indian master's degree in computer science and spent four years working at Oracle; he took a Stanford-based Machine Learning course to assist him in starting a business. Dennis Cahillane, twenty-nine, found no work as an attorney despite holding a law degree from the University of Chicago. So he embarked on an intensive self-study of Stanford computer science classes, as well as an internship at a nonprofit, and was employed as a computer programmer within nineteen months.

These are wonderful success stories. But broad-access institutions by definition serve the majority of students, not merely the most self-directed and motivated, let alone those who already have a degree. For most students free online courses, while exciting, do not constitute a complete solution to the problem of rising college costs. For one thing, every MOOC platform has reported attrition rates of 75 to 95 percent for individual courses—not too much worse than most community colleges but still a troubling statistic. And the courses are not yet organized into full curricula. Besides, "free" MOOC platforms are currently supported by a combination of venture capital and investments from participating universities. They are beginning to implement business models, which may include advertising, data collection on students, or charging students a fee of $50 to $100 to certify completion of a particular course.

That said, paths from MOOC to college credit for nontraditional students are already clearly marked. In November 2012, Coursera announced that the American Council on Education would evaluate and recommend a selection of courses through their College Credit Recommendation Service, meaning students will be able to redeem Coursera courses, in theory, for credit at thousands of institutions (Coursera, n.d.).

Soon we will see more broad-access institutions leveraging their campus resources to guide, motivate, support, and certify students participating in free online courses, and adopting free best-of-breed MOOCs as a supplement, extension, or substitute for their own curricular development. "Does it really make sense to have thousands of community-college instructors developing the same courses?" asks Daphne Koller, Stanford professor and founder of Coursera. "We see this as an easy, very natural direction for the world to take" (Kamenetz, 2012b).

Completion

Thirty-seven million Americans have some college credits and no degree. Open learning resources present a chance to glean tens of millions of new graduates at the lowest possible cost by offering flexible reentry points for adults who have already begun their educational journeys.

In 2011, the nonprofit Council for Adult and Experiential Learning (CAEL) launched LearningCounts.org as a national service for prior learning assessment (PLA). Anyone can call and speak to an advisor to learn about their options for receiving college credit for prior learning, either through an exam program like the American Council on Education's credit recommendation service, the College-Level Examination Program (CLEP), or directly through LearningCounts' online portfolio class. Their six-week course costs $500 plus

$50 for each credit you want to have evaluated. LearningCounts.org has partnered with hundreds of universities that agree to accept their credits to enhance their use of prior learning. (For the LearningCounts.org company profile, see Council for Adult and Experiential Learning, n.d.)

Prior Learning

Prior learning assessment (PLA), the awarding of college credit through exams or portfolios, has been around for decades but is rarely used outside the advanced placement (AP) exam. A 2010 CAEL study of over sixty thousand students at forty-eight colleges and universities found that participation in prior learning assessment has a dramatic effect on graduation rates and time to degree (Council for Adult Experiential Learning, 2010). The students saved between two and a half and ten months in their time to graduation through PLA. Even those who did not graduate accumulated more credits than non-PLA students. Most PLA participants earned a degree within seven years, compared to 21 percent of non-PLA students. The differences persisted after accounting for the level of academic preparation, the income levels of the students, and the type of college. Other studies have found that students who create portfolios gain insight into how they learn best and confidence that helps them become more engaged and successful students.

Prior learning assessment is a ready path for colleges to domesticate the free and wild learning going on in open provinces of the web. Wayne Mackintosh directs the International Center for Open Education at Otago Polytechnic in New Zealand and is the founder of the Open Educational Resources University (OERu). OERu is committed to developing assessments and accreditation for learning accomplished through the use of open educational resources. "It's a simple concept aimed to provide free learning for all students worldwide and start tackling the obstacles," says Mackintosh (Kamenetz, 2011b). "Given the technology we have combined with free content licensing, it's certainly possible to provide learning materials for degree programs for free." So far, OERU counts eighteen anchor partners on five continents, including SNHU, Empire State College, and Thomas Edison State College in the United States (WikiEducator, 2012).

Getting rusty or reluctant learners back into the college system will take finesse and a redeployment of human resources into coaching, mentoring, and motivation. Part of the public college system of New York, Empire State College is a national leader in prior learning assessment and an instructive model for broad-access institutions that seek the hybrid path. It offers both online and on-campus programs in several locations around the state. Of Empire State's twenty thousand students, 5 to 10 percent a year participate in prior learning assessment (Kamenetz, 2011e).

Students have earned college credit for running a business, military training, professional licenses and certifications, or even hobbies such as gardening or theater. Students who want this kind of credit must take an online workshop where they reflect on their learning and create a "portrait" of their experiences, which may be a written essay or multimedia presentation documenting what they have learned and how it satisfies the college's requirements. Adjunct faculty mentors earn $100 to $150 for working with a student to create a portfolio and then evaluating it, and outside experts may review it. An adjunct might earn $2,000 for teaching a four-credit course, so if there are fewer than twenty students in that course, PLA is cheaper. That savings is passed on to the student, who pays $80 to $100 when seeking four credits through PLA (Kamenetz, 2011e).

Badges and Microcertifications

A badge, familiar to all scouts, is defined as any recognition of a specific skill, competency, or achievement. In the past decade, there has been increasing interest in badges that recognize the learning going on in informal and especially digital domains. The Mozilla Foundation's Open Badges project was initially developed to salute web development skills (Mozilla, 2011). It is now building a shared, free open-source infrastructure to enable libraries, museums, after-school programs, labor unions, and other providers or verifiers of learning to create badges that can be earned and displayed by anyone across the web. A badge could be awarded based on challenges created by the issuer or by peer assessment, or it could be self-verified by being linked transparently to the accomplishment itself. In 2012, the MacArthur Foundation, in partnership with Mozilla, sponsored a national competition for badges for lifelong learning (MacArthur Foundation, 2012). One winner was the Department of Veterans Affairs BadgesWork for Vets program, created to "help veterans leverage their military training and unique skill sets by developing badges that visually represent their military training while serving in the US military" (Humanities, Arts, Science, and Technology Alliance and Collaboratory, n.d.).

While badges represent an edge case, they are not the first or only alternative postsecondary credential. States and hundreds of nonprofit industry associations in the United States offer thousands of licenses and certifications to qualify people in specific careers, from state-licensed massage therapist to LEED-certified green building specialist. These vary widely in quality and their value in various professional circles, but an open digital infrastructure where they could be compared along various dimensions could go a long way toward enhancing their visibility, transparency, and interoperability—and therefore their value to nontraditional learners.

Hurdles to the Finish Line

The tens of millions of Americans who have started college and not finished it constitute our best hope for improving the national graduation rate. The current edifice of higher education blocks the "swirling" of these millions in their path toward a degree. The rigid conformity to a vanished population who entered college at age eighteen and exited at twenty-two is not helping students as they are today.

Prior learning assessment and other kinds of competency-based assessments are at odds with a regulatory system based on the credit hour, which is now loosening. "The traditional system has been a barrier," says President Chris Bustamante at Rio Salado Community College (personal communication, October 1, 2012). "We'd like to see more opportunities for prior learning assessment, where we can cut the time to a degree or certificate, and especially in the developmental education mode—being able to diagnose and modularize curriculum to address gaps in learning rather than starting from A."

The first round of grant winners in the $2 billion Department of Education grant previously mentioned seek to improve efficiency. For example, every community college in Arkansas is banding together in a consortium to accelerate program completions by 15 percent by restructuring 146 certificate and associate degree programs (Arkansas Association of Two-Year Colleges, 2012). The twenty-two colleges, led by Northwest Arkansas Community College in Bentonville, plan to work together to streamline the programs to reduce time and credit to completion rates, and improve student advisement so students can make better choices and achieve their goals more efficiently.

Customization

While the stereotypical eighteen-year-old, upper-middle-class, high-scoring college freshman might be expected to conform to the requirements of an

institution, broad-access institutions are charged instead to meet the requirements of their students. The Platonic ideal in higher education is a close relationship between a tutor and student where a young mind is kindled and
drawn out, developing a personal philosophy and view of the good life. Unfortunately, the budgetary constraints of mass higher education have led to its expansion along industrial lines: large classes and standardized assessments that
leave little room for the idealized human encounter.

For thirty years or more, broad-access institutions have been spending less
money on instruction, cutting costs by increasing class sizes or putting less
experienced, lower-paid teachers in front of students. By contrast, the web
offers students infinite office hours at no additional cost—the opportunity to
seek multiple explanations of a stubborn math or science concept, via anima-
tion, text, audio, and video, until comprehension dawns. Many learning platforms offer embedded assessment to provide immediate feedback, prompting
spaced recall, which has advantages for memorization. And artificial intelligence informs digital textbooks that learn as the student interacts with
them, offering material and exercises at an individualized pace and sequence.
Finally, software systems can aid college counseling staff in assessing, tracking, and responding to students' needs. Digital resources can free up humans
to offer a more personal experience to students.

Mass customization is a paradox that the web nonetheless supplies almost
effortlessly in every area of our lives, from movie suggestions to finding a
nearby restaurant recommended by your Facebook friends. A digital lecture
can be paused and rewound again and again. You can move through the material as quickly or slowly as you like. And reams of supplemental material are
only a click away.

Daphne Koller, founder of Coursera, told me why she believes the online
MOOC learning experience is preferable to the large lecture courses she was
used to teaching at Stanford. "When you're giving a lecture and you stop to
ask a question, 50 percent of the class are scribbling away and didn't hear you,
another 20 percent are on Facebook, and one smarty-pants in the front row
blurts out the answer and you feel good" (Kamenetz, 2012b). By contrast, on
Coursera, when each video lecture chunk comes to the end, the viewer must
answer a few multiple-choice questions to continue. Koller and her cofounder,
Andrew Ng, drew on neuroscience research showing that these instant-
retrieval questions enhance memory and comprehension more than complex
questions answered later. And with the Coursera course, there is no sitting

in the back. "This way," Koller says, "every single person needs to answer the question and retrieve the information."

Adaptive Learning: Computer as Tutor

Adaptive learning designates software that takes in data on the learner as he or she views content and answers questions, much as a video game moves the player on to harder and faster levels. An adaptive learning platform can offer hints and encouragement, much like a tutor, while storing information on the pace at which you learn and which specific concepts you have trouble with, for your own insight and that of a professor or curriculum developer. Knewton is a leading for-profit company in the adaptive learning field. What founder Jose Ferreira calls a "data interoperability engine" promises to take any kind of educational content, break it down to the concept level, and present each concept to students at exactly the sequence and pace they need while giving detailed feedback on performance to students, professors, and curriculum designers (Kamenetz, 2011d).

Using content from large textbook publisher Pearson, Knewton built a math "College Readiness" course that is both remedial and diagnostic (Knewton, 2011). It is online and self-paced. Students can take it before registration, with the goal of placing into a regular college math class, or in their first semester. Tens of thousands of students at Arizona State, Penn State University (PSU), University of Nevada, Las Vegas (UNLV), the State University of New York (SUNY), and the small private Mount St. Mary's University tried "College Readiness" for the first time in the fall of 2012 (Knewton, 2011).

Customized Paths: Computer as Advisor

The new normal for students is transferring from institution to institution, stopping out or dropping out more than once along the way to graduation. Technology can help manage and clarify these movements, handling transfer credits and articulation issues that our educational bureaucracies do not find easy, and mapping the path to graduation more clearly for students. Software systems based on customer relationship management can also support counseling and advising services, providing a more personal level of contact that can help students succeed.

Rio Salado Community College in Arizona has forty-two thousand online students, making it the largest online public community college, plus twenty-seven thousand students "on the ground" (V. Smith, 2011). Their students are

100 percent nontraditional, predominantly lower-income, Hispanic, and first-generation; they partner with high schools and serve adult GED learners and even prisoners. They have created RioLearn, a customized course management and student services system, which alerts faculty when a student's attendance slips or he or she misses assignments and sends the students text message reminders. This year, a redesign to the system offers integrated news, alerts, and new social networking features, and a single sign-on for all campus systems. They are currently testing a program called PACE (Progress and Course Engagement) that can predict with 70 percent probability which students are likely to drop out within the first eight days of class (Parry, 2012).

Diana Oblinger of Educause, in her book *Game Changers* (2012), cites the STAR program at the University of Hawaii, Degree Compass at Austin Peay State University, Valencia College's LifeMap, and Central Piedmont Community College's Online Student Profile system as the best examples of the applications of IT to drive better student decision making, by recommending courses, transfers, majors, or degrees based on the choices of other students.

Connection

Distance education does not exist. I have interviewed dozens of students in online, traditional, and hybrid programs over the years, and without exception they did their learning while seated in a physical place, mere inches from the course material. While I have been responsible for promulgating the term *DIY U*, I likewise never meant to imply that learning is a solitary activity. From the time we speak our first words, the motivation to learn is social. Broad-access education that is scalable and adaptive depends more than ever before on strong relationships between students and their professors, their peers, and local and professional communities. This is especially true for nontraditional students, who are more likely to need higher education for social mobility, which means forming new connections beyond their existing families, friends, and communities. The DIY community itself is a great example of how learning advances through connections.

Connections with Peers: The Crowdsourced TA

Open learning environments are making the key role of peers in learning ever more visible. Coursera is the first major MOOC platform to offer humanities courses alongside technical topics. Founders Daphne Koller and Andrew

Ng considered and swiftly rejected the notion of "robo-grading" of essays and other written assignments. Instead they have pioneered and tested a method called *calibrated peer review*. My aunt took the MOOC Modern American Poetry, taught by Al Filreis at the University of Pennsylvania. She wrote a paper, submitted it, and received four other students' papers for grading. Each of the forty-thousand-odd students in the course will have their papers graded by four classmates. Software programs will compare and track the grades to try to resolve discrepancies, and human sampling by teaching assistants (TAs) will provide an additional control on the process. Meanwhile, students like my aunt are learning even more by reading other students' work.

Over the past few decades, much research has shown that cooperative small-group learning can make the difference in students' success or failure in a variety of contexts and subjects. Asking and answering questions is a fundamental human activity; "How to" is one of the most popular query strings on Google and YouTube. Sites like Stackoverflow.com and Mathoverflow.com are like buzzing hives where practitioners and students post and reply to questions, collectively advancing their knowledge. Websites like OpenStudy and Peer 2 Peer University offer the chance to convene study groups on particular topics or assignments for the length of a course or for an afternoon. Message boards and wikis are key to the success of MOOC platforms; students use them to arrange study groups in various languages and time zones, and the platforms reward students for participating and answering each other's questions. In one iteration of a Coursera course, students received responses to their questions in the forum from other students within an average of twenty-two minutes—responses that, the program showed, helped them arrive at the correct answer. Most students in traditional programs, meanwhile, resist the clunky interfaces provided by enterprise learning management systems such as Blackboard and seek support from each other via Facebook.

Connected Teaching: Collaborating with Watson

An emerging theme across the economy is the use of people to do what only people can do, while technology does what it does best. The majority of costs for public colleges is in salaries; a likely trend over the coming decades is for salaries to remain static while job titles and descriptions change greatly. Large numbers of web developers with curricular expertise will be required to create and update software systems for learning, counseling, and administration.

When information becomes a commodity and course materials can be delivered in multimedia, often that means the best use of faculty resources is not in professorial expert mode but in the supporting roles of mentor, advisor, librarian, and coach—all of whom will use software to do their jobs better.

Mentors take a warm ongoing interest in learners, helping them develop a plan, stick to it, and overcome obstacles. Advisors relate students' interests to the formal requirements of schools and workplaces. Librarians help people frame their own research questions and acquaint them with the resources available for pursuing them. Coaches are experts in motivation, goal-setting, and helping teams form and function.

At Empire State College, enrolling students begin with an initial two-hour phone conversation with a mentor to plan an individualized degree program based on their goals, experiences, and needs.

The mentor helps students match their goals and interests to the framework of academic programs offered by Empire State to create a personal degree plan. This may be designed around a problem in society such as suicide or local food supplies. Assuming that most students come with previous courses and other experience, the mentor can help the students figure out where this fits into the new degree plan. The college is investing its resources in building closer one-on-one advising relationships.

At Western Governors University, there are no traditional professors. Students make their way through material with the help of PhD expert "course mentors" and personal "student mentors." While the software systems give them insights into the students' progress, it is the student mentors' job to cheerlead and handhold via Skype, phone, or e-mail. These professionals are rewarded based on their students' performance. Assessments are graded by an outside group to ensure the integrity of the process.

At SNHU's online COCE program, faculty advisors stay with students from their first application throughout their careers. The advisers use a software system that tracks a slew of factors predictive of student success, from the amount of time since their last college class to the length of an average post on a class discussion board. The same system is used to evaluate the performance of professors: Do they respond to student posting? Are they present for their virtual office hours? Since the software and advising system was adopted, retention from the first to second year has doubled since 2008, up from 35 percent to 69 percent (Kamenetz, 2012c).

Inside Track is a freestanding for-profit that offers coaching by telephone as a service to students at several dozen institutions, divided evenly between four-year institutions serving traditional-age students, nonprofit institutions serving working adults both online and on campus, and for-profit, online institutions. No matter the setting, "ultimately what we're focused on is making sure the student is able to articulate a vision for what they're getting out of school and where they want to be when they graduate," says Dave Jarrat, Inside Track's vice president of marketing, "helping them develop some contingency planning for what might get in the way, and ongoing support and encouragement to get them through the tough times" (personal communication, September 6, 2012). Planning may include things like arranging backup child care or transportation or researching the best way to transfer from an associate to a bachelor's degree. In over fifty-five studies, Inside Track's services have been shown to improve graduation rates by an average of 15 percent (Bettinger & Baker, 2011).

Concentrating on coaching, advising, and mentoring brings to the forefront the emotional dimension of the mission at broad-access institutions. "There's a lot of fear" among adult, low-performing, and returning students, says Yvonne Simon at SNHU. "Targeting the underserved market means figuring out how to reach those folks who had a bad experience with education in first grade" (personal communication, 2012).

Community Connections: Microfinance Model of Education

In 2006 Muhammad Yunus won the Nobel Peace Prize for his work founding Grameen Bank. He empowered the poor, uneducated, and disenfranchised women of Bangladesh by extending capital where large banks were unwilling to go. He ensured that his loans would be paid back by leveraging the women's existing social capital: women joined groups that were collectively responsible for the debts of each member. This model has been followed throughout the field of microfinance. It is starting to emerge as a new hybrid prototype of digital education: education that starts in the workplace and uses employers and other social ties to provide the connection, support, and motivation a nontraditional learner requires, while the digital resources are provided centrally at low cost.

SNHU president Paul LeBlanc started the Innovation Lab, known as the I-Lab, to create the business model that would put his own university out of business. His new online competency-based degree program, College for America, is designed for students to access multiple kinds of support: peers and faculty experts online, employers and coworkers who are fellow students in person. "You're a line worker at Stonyfield Farm taking a math course trying to finish your college degree," LeBlanc offered by way of example. "We will work with Stonyfield to have someone in its accounting department do brown-bag-lunch tutoring" (Kamenetz, 2012c).

SNHU's campus also hosts the third chapter of College Unbound, a new program that anchors the learning experience for nontraditional students with strong connections to peers, mentors, and a workplace all at once. Working intensively with faculty mentors and their peers in a small group of twelve or fifteen, College Unbound students create a personalized learning plan tailored as much as possible to a personal passion and designed to dovetail with a job. Students can work full time while participating in the program—College Unbound was founded by Dennis Littky, who also founded the Big Picture network of charter schools, which use a similar community placement model. In three to four years, the students, who are primarily in their mid-twenties to early thirties and the first in their families to go to college, will earn a bachelor's degree accredited by either SNHU or Roger Williams College in Rhode Island. The cost for the program, all told, is $10,000 per student.

The hybrid aspect of College Unbound comes from the individualized research and exploration each student must do, a great deal of which happens online. "Unlike a traditional classroom, where the teacher gives you the textbooks and the assignments, we have to frame our own essential questions and get all the information we need on our own," eighteen-year-old Ebony Byas, an SNHU College Unbound student who is exploring child psychology while interning at an Easter Seals day-care center, told me (Kamenetz, 2012c).

One can easily imagine a public university operating like a digital Oxford, in which faculty mentors, advisors, or coaches focus their efforts on helping students build a personal learning plan, relate their studies to a broader academic framework, and form teams for mutual support and ongoing feedback and evaluation.

Call it the microfinance model of education: an online curriculum coordinated and supplemented with structured support from students' existing employers, community organizations, and family and friends. It is a lower-cost model that concentrates resources in supporting students' personal growth. With its state chapters, WGU is already working to help students form real-world connections; their Texas chapter held ice cream socials across the state this past year so that students and mentors could meet each other for the first time. LearnerWeb, an adult basic education program out of Portland State University, and HOPE, a network of K–12 charter schools, each combine an on-line curriculum with in-person mentorship by community groups, churches, and charities. Portmont College at Mount St. Mary's, funded in part by the Gates Foundation, also combines an online curriculum with periodic visits to campus to participate in group projects and presentations and to bond with mentors and classmates. Starting in Denver, the college plans to grow nation-wide through a network of local on-the-ground partners. Kepler University, a project of the nonprofit Generation Rwanda, combines in-person seminar-style teaching in a small, supportive learning community with a competency-based degree program built on a backbone of MOOCs to offer a university education to young Africans at $1,000 a year.

We already see nontraditional students struggling to juggle low-wage jobs with their educations; what if the various threads of their lives could enhance each other, rather than working at cross-purposes?

What distinguishes this from traditional tuition benefits is the idea of companies—or trade unions or other labor market intermediaries or com-munity groups—using their existing social networks to promote learning and success. Starbucks, for example, is partnering with LearningCounts, pro-viding tuition assistance, while the organization provides career and educa-tion advising, plus assessments that can allow baristas to earn course credit for their training in restaurant hospitality, basic health, even coffee roast-ing (Council for Adult Experiential Learning, 2010). They could take a step further and provide their employees an opportunity to form small learning groups together, plus free coffee and Wi-Fi and a place to study.

Reputation-Based Networks

For nontraditional students, the foremost aim of higher education is a better life, and more often than not a better job. To this end, a diploma and a résumé are no longer sufficient. They are inert documents whose usefulness declines with each passing second.

Instead people need a way for work to find them. When their name is typed in a Google search bar, it needs to return a rich story about skills and character. Students must express themselves artfully on reputation-based networks, sites where people immerse themselves in enthusiasms and exhibit their accomplishments: writing, computer programs, photography, web de-sign, and international development. One leading example is Behance, where creative workers such as photographers, graphic designers, and illustrators can upload multimedia portfolios. These are seen, commented on, and voted up or down by the community. Portfolios that get the most recognition are easier to find. Advertising and consumer companies like Saatchi and Saatchi, JWT, R/GA, Crispin, Ogilvy, Nike, Apple, Facebook, Zappos, Target, and Netflix all actively recruit from the site (Kamenetz, 2011c).

A second reputation-based network is GitHub. The largest software code-hosting site in the world, GitHub was created as a place for open-source programmers to work together on code (see GitHub, n.d.). It now has two million members. Companies such as Twitter recruit developers from GitHub. Instead of just looking at a résumé or school transcript, they can use the site to get far more detailed information about a person's skills and interests by looking at their actual record of work and collaboration. Stackoverflow, mentioned earlier in this chapter as a peer learning forum, also works as a reputation-based network. Engineers gain credit with their peers by being helpful in answering questions, which can lead to employment.

Yet another fascinating network that has emerged as an alternative path to legitimacy for thousands of creative professionals is Kickstarter. Anyone can post a project or product and request pledges from donors. If you do not meet the goal you have set by a deadline, the money is not collected. This enables an individual with a good idea to find funds without having to go through a grant maker or other institution. Indeed, Kickstarter facilitated more funding directly for the arts than the National Endowment for the Arts in 2011 (Franzen, 2012).

On reputation-based networks, people connect based on shared interests, not shared backgrounds. They are rich in the type of "weak ties" that have been shown to be most useful in finding employment. Simply by joining one, aspiring professionals in any field can have access to what theorists call *legitimate peripheral participation*, learning the language and concepts that are part of the implicit information needed to negotiate a particular community of practice.

Careers from the Cloud

Broad-access institutions would benefit from partly outsourcing their career services to the cloud, making participation on reputation-based networks a necessary part of their curriculum and requiring students to publish work for evaluation by the open web. Some institutions are even using artificial intelligence to forecast workforce needs. Jobs for the Future, a nonprofit dedicated to expanding opportunities for low-income youth through education, has an initiative called Credentials That Work. They commissioned a software engine to crawl job websites like Monster.com, CareerBuilder, and LinkedIn looking for phrases that map to key skills and competencies. The idea is to get labor market information in the hands of community colleges more quickly so they can share it in turn with job seekers and use it to update credentials and programs. "There's no question that any training institution is up against a more dynamic, fast-moving economy," says program director John Dorrer. "In the past, the data was aged and we were looking in the rear-view mirror. That doesn't work for the active job seeker today" (Kamenetz, 2012a).

Conclusion: The Constantly Arriving Future

The phrase *digital divide* expresses a legitimate fear: that the latest consumer iGadget, with its several-hundred-dollar price tag and six-month obsolescence cycle, will burnish the prospects of elite students who already have every advantage while leaving the majority further out in the cold. This chapter has provided a flock of examples to counter this perception. Digital technology, carefully designed, can address the prime needs of the nontraditional student and thus may redress the significant social and economic problem of equitable access to higher education in the United States.

To accomplish this aim, public and nonprofit institutions must take the lead as they always have in extending the franchise of education. They must dedicate themselves to designing, adopting, and testing the best technologies and collaborating with for-profit companies and nonprofit foundations that are doing the same. The good news is that with our completion rates currently so low, and spending on higher education so high by international standards, there is a lot of headroom to improve outcomes without greatly increasing overall spending. The focus should be on reallocating resources to investments in the future, not on finding new sources of money that will not be forthcoming in the current climate.

Each of the innovative institutions mentioned in this chapter—and there are many more—is working to keep costs low, keep educational standards high (which often requires, first, better defining and measuring these standards), and maintain a professional team flexible enough to be open to what is next. The hybridization of higher education requires more than a particular set of tools—those will change again nine months from now. It requires a new mindset that can preserve the ideals of the past in a constantly evolving future.

3

BOOM, REGULATE, CLEANSE, REPEAT

For-Profit Colleges' Slow but Inevitable Drive
Toward Acceptability

Paul Fain and Doug Lederman

For-profit colleges are not new. Small business and secretarial colleges date to the 1800s and in some ways resemble today's neighborhood cosmetology schools. But national, degree-granting for-profit chains with scores of office-park campuses and huge online enrollments are a comparatively recent, and controversial, addition to the field of U.S. higher education.

The modern for-profit college and their mom-and-pop relatives differ from traditional higher education in one crucial way: they pay taxes and return profits to their owners. Most of the major chains are publicly traded and have access to Wall Street capital. Others, particularly regional for-profits, are privately held, with venture capital and equity firms having a big stake in both varieties. This new breed of for-profit emerged in earnest during the last forty years, and the growth has been particularly dramatic in the most recent decade, largely because of the increasing feasibility of online education, a huge influx of federal aid, and deregulation during the George W. Bush administration. As recently as 2000, the number of students enrolled in degree-granting for-profit colleges and universities was 450,000, less than 3 percent of the total domestic enrollment. Today those figures stand at nearly 2.4 million and roughly 10 percent, respectively—with one in every four students pouring into higher education over that decade enrolling at a for-profit institution. Between 2007 and 2010, one of every three new college students enrolled at a for-profit (Knapp, Kelly-Reid, & Ginder, 2012). As seen in Figures 3.1 and 3.2, the for-profit share is even greater when one looks at all students enrolled in

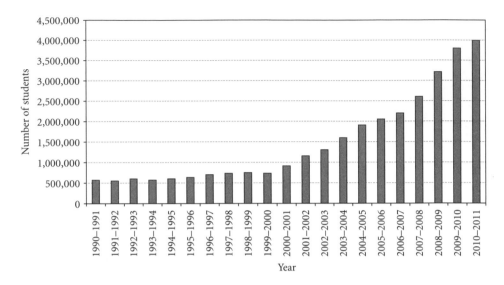

FIGURE 3.1. For-profit enrollment, all Title IV–eligible colleges, 1990–1991 to 2010–2011. Source of data: IPEDS database.

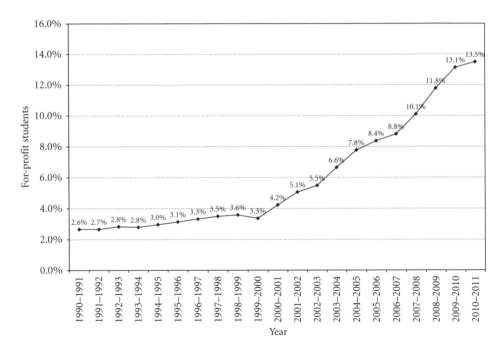

FIGURE 3.2. For-profit students as proportion of all enrollees in Title IV–eligible colleges. Source of data: IPEDS database.

institutions eligible to award federal financial aid, with for-profit colleges enrolling a full 13.5 percent of all postsecondary students.

For-profit colleges are far from alone as powerful corporate entities in higher education; technology companies and major publishers, among others, also wield significant influence. As the roles some of these companies play shift, and in many cases grow—with former textbook publishers like Pearson now developing and hosting online course material, often powered by "adaptive" learning capabilities—some of them attract scrutiny, with concerns about their ownership and potential misuse of student data. But they largely fly under the radar compared to for-profit colleges, at which much more scorn is directed—the result of a mix of misbehavior by those institutions, competitive fears among traditional colleges, and an intense philosophical objection in some quarters that education and profit do not mix.

Still, there is little dispute that proprietary businesses are likely to continue to expand their share of the higher education field. The proprietary sector's explosive growth—as well as concerns about how that growth has been achieved and the quality and value of the education that students in the sector receive—have combined to put a bull's-eye on the back of the enterprise known (in the typically oversimplified fashion that characterizes much of our discourse) as for-profit higher education. Whereas supporters of the sector argue that the growth has been driven by market demand, institutional flexibility, curricular innovation, and a laserlike focus on students' needs, critics attribute it to hyperintensive marketing, an if-you're-breathing approach to recruitment and admissions, and a steadily growing supply of federal financial aid dollars, often a result of laissez-faire federal regulation. All of these have at times been true, to varying degrees.

The result has been a bumpy ride for the colleges, marked by a recurring cycle of growth and retrenchment. For-profits tend to rapidly increase their share of the higher education market and then recede when the feds tighten the rules. The sector is currently experiencing steep declines in enrollment and revenue. This multiyear slump is because of the recession, stepped-up competition by nonprofit colleges, and pricing problems for relatively expensive for-profits, as well as the continued scrutiny of the industry by the regulation-minded Obama administration and other federal lawmakers.

The repeated ebbs and flows have had a partisan flavor, with the industry benefiting when Republicans hold the reins and then warding off crackdowns led by Democrats. That arc has been developed through several cycles (and likely more to come) in which booming growth in enrollments and revenue are followed by intensified regulation that weeds out some of the weaker players but leaves those remaining, and the enterprise as a whole, ultimately stronger and edging closer in form and quality to the rest of higher education.

Not Your Father's For-Profit Sector

The looks on the faces of the lobbyists for the major associations of colleges said it all on a July 2005 day in a congressional office building. The House of Representatives higher education subcommittee had just approved legislation to renew the Higher Education Act, and while the representatives of public and private nonprofit colleges looked stricken, the lobbyists for for-profit colleges beamed. "It was a good day for us," said one. "We got almost everything we wanted" (quoted in Lederman, 2005).

The legislation approved that afternoon included provisions that would have softened the rule that requires for-profit colleges to derive at least 10 percent of their revenues from sources other than federal student aid and another that created a "single definition" of a postsecondary institution in federal law, ending a segregated approach that treated for-profit and nonprofit colleges differently. Some of the changes approved that day did not survive the negotiations that unfolded over the three additional, excruciating years it took to renew the Higher Education Act in 2008. But as a symbol of the political clout that for-profit colleges had accumulated since the sector took shape, through a mix of success, persuasion, and campaign contributions, that July day arguably represented a high-water mark.

The story of for-profit higher education is a financial story, a political/public policy story, and—oh, yes—an education story. Which of those prisms dominates the tale varies at different times of the sector's development and, of course, varies based on who is doing the telling. None can be ignored, but if one dominates heavily over the years, the picture probably is not fair or complete. The policies adopted by federal, state, and other regulators have irrevocably shaped—sometimes positively and sometimes negatively—the institutions' ability to educate their growing legions of students. And the colleges' success in persuading Wall Street and other investors (as well as employers who finance their workers' education) that private sector colleges can better educate adults and others long ill-served by traditional higher education has undoubtedly driven their growth. But in the long term, the success and viability of for-profit colleges—like their nonprofit peers—will ultimately be judged by how well they train and develop their students and the value they provide. That is the realm, though, that we have been (and to some extent continue to be) least able to judge.

Talking about "for-profit higher education" as a coherent entity is almost as misleading as assuming that all "private nonprofit colleges" or all "public colleges" are the same. The publicly traded Apollo Group, with its 270,000-student University of Phoenix (Apollo Group, 2013) and the 700-student Refrigeration School, Inc., on the outskirts of Phoenix, arguably have less in common than do UC-Berkeley and Laredo Community College, or Stanford University and West Virginia Wesleyan College. For-profit higher education has been around, in one form or another, for well more than a century, but over the last forty years it has developed into a diverse, complex sector with the same sorts of shadings that mark the parts of higher education with which Americans are more familiar.

Institutions like Bryant and Stratton College and Strayer's Business College cropped up in local communities to fill specific niches closely tied to economic needs, often in the form of business or secretarial schools. Federal funds first flowed to students at the institutions in the original GI Bill, and the number of for-profit institutions grew sharply over the next decade, as did concomitant concerns about their performance. But the story of today's recognizable for-profit higher education sector is more clearly traced to the early 1970s, when for-profit colleges first became eligible to award federal student grants and loans. For context, in 1970 eighteen thousand students were enrolled in degree-granting for-profit colleges (Aud et al., 2012, Table A-10-1).

The 1970s and 1980s saw the beginning of the boom-regulate-cleanse-repeat patterns that have taken hold since then. Significantly more enrollment and institutional growth occurred in for-profit colleges during those decades than elsewhere in higher education. Enrollment in the institutions roughly doubled every five years (on an admittedly small base), while it rose sharply (but proportionally far less) in public and private nonprofit institutions, to the point that by the late 1980s roughly 2.6 percent of all postsecondary students were enrolled at for-profits.

That initial big boom started the first of several major cycles of perceived abuses and very real crackdowns that for-profit higher education has experienced in recent years. Reports that a slew of fly-by-night schools had cropped up to try to tap into the federal student aid that attached to many low-income and minority students drove a high-profile investigation in 1991 by a U.S. Senate committee led by Georgia Democrat Sam Nunn. A series of hearings featured one trade school official in leg irons and others citing their Fifth Amendment right not to self-incriminate and produced evidence of students' heavy loan debt and disproportionately high default rates (Burd, 2009).

As enrollments at for-profit colleges began climbing much faster than those at other types of institutions, the questions of who was enrolling—and why—became more central. Throughout their existence, the institutions had been portrayed—and portrayed themselves—as focused on adult, working students whose schedules and life situations did not permit them to further their educations at traditional colleges with traditional curriculums offered in traditional formats. In many cases employers paid their tuitions. Night classes and the ready availability of parking spaces were key elements of the draw.

But over time, as the availability of federal student aid grew and the institutions became eligible to compete for more pots of it, they increasingly set their sights not just on the working adults who had historically been their targets but on other population segments that have historically been underserved by higher education—notably students from low-income families and underrepresented minority groups.

Since around this time, for-profit-college leaders have been able to point to data showing that they provide access to such students at greater rates than most other colleges. But whether the institutions serve those students or prey on them has been a perpetual argument. Are low-income students flocking to for-profit colleges because they have washed out of community colleges where they received little nurturing and guidance, or because they are bombarded with advertising from institutions that spend as much as a third of their budgets on marketing? Does the fact that minority and low-income students enroll at for-profit institutions at increasing rates mean that they are making sound decisions based on how they can expect to fare, or are they being taken advantage of in a marketplace in which data on outcomes and value (for all types of higher education institutions, not just for-profits) are imperfect, to be kind? Iterations of that argument intensified in this era and have not abated.

The findings of Nunn's investigation led Congress, in renewing the Higher Education Act in 1992, to impose new requirements on for-profit institutions, including a demand that they derive no more than 85 percent of their revenues from federal student aid, a prohibition on incentive-based compensation for student recruiters, and a new mechanism of severe penalties for colleges where significant proportions of student loan borrowers defaulted on their loans. Another provision, which reflected skepticism about new providers of higher education regardless of their tax status, prohibited institutions from awarding federal financial aid if more than half of their programs or students were online.

Nunn's investigation and the new rules produced some of the cleansing that policy makers hoped for, driving hundreds of low-quality providers out of the federal student aid programs or out of business entirely. Leaders of for-profit colleges complained that the rules also drowned many legitimate institutions, but it was inarguable that the changes pruned the industry in ways that left it stronger. Those who might have hoped to snuff out for-profit higher education entirely—and surely some wanted that—did not get their wish. Several of the largest for-profit companies, including Apollo Group's University of Phoenix and DeVry, used newfound investment capital from going public to increase their degreed offerings for working adults, and expanding their reach in some cases (as with Apollo's short-lived Axia College) to traditional-age students in general education programs. Significant consolidation also occurred, with a group of massive holding companies such as Career Education Corp., Corinthian Colleges, Inc., and Education Management Corp. buying up smaller chains and joining early pioneers Apollo and DeVry in creating companies on the publicly traded stock market.

Numbers help tell the story. After a few flat years in the wake of the new federal rules, for-profit enrollments began booming once again in the mid-1990s, rising from 576,000 in 1993–1994 (when they made up 2.8 percent of all students enrolled in Title IV–eligible institutions) to nearly 1.6 million (and 6.6 percent) in 2003–2004.

The growth did not stop there, with tacit encouragement from business-friendly lawmakers and, beginning in 2000, a Bush administration that the for-profit industry lobbied (and infiltrated) heavily. Between 1998 and 2002, several of the restrictions imposed in 1992 were rolled back, with the maximum proportion of revenues that an institution could derive from the government rising to 90 percent from 85 percent and the ban on incentive compensation being significantly watered down.

In 2006, the so-called 50 percent rule—the requirement that no more than 50 percent of an institution's students or programs could be online—fell by the wayside, and in 2008, the 90/10 rule was further liberalized (Dillon, 2006). That rule was obviously aimed at for-profits, which until recently have been synonymous with "online colleges" in the minds of both policy makers and the general public. This is no longer the case, however. And some nonprofits with large and growing online programs would have run afoul of the old 50 percent rule, including Liberty University and Southern New Hampshire University, among others. Those institutions owe much of their success online to the for-profits' playbook, and some nonprofit college leaders admit (grudgingly) to having studied Phoenix's approach, particularly its strategies for student support and the academic calendar, in terms of timing of course offerings and the length and frequency of terms (more on this later). Others have poached employees from for-profits, particularly these days as much of the sector has fallen on hard times.

Another set of changes that fueled the for-profit industry's growth during the last decade of the twentieth century occurred in another regulatory sphere, the world of higher education accreditation. To qualify for federal student aid, all institutions must be accredited by an agency recognized by the U.S. Department of Education, and for-profit colleges are no exception. For most of their history, though, the institutions were accredited by a set of agencies focused specifically on career-related training, rather than by the regional agencies that accredited most public and private nonprofit colleges.

A handful of major for-profit institutions, including the University of Phoenix, were granted accreditation by regional agencies as early as the late 1970s, but most chose not to seek it or were discouraged from doing so. In the mid-2000s, though, several for-profit colleges bought failing nonprofit campuses with the goal of turning them into launching pads for massive online programs. The most visible of those was Bridgepoint Education's 2005 purchase of Franciscan University of the Prairies, in Iowa (more on that to come later), but the practice was widely seen as an attempt by some for-profit providers to "buy" regional accreditation. (Some recruiters at for-profit colleges with regional accreditation have been known to boast that they offer students the "same accreditation as Harvard," a technically true statement.)

For-profits' business model also helped their competitive advantage during this recent period of growth, because the sector is set up to squeeze plenty of productivity out of its labor force. Tuition hikes have outpaced inflation for decades, and higher education has faced increasing pressure to control costs. That's not easy to do at traditional colleges, which typically have tenured professors and strong unions. For-profits lack both. So while nonprofit colleges have gradually converted their faculty mix to feature more lower-paid adjunct professors, amid plenty of controversy, for-profits have continued to hum along with cheap labor costs.

On a related note, for-profits have used economies of scale in curricular design to boost efficiency. Standardization is the name of the game at most major for-profits, where a course is devised centrally and then taught with relative uniformity by armies of adjuncts. While this mass-production style of course design has often been criticized for not standing up to the traditional ideal of giving control to professors and allowing them to play up to their strengths in teaching, it is inexpensive and replicable and works well online.

For-profits also led the way in catering to adult students with convenient academic offerings and support structures. The sector was the first to widely adopt new class "starts" all fifty-two weeks in the calendar, abandoning a se-mester schedule that is geared to traditional-age college students. For-profits have also been aggressive in offering night and weekend class times or even asynchronous online offerings. And Phoenix and others helped pioneer the online peer group model, where students work together on course material—a cost-effective way to boost online engagement.

These innovations, controversial as some may be, have increasingly mi-grated to the nonprofit sector. Take Western Governors University (WGU), a nonprofit that serves adult students and has seen impressive growth in recent years. Students enrolled at WGU work at their own speed on packaged online material. Faculty members are essentially tutors at Western Governors, and the coursework tests students' mastery of "competencies" rather than issuing them subjective grades. This model, dubbed competency-based education, is in vogue among policy makers of both stripes, with Arne Duncan, secretary of education for the Obama administration, saying he wants the approach to be the "norm" in higher education, and the administration giving an en-couraging boost to the concept in the spring of 2013 (Fain, 2013a). Ironically, given the Obama administration's antagonistic relationship with for-profits, competency-based education owes much of its creation to ground broken by for-profits, which pioneered a focus on students covering standardized learn-ing objectives.

The Obama Years

The summer of 2012 was a major turning point in the debate over for-profits, with the long-awaited arrival of two centerpieces of the latest round of federal crackdowns. First, in June, Senator Tom Harkin released the damning results of his two-year investigation of the industry. A few weeks later the U.S. Department of Education disclosed the first findings from "gainful-employment" regulations, which are the crown jewel of a broad, controversial tightening of the rules on for-profits. While both releases were highly publicized hits for the industry, neither was a home run. And a ruling by a regional accreditor, also released in the summer, may have more influence in future regulatory battles.

The report from Harkin, who is chairman of the Senate Committee on Health, Education, Labor, and Pensions, failed to get a single cosigner, even among fellow Democrats who have joined him in criticizing for-profits. And the sector fared better than expected in their performance in the debut batch of gainful-employment data, although the standards for failure under those rules are hardly stringent. And even those who fell below that line got a reprieve when, just a week later, a federal judge struck down the regulations.

Perhaps more important than the substance of the twin rollouts is what they signaled about the next stage of for-profit regulation. Critics of the sector will continue to push reforms. But both gainful employment and Harkin's report suggest that the elimination of for-profits is no longer on the table, if it ever was. After hitting a peak of more than 3.2 million students in 2009 (4 million if you include non-degree-seeking students), the industry now accounts for more than 10 percent of higher education's total enrollment. It may indeed be too big to fail, at least the bulk of it. And while Harkin and fellow Democrats continue to criticize the sector—and to target its reliance on federal aid for military service members and veterans—attacks on the profit motive and business model no longer seem as resonant, particularly now that politicians and the general public are asking increasingly tough questions about the price and value of degrees from traditional colleges.

Furthermore, for-profit education companies of a different sort enjoy newfound acceptance in the academy. One of the most notable—and hyped—developments in 2012 was the emergence of massive open online course (MOOC) providers like Udacity and Coursera, both of which are private companies supported by venture capital. With these for-profit, online course providers partnering with the most elite of universities, it might be tougher for traditional higher education to thumb its nose at the notion of profit peacefully coexisting with the academy.

If there is a definitive case against for-profit colleges, it is probably the Harkin report, which condemns the industry for putting profits ahead of students (Senate Committee on Health, Education, Labor, and Pensions, 2012). The four-part broadside includes thousands of pages of critical findings about the industry, based on six congressional hearings, three previous reports, and voluminous document requests. It also goes in-depth with individual sections on thirty companies. Among its most damaging findings were high dropout rates among the examined for-profits, including a 64 percent overall withdrawal rate in associate degree programs. And the report links dropout rates to the relatively skimpy spending by for-profits on students.

For example, in 2009 the companies spent $4.1 billion (22.4 percent) of all revenue on marketing, advertising, recruiting, and admissions staffing, according to the report. They also spent $3.6 billion (19.4 percent) of revenue on profit distributions. In contrast, the group of for-profits spent $3.2 billion (17.7 percent) on instruction.

Any accumulation of data as sweeping as Harkin's is inevitably going to gain attention in a landscape in which information—truly good and useful information—about the performance of colleges and their students is so hard to come by. Higher education as an industry is notoriously data poor—or, more accurately, lacking in data that help educators and policy makers really assess what's happening in classrooms and to graduates in the workplace. While the research effort aimed at capturing and analyzing educational outcomes is gaining steam, it may be some time before we can begin to answer questions about how well for-profit colleges educate and train their students, among the many other vexing questions in higher education.

The Harkin report is dubbed "For Profit: The Failure to Safeguard the Federal Investment and Ensure Student Success." That title could also be shorthand for the underlying goals of the Obama administration's pursuit of the sector. The most ambitious of the Department of Education's pursuit of for-profits under Obama are the gainful-employment regulations, which were introduced after a bruising and politicized battle. The department also tightened other "program integrity" rules for institutions that are eligible to participate in federal aid programs under Title IV of the Higher Education Act. Those new rules include a definition of the credit hour and a requirement that online colleges are authorized to operate in each state where they enroll students. The department acknowledged that gainful employment and program integrity regulations were aimed primarily at for-profits. But gainful employment was the most hotly contested of the bunch, by far.

The gainful-employment regime, which was enacted in 2011, required colleges to report the loan repayment rates and debt loads of graduates of vocational programs. When the first round of data was released, about 5 percent of academic programs at for-profits failed all three of the minimum benchmarks established by the regulations. Those benchmarks include a 35 percent debt repayment rate and two tests based on debt-to-income ratios. The first round of findings was only informational, as final data were not due until 2013. Serious penalties, such as colleges having their federal aid eligibility nixed, would not kick in until 2015.

Gainful employment's future got a little cloudier a week later, when Rudolph Contreras, a judge with the U.S. District Court in Washington, D.C., struck them down. The loan repayment standard under the rules was arbitrary, Contreras wrote, because the department had not used expert studies or industry standards to determine it. As a result, the standard "was not based upon any facts at all," he said (*Association of Private Sector Colleges and Universities v. Duncan*, No. 11-1314 [D.D.C. March 19, 2013]). That finding took down the entire set of regulations, because the judge found that the three standards were intertwined. The ruling also suspended the reporting process, meaning that colleges do not need to give the feds data on gainful employment, for now.

For-profits and their advocates celebrated the victory. But gainful employment is not dead. The judge ruled that the department was well within its rights in trying to address a "serious policy problem" of underperforming vocational programs. And in the fall of 2013, as expected, the Obama administration took another bite at the apple, holding a series of negotiations to try to craft a new set of gainful-employment regulations that will pass legal muster. The negotiations failed to reach consensus, leaving the Department of Education free to impose its own, tougher vision of the rules on vocational programs.

The chief architect of Obama's tougher stance on for-profits was Robert Shireman. After founding the California-based Institute for College Access and Success (TICAS), Shireman helped shepherd gainful employment as an undersecretary at the Department of Education. He was canny and aggressive at the department and succeeded in moving policy further than many had predicted. So it is a sign of the times that even Shireman and Harkin now have some nice things to say about for-profits, albeit in nuanced statements. Both acknowledge that the industry is not monolithic, and that there are big differences between "bad actors" and some of the better-performing for-profits.

For example, Shireman has returned to California, where he is running a nonprofit group called California Competes. His current cause is advocating fixes for capacity problems at the state's public colleges (especially two-year colleges), which are largely budget driven. Shireman has said one possible part of the enrollment solution in California could be New Charter University, an upstart for-profit that plans to keep tuition down by not participating in Title IV financial aid programs. "If the community colleges aren't going to get creative in this crisis in figuring out how to serve the students who need courses and training, we need others stepping in to fill the gap in a way that doesn't put the students into the poorhouse," he told us via e-mail (September 13, 2012).

As for Harkin, at the Capitol Hill release of his report, the Iowa Democrat said for-profits are here to stay and will continue to help more disadvantaged and nontraditional students attend college. "Their success is in the national interest," he said and then singled out several colleges for praise, a likely first for the industry's most powerful antagonist. Harkin said American Public Education, Strayer Education, Walden University, and National American University had largely risen above problems found in the report. Receiving more watered-down compliments were Kaplan Higher Education, DeVry, and Apollo, all of which have had "very serious problems" in the past, according to Harkin, but are now moving in the right direction (Fain, 2012a).

Praise for Kaplan was surprising, given how the company has often been a target of federal regulators. But Harkin is not alone in his softer take on Kaplan: Bill Gates made flattering references to the company in 2012. Gates, who through his foundation wields a tremendous influence over higher education policy, appears to take a shine to some of Kaplan's strategies. He wrote a positive review for a book by Andrew Rosen, Kaplan's CEO, and hosted a Kaplan official on a panel about innovation in higher education.

When Gates, Shireman, and Harkin all say for-profits will play a role in educating lower-income and adult students, it is a safe bet that at least part of the sector is on firm ground.

For example, one for-profit that has quietly become a global higher education player, even as others have struggled in recent years, is Laureate Education, Inc. The Baltimore-based chain now enrolls more than eight hundred thousand students at seventy-eight institutions in thirty countries. The privately traded company is unusual, in part because of its heavy international focus. Laureate has also managed to avoid much of the negative publicity that has dogged other for-profits. But it employs a global version of the familiar for-profit playbook: acquire struggling nonprofit colleges, use significant capital infusions and economies of scale to create degree offerings, develop online programs, and grow enrollment (Redden & Fain, 2013).

Despite the thaw in rhetoric about for-profits, a further regulatory shake-up seems likely, even inevitable. The best place for policy makers to seriously take on the industry is probably the reauthorization of the Higher Education Act, which was due to occur this year but is unlikely to advance in the deeply divided Congress. Most insiders predict 2015 at the earliest for that laborious, and often bruising, process. As a result, state policies are where much of the action is right now, particularly in California. And the biggest threats to for-profits these days might be accreditors and the recession's lingering effects.

Bridgepoint Education Inc. was the first major for-profit to feel the heat from accreditors. The publicly traded company's Ashford University was trapped in a serious vise in 2013 and had to scramble to keep its regional accreditation while simultaneously applying to move its accreditation base to a different agency. However, Ashford appears to have walked the gauntlet successfully, having made the required improvements and gotten a green light from its new accreditor. Some changes were not easy, such as the university's laying off of hundreds of adjunct instructors, who were replaced by more-expensive full-time faculty members (Fain, 2013b).

Bridgepoint's rapid growth helped lead to its being in the crosshairs. The company, which also owns the University of the Rockies, rode Ashford's enrollment boom to Wall Street riches. Only five years ago, ten thousand students attended Ashford, almost all of them fully online. At its peak more than ninety thousand were enrolled there. Ashford is also the poster child for one of for-profit higher education's most controversial practices: the purchase of a struggling nonprofit college—usually a Christian institution—along with the college's regional accreditation. Critics have likened that strategy to buying a taxi medallion.

With financing from Warburg Pincus, Bridgepoint in 2005 bought the foundering Franciscan University of the Prairies and renamed it Ashford University. The purchase came with both a traditional residential campus and regional accreditation with the Higher Learning Commission of the North

Central Association of Colleges and Schools, which is one of six regional accrediting agencies. But while Ashford has a football stadium and residence halls, almost all of its operation is online. In 2011, the university enrolled only 973 students on the campus.

Ashford's sparsely populated physical campus became a symbol of the perceived excesses and hollow promise of for-profit education. And it probably did not help that the campus is located in Clinton, Iowa, which is Harkin's backyard. The company's corporate headquarters, however, are in San Diego. Harkin commissioned a special investigation of Bridgepoint, torching it during a 2011 hearing on the Hill. He criticized the university's explosive growth online, apparent shell campus, and heavy reliance on federal aid, calling Bridgepoint a "scam, an absolute scam" (quoted in Lederman, 2011).

But the real impact of Harkin's denunciations was more indirect. He also called out the Higher Learning Commission for blessing the company's original purchase of its campus—and by extension its accreditation. And that stinging criticism—along with a changeover in leadership—appears to have contributed to a stricter approach by the commission, which had formerly been among the friendliest to for-profits.

The Harkin hearing on Bridgepoint was billed as a case study on for-profit regulation, which focused heavily on how regional accreditors function as outsourced government contractors to decide which companies should be eligible to participate in federal aid programs. That can be a tricky task, particularly with companies backed by private equity that do not exactly relish opening their books to regulators. Harkin said the accreditors lacked the resources and expertise to keep tabs on the fast-growing for-profit sector, particularly the Higher Learning Commission, which is tasked with overseeing nineteen states. He did not mince words.

Bridgepoint's founder and CEO, Andrew S. Clark, opted to skip the hearing. So Sylvia Manning, the commission's president, was in the hot seat. "The question I would ask is, in their current state, are our accreditation agencies equipped to oversee billion-dollar, multi-state corporations?" Harkin asked Manning. He then answered the question for her: "I don't think so. I don't think the accrediting agencies have the wherewithal" (Lederman, 2011).

Despite the hearing's theatrics, the commission had already begun taking a harder line on for-profits. Manning took over the lead role at the Chicago-based commission in 2008. She had been publicly skeptical about the industry and promised to better vet for-profits. Perhaps the most visible example of a change came in 2010, when the commission rejected two for-profits' attempted purchases of failing Christian colleges, which has had a broad chilling effect on accreditation shopping nationwide.

That year Manning's group turned down a new for-profit entity's bid to purchase Dana College, a Lutheran institution in Nebraska. Without a buyer, the college was forced to close and was eventually subsumed by Midland Lutheran College, which changed its name to Midland University. Also in 2010, the commission nixed a continuation of accreditation for Rochester College, located in Michigan, which was in the midst of a planned buyout by University Education, a publicly traded for-profit with a specialty in online education.

The commission did not release detailed information on those decisions. That relatively secretive approach has been the norm among regional accreditors, until a recent shift by the Western Association of Schools and Colleges senior college commission. But the commission disclosed that it had new, stricter rules for changes of ownership and would now require buyers to demonstrate that they would maintain certain characteristics of purchased colleges. Manning said at the time that the basic standard was an "extension of the mission, educational programs, student body and faculty that were in place when the commission last conducted an onsite evaluation of the affiliated institution." As a result, a for-profit can still buy a college and go for a full face lift by taking a residential, religious campus and creating a mostly online university that caters to adult students—akin to what Harkin calls Ashford's "radical reinvention." But existing accreditation will no longer be part of the deal in that scenario, Manning said, and the company would need to apply for the college to be a candidate for initial accreditation (Jaschik, 2010).

Meanwhile, as for-profits everywhere came to grips with not being able to buy regional accreditation, Ashford continued its rapid expansion with a campus base deep in the heart of Higher Learning Commission territory. That now looked dicey, with the commission now requiring colleges to have a "substantial presence" in their region. So the company started looking for a new home for Ashford and began the application process for accreditation with the Western Association. The verdict would have high stakes, for both Bridgepoint and the industry more broadly, with Harkin and other for-profit critics joining investors in watching closely.

The Western Association brought in a group of heavy hitters in higher education to review Ashford's application, with a twelve-member site visit team led by Stanley O. Ikenberry, a professor and president emeritus of the

University of Illinois and former president of the American Council on Education. The final report, which went live in July 2012, was the first major review that a regional accreditor released to the public. The seventy-three-page document was a stinging blow to Bridgepoint, arguing that the university fell short in several measures of quality. And behind most of the university's problems was its emphasis on growth, according to the report.

"The challenges that this rapid growth and enrollment model present to management, quality and student success cannot be overstated," said Ralph A. Wolff, the association's president, in a letter to Elizabeth Tice, Ashford's president and CEO. "Although the team found that Ashford has sought to keep pace by building its infrastructure to support this large number of online students, many of its promising initiatives are recent, some only undertaken within the last year" (Fain, 2012c).

The accreditor found that Ashford lacked a "sufficient core" of professors, with 56 full-time faculty members in 2011, 2,458 part-time faculty, and 875 other instructional staff. Those numbers do not cut it for ninety thousand students, the report said. Other identified problem areas were questionable academic rigor in some programs and inadequate student-support services. And these deficiencies all contribute to an "unacceptable" dropout rate, according to the report. It found that 128,000 students withdrew from the university over the last five years, a time during which Ashford enrolled 241,000 new students, meaning that more than 50 percent dropped out.

The Western Association rejected Ashford's first bid. But the for-profit succeeded a few months later with a second attempt. Its share price took a beating in the meantime, with the former high-flier bottoming out at less than a third of its peak market value only one year earlier. Ashford also laid off 450 admissions reps and reassigned another 400 to student services as it tried to comply with the commission. And while those dark days are over, the university still faces plenty of uncertainty. Most importantly, it is not clear how many students are ready to fork over $413 per credit for Ashford's online tuition, particularly given the rise of less expensive, nonprofit competitors like Western Governors University and Liberty University.

Bridgepoint is hardly the only for-profit facing an existential challenge. In fact, American Public Education and Grand Canyon University are the only major, publicly traded for-profits that are still growing. The rest are coping with tumbling enrollments and at least some possible regulatory heat. Overall,

Department of Education data show that the sector's enrollment declined by nearly 3 percent from fall 2010 to fall 2011 (Lederman, 2012), and reports suggest that further dips have occurred since then. For example, the National Student Clearinghouse Research Center found that fall enrollments at four-year, for-profit institutions dipped by 9.7 percent in just one year. Enrollments at two-year for-profits were down 3.1 percent (National Student Clearinghouse Research Center, 2013).

The industry's deep slump has been jarring to its advocates and investors, who made lots of money in the wake of Bush-era deregulation. The model worked in part because of multimillion-dollar marketing aimed at potential students who might otherwise have attended community colleges or not considered going to college at all. For a while there was no end in sight to the growth, which made for-profits the darlings of Wall Street. But much of the industry's quick expansion was fueled by lesser-prepared students who were unlikely to graduate and racked up big debt along the way. Those students now come with potential regulatory and PR risks that may outweigh potential payoffs.

One sign of that shift was the end of federal financial aid for "ability to benefit" students, who wanted to attend college but lacked either a high school degree or GED. This group used to be able to qualify for federal aid by taking a basic skills test or by successfully completing six college credits. For-profits were the likely destination of these students. But with annual federal expenditures of Pell Grants expected to hit $40 billion, Congress shut off the ability-to-benefit funding in the summer of 2012.

At the same time, the relatively expensive tuition of most for-profits has begun to look like a riskier investment. Job seekers tend to attend college during an economic downturn. But years of high unemployment rates tend to have a chilling effect on higher education. Even with huge marketing budgets, for-profits increasingly struggle to entice students. Some financial analysts say the industry may have already churned through most of its potential student markets.

For-profits were the first to target adult students with convenient, online academic offerings. No longer, as the marketplace is getting increasingly crowded with upstart nonprofits like Western Governors University, the University of Maryland University College, Liberty University, and Southern New Hampshire University, all of which have national reach with fast-growing online programs.

With limited exceptions, for-profits can expect modest enrollment and revenue growth over the next few years, at best. And for those that grew too big, a painful period of shrinking will come first. Some for-profits are not waiting for that to happen and have proactively lopped off some of their market share. Others have begun to imitate nonprofits by discounting their tuition to help attract students. Strayer, ITT, and Grand Canyon all have substantial scholarships in place. ITT, for example, introduced a 20 percent tuition discount for new students in its associate degree programs in October 2012. And in May 2013, Strayer announced that students can earn a free course credit for every three they successfully complete. The new scholarship pays for a 25 percent discount on degrees as long as students do not take two consecutive quarters off.

Phoenix and Kaplan were among the worst offenders in courting students who had little chance of earning a credential. But the two institutions have also taken the lead with the most visible of intentional enrollment sacrifices, which have landed them praise from even strident for-profit critics. Both institutions recently introduced trial periods for students, which allow them to either quit or get the boot without spending anything. Phoenix has a free three-week orientation for students, while Kaplan only charges an application fee for its five-week trial period.

Both such programs have been expensive. About one in four students wash out at Kaplan during the introductory session, only 40 percent of them voluntarily. The university asks the rest to leave after determining that they are not performing well enough. The trial period cost the university $27 million during a six-month period in 2011. Kaplan has felt the sting, and in 2012 it closed nine campuses and consolidated four others.

The University of Phoenix remains the most visible for-profit by far. Its name is still a stand-in for "online" and "for-profit" to policy makers and the general public. But the Apollo-owned flagship has been buffeted of late, and its woes have prompted many to predict that for-profits are on their way out. With a double-digit annual decline in both enrollment and revenue, critics of for-profits were ready to dance on Phoenix's grave.

But do not count the university out just yet. With some self-inflicted and purposeful wounds, Phoenix is reloading as part of a broad "re-engineering" that could position it for a next stage in the evolution of for-profit higher education. The university is likely to be among survivors that cut or maintain their prices, improve selectivity, and develop stronger ties to employers, even shaping their curriculums around workplace-determined competencies.

With 270,000 students on a degree track, Phoenix is the largest for-profit. However, that enrollment number is just 57 percent of the university's peak level in 2010. And its operating expenses remained unchanged since those salad days. So in October the university announced $300 million in planned cuts, with layoffs of eight hundred nonfaculty employees and the shuttering of twenty-five campuses and ninety smaller learning centers. The closures represent about 40 percent of the university's physical footprint. Phoenix is cagey about disclosing which percentage of its students are fully online, versus the hybrid variety who rely on campuses for classroom-based learning and their IT needs. But most are fully online, according to company officials. So the closed locations will affect only about thirteen thousand students, many of whom live within twenty-five miles of another Phoenix spot.

The university was the first to go nationwide in serving working adults with vocational programs. That business model, which goes back forty years, needed updating, Apollo group executives say. Financial analysts agree, saying the attempt to "right-size" the university was overdue.

The larger challenge may be what company officials call Phoenix's "value proposition." Tuition rates vary at the university but generally hover around $420 per credit. That is a fairly average price for the for-profit sector but much more than competitors like Western Governors, with self-paced, competency-based programs that run about $240 per credit. Rio Salado College, an Arizona-based online community college, charges $76 per credit for local students and $317 for out-of-state students. As a result, Phoenix's leaders say they realize the university must demonstrate more bang for students' tuition buck.

So in addition to shrinking, Phoenix in September 2012 announced a university-wide tuition freeze for all current and incoming students. And as a further sell, the university is doubling down on career services, with a slick new advertising campaign about the push. That effort includes bulked-up partnerships with corporations, including Microsoft, Hitachi Data Systems, and Rubbermaid. And Phoenix is working with nonprofit trade groups that represent industries, such as the manufacturing and energy industries, to create tailored degree programs and to help students find jobs. Dubbed "Let's get to work," the campaign's ads tout that Phoenix is ramping up career planning services to help students "get ahead" in their careers.

"This is a more competitive industry today," Gregory W. Cappelli, Apollo's CEO, told investors in October 2012. "We've been preparing for this for some time. We want to be the university of choice for working learners" ("Apollo Group," 2012).

Looking Forward

California may give a glimpse of the future for the for-profit industry. The state is often ahead of the curve, but in this case desperation may be as much of a driver as innovation. After years of deep budget cuts, California's 112 community colleges and the California State University system have struggled to meet demand and have been forced to turn away hordes of students—as many as three hundred thousand in 2012 for community colleges alone.

Somehow California has to find a way to educate and train its workforce, and for-profits are certain to be part of the solution. It might also be hard to tell which of the next generation of for-profits in California are actually for-profits.

Take the recently launched Ameritas College, which is aimed at serving Hispanic students. Ameritas will charge roughly $400 per credit, with a teaching model of a single three-hour course per week bolstered by two and a half hours of online coursework. The new college will be jointly operated by Brandman College—an entrepreneurial nonprofit college that is itself a spin-off of the Chapman University System—and by the University Ventures Fund, a for-profit investment group with a college completion mandate written into its charter. Ryan Craig is the fund's founding partner. He has also been a Bridgepoint director since that company's founding, having previously worked at Warburg Pincus, which helped bankroll Ashford's creation. Brandman and the fund co-own Ameritas College Educational Services, a corporate entity that will provide money, research, and administrative services to Ameritas College. So is Ameritas a for-profit? A better question might be: Who cares?

Not all for-profits, however, will keep their seat at the table in California. An early battle has been over Cal Grants, the nation's most generous state-based financial aid program, which ran up a bill of $1.6 billion last year. As a result, the California Student Aid Commission decided to tighten the rules about which colleges can qualify to receive Cal Grants. State officials clearly targeted the for-profit sector and came up with some novel ways to eliminate low-performing colleges. The new requirements are tighter than the federal gainful-employment regulations.

For example, colleges must have three-year loan default rates of less than 24.6 percent to be Cal Grant–eligible. That is a much higher bar than the 35 percent loan repayment rate under gainful employment, which means that 65 percent of graduates can be in default. When announced, the new rules appeared likely to lead to the shuttering most of the Corinthian Colleges–owned Everest College locations in California.

However, the Cal Grant crackdown will not be a problem for the for-profit UniversityNow, an investor-backed enterprise that opened its New Charter University in 2012. The startup will lean heavily on self-paced, online, and competency-based learning—the troika of hot ideas in higher education. And it has received a decent chunk of funding to get started, including a grant from the Bill & Melinda Gates Foundation. Students will pay $199 a month to take as many classes as they want at New Charter, which will rely on a "disaggregated coaching model" of teaching to keep costs down. Also helping on that front will be the university's decision to opt out of participating in federal financial aid programs, a process that comes with a load of red tape and administrative costs.

UniversityNow got some good news last summer from the Western accrediting agency. On the same day that the regional accreditor rejected Ashford's bid, it accepted UniversityNow's purchase of Patten University, a struggling nonprofit college in Oakland. Accreditation buying is still alive, apparently, but with a twist. UniversityNow plans to make a degree from Patten inexpensive—really inexpensive. Tuition will be a flat fee of about $1,300 a month. And an online bachelor's degree will run just over $10,000, said Gene Wade, UniversityNow's CEO (Fain, 2013c).

So it does not really matter that Patten also got tossed out of the Cal Grant program, because students will not need Cal Grants to attend. And the university's new owners said they are transitioning it out of being Title IV eligible as well. "This current rule change will have little negative impact on Patten," Wade said when asked about the tightened Cal Grant regulations. "However, it should lead to increased demand since more students will need affordable private options" (Wade, 2012).

It is hard to argue with potential solutions to the capacity problem in California. Profit, it seems, is not the issue in the state. If colleges can offer a high-quality, low-priced product, they will probably be welcomed in California, regardless of tax status. And that litmus test will probably spread to other states, where public funding for higher education is unlikely to return to pre-recession levels anytime in the foreseeable future.

Of course, colleges will need to graduate decent proportions of students to stay in favor, whether in California or elsewhere. Deborah A. Santiago is cofounder of Excelencia in Education, a group focused on Latinos in higher education. She likes the mission of Ameritas, saying it is sorely needed in California. And Santiago is unfazed by the college's for-profit ties. Proof that the model works, she said, will be in graduation rates. "The devil in the details is really the issue of completion" (Fain, 2012b).

4

THE CLASSIFICATION
OF ORGANIZATIONAL FORMS
Theory and Application to the Field
of Higher Education
Martin Ruef and Manish Nag

In 1973, the Carnegie Foundation for the Advancement of Teaching (CFAT) first published its basic classification of degree-granting colleges and universities in the United States. Building on a long history of earlier efforts to survey and evaluate the diverse organizational forms in American higher education, a commission under the leadership of Clark Kerr sought to differentiate these institutions into five broad categories, as well as a number of more nuanced subcategories (Carnegie Commission on Higher Education, 1973). Kerr's philosophy, adopted from Thomas Jefferson, was to create an "aristocracy of achievement arising out of a democracy of opportunity" (Lagemann, 1992, p. 230). Practically speaking, this meant that the classification offered by the commission would continue to distinguish the traditional "elite" universities, such as Harvard, Princeton, Stanford, and Berkeley, while encouraging systemic expansion—and greater access—at lower levels of postsecondary education.

The Carnegie Classification emerged at a time when scholars of institutions and organizations had come to appreciate the increasing complexity and profound change that was evident in the field of higher education (Clark, 1972; Hodgkinson, 1971; Parsons & Platt, 1973). The population of colleges and universities expanded rapidly over the preceding century, with merely 250 schools in the United States at the time of the Civil War and roughly ten times that number by 1970. The growth of the academic profession was especially pronounced in the period leading up to the commission's activities, doubling between 1960 (260,000 faculty members) and 1970 (530,000, including 383,000 full-time instructors) (Oakley, 1997, p. 47; Thelin, 2004). More subtle changes in the culture of the American university were also evident. While students in nineteenth-century and early twentieth-century institutions of higher learning were relatively insulated from broader societal developments, the social movements of the 1960s and the decline of in loco parentis norms created far more permeable organizational boundaries (Aldrich & Ruef, 2006, p. 128). A proliferation of coursework and academic units in the social sciences, natural sciences, and applied fields undermined the traditional emphasis on humanities as the academic core of the university (Frank & Gabler, 2006). Changes in admission policies produced a more diverse student body (in terms of gender, ethnicity, and class), even at elite institutions (Karabel, 2005). The CFAT's classificatory schema could thus be seen as one concerted effort to impose order on an expanding and increasingly heterogeneous array of campus settings.

With the growth of American higher education over the succeeding four decades, the CFAT has repeatedly issued new classifications. The most recent system (issued in 2010) represents the sixth update to the original schema and features thirty-three categories in its basic classification. As this volume highlights, the ecology of higher education in America has increasingly moved away from the "traditional" college experiences that the foundation helped us to analyze and understand. The new organizational models in the sector, which rely less on physical campuses, offer vocational and professional training rather than liberal arts pedagogy, and tend toward for-profit ownership, have generated a particularly strong impetus to modify the categories of higher education that were in use until the end of the twentieth century (Carnegie Foundation for the Advancement of Teaching, 2011).[1]

The benefits of these evolving categories for understanding higher education have been decidedly mixed. One historian of education, John Thelin, has commented that the CFAT's "attempt at creating order actually increased the chaos among institutions," insofar as a descriptive device for analyzing the field of higher education was converted—by both the public and some university administrators—into a "hierarchical ranking scheme" (2004, p. 320). The heuristic distinctions drawn by the foundation became an invitation to game the classification, especially for some organizations that appeared in the lower rungs of the hierarchy and sought to pursue a more prestigious status. This dynamic was pernicious given the early goal of the Carnegie Commission to promote diversity in postsecondary education by encouraging the founding of more accessible community and comprehensive colleges (McCormick & Zhao, 2005). It has become even more problematic as the highest tiers of the academic status system, topped by "research universities and liberal arts colleges as the ideal expressions of higher education" in the twentieth century, serve a shrinking proportion of students in the twenty-first century (see the introduction).

Another important challenge for the classification of organizational forms in higher education involves the social scientific validity of these efforts. Beginning in the 1960s, a substantial literature in organizational studies developed methods to elicit taxonomies of organizational types and practices. Many of these approaches have been a posteriori, allowing salient categories to emerge from detailed information on activities, structures, membership, and expressed identities within organizations. By contrast, an early critique of taxonomies of administrative structures lamented that typologies up to that point had been "*a priori* classifications, based on wide generalizations derived from common knowledge and common sense, the only concession to empirical complexities being the admission that they are in some sense pure, ideal, or archetypal" (Pugh, Hickson, & Hinings, 1969, p. 115; see also McKelvey, 1982).

While the classification efforts of the CFAT—as well as similar schemata issued by the Southern Regional Education Board and American Association of University Professors (AAUP)—have been resolutely empirical, they continue to rely on the a priori approach, in which an analyst or commission comes up with mutually exclusive categories that structure distinctions among universities and colleges, rather than allowing data to drive those categories. This raises a number of concerns. First, classification in higher education has become decoupled from recent organizational scholarship, which offers a range of theoretical perspectives and inductive tools for understanding the landscape of American colleges and universities. Second, the top-down, a priori imposition of categories may be particularly ill-suited to capture new or emergent organizational forms (e.g., alternative medical schools, for-profit universities, work colleges, and education based on massive open online courses), owing to the institutionalization and taken-for-grantedness of existing classification systems. Third, an important development in recent work on organizations has been to recognize that membership in categories is often fuzzy and partial (Hannan, 2010), rather than conforming to the crisp boundaries proposed by traditional approaches to classification. This holds true especially when organizational fields are in flux and audiences struggle to make sense of new organizations. Finally, existing approaches to classification in higher education are based on the intuitions of experts, rather than rigorous statistical models. A crucial goal of the Carnegie Classification, as stated by Kerr, was to generate categories that were "relatively homogeneous with respect to the function of the institutions as well as with respect to characteristics of students and faculty members" (McCormick & Zhao, 2005, p. 52). Only a quantitative model can systematically assess the homogeneity of underlying categories or themes that are applied across several thousand organizations and, possibly, several hundred attributes.

To confront these shortcomings, this chapter offers a new approach to classification in higher education that is grounded in contemporary organizational theory. We begin by surveying the literature on the development of organizational taxonomies, considering four distinct perspectives on the empirical basis of categories: (1) internal functions, routines, and structures; (2) resource niches that support an organizational form; (3) the identity claims advanced by organizational leaders and members; and (4) the external attributions applied to organizations by field participants and the general public. For each perspective, we consider both how it has been applied to organizations in general and how it has been used more specifically to understand developments in the field of education. The latter half of the chapter then introduces a statistical model that provides a formal basis for implementing some insights from these perspectives on organizational classification. The intuition behind the model, termed latent Dirichlet allocation (LDA), is that organizations may have partial membership in a number of different categories, that those categories are not observed directly, and that there is a generative process whereby the observed attributes of organizations are produced by their membership in categories (Blei, Ng, & Jordan, 2003).

To bring our inductive model into dialogue with the Carnegie Classification of institutions of higher learning, we rely on the same data set that informs those efforts, the Integrated Postsecondary Education Data System (IPEDS). IPEDS now provides a directory of over sixty-eight hundred postsecondary schools from a survey of Title IV institutions (and roughly two hundred non–Title IV voluntary submitters) and is collected annually by congressional order. Drawing on IPEDS, we illustrate how our inductive model can be used to derive new sets of categories for the population of American colleges and universities and how those categories vary depending on the theoretical perspective used to understand differences among these institutions.

We conclude by contrasting the classification systems derived inductively with the Carnegie Classification itself.

Approaches to Defining Organizational Forms

While common labels for organizational forms in the field of education—such as *Ivy Leagues, community colleges,* or *state universities*—suggest a well-established and intuitive understanding of the ways that higher education is structured and the distinct student populations that it caters to, the history of the Carnegie Classification reveals considerable contestation around the basis for differentiating colleges and universities. The history of classification in organizational theory is no different. When researchers in the 1960s first proposed empirical approaches to deriving taxonomies of organizational forms (Haas, Hall, & Johnson, 1966; Pugh et al., 1969), they confronted an older tradition that had primarily been oriented toward understanding organizations in terms of ideal-types. The newer empirical approaches to studying organizational forms soon manifested their own points of divergence. Following Aldrich and Ruef (2006, Chapter 6), these approaches can be distinguished along two dimensions. The vertical dimension shown in Table 4.1 addresses

TABLE 4.1 Inductive approaches to defining organizational forms

Focus with respect to role of perception	*Focus with respect to organizational boundaries*	
	Internal	*External*
Objective	**Blueprints** *Typical method:* Surveys of internal structures and routines *Examples:* Haas et al., 1966; Pugh et al., 1969; Brint, Riddle, & Hanneman, 2006*	**Resource Niches** *Typical method:* Analysis of conditions or relationships supporting organization *Examples:* McPherson, 1983; DiMaggio, 1986; Renzulli, 2005*
Subjective	**Identities** *Typical method:* Interpretation of mission statements and self-depictions *Examples:* J. Martin, Feldman, Harch, & Sitkin, 1983; Albert and Whetten, 1985; King, Clemens, & Konty, 2011*	**Cultural Codes** *Typical method:* Analysis of public discourse or external classifications *Examples:* Zuckerman, 1999; Ruef, 2000; Hannan, 2010*

SOURCE: Adapted from Aldrich & Ruef, 2006, p. 115.
NOTE: Asterisks (*) identify analyses that are oriented toward the field of education.

the role of perception and considers whether a theoretical perspective treats organizational attributes as objective features or subjective interpretations on the part of observers. The horizontal dimension addresses the analyst's focus with respect to organizational boundaries, considering whether a perspective primarily employs a "closed system" approach, emphasizing attributes that are internal to an organization, or an "open system" approach, emphasizing the relationship of the organization to its broader environment (see also Scott & Davis, 2007).

Organizational Forms as Blueprints

The earliest approaches to defining organizational forms inductively can be placed in the upper left-hand cell of the table. Drawing on interviews with managers of fifty-two enterprises near Birmingham, England, the British Aston Group sought to sort organizations based on features of their internal human resource practices, especially those related to the concentration of authority, the degree of formal structure in activities, and the line control of workflow (Pugh et al., 1969). Analyzing clusters of these features, the Aston group identified seven distinct categories of workplace structures, many of them deviating from the Weberian ideal-type of formal bureaucracy. Using a somewhat broader sample of organizations, a similar research effort was undertaken by Richard Hall and his colleagues in the United States (e.g., Haas et al., 1966). An emerging method with respect to organizational taxonomy thus appeared, emphasizing the inductive derivation of categories based on surveys of internal practices across samples of organizations and multivariate analysis (see McKelvey, 1975, for an overview and critique).

In a highly influential paper, Hannan and Freeman (1977) provided a theoretical rationale for this taxonomic approach. Arguing that organizational theorists had focused for too long on the adaptation of individual organizations, they called for a shift in the unit of analysis to organizational populations. The shift required that scholars "identify classes of organizations which are relatively homogeneous in terms of environment vulnerability" (p. 934). In an analogue to the study of genetic structure among population biologists, they suggested that the key to identifying these classes of organizations was to look inside organizations and study empirical differences in organizational form. For Hannan and Freeman, "an organizational form is a *blueprint* for organizational action, for transforming inputs into outputs" (p. 935). They went on to identify various internal features of organizations that might allow analysts to infer blueprints, including an organization's formal structure, routines, and normative order, where the latter feature was thought to be encoded in claims regarding the history of an organization, its politics, and the like.

The idea of classifying organizations in terms of internal, objective features has been carried forth under various labels, including the study of "dominant competencies" (McKelvey, 1982), "grammars of action" (Pentland & Rueter, 1994), and "organizational genealogies" (Phillips, 2002).[2] In the field of higher education, the application of such perspectives to classification is of a relatively recent vintage. Brint and colleagues (2006) launched an effort to map the "objective structure" of American colleges and universities, employing a cluster analysis to identify relatively homogeneous categories. Drawing from the Institutional Data Archive on American Higher Education (IDA), a survey of four-year university presidents, they considered such internal characteristics as the form of institutional control (e.g., public, nonprofit, religiously affiliated, independent), student selectivity, tuition, operating budget, and the extent of vocational training (percentage of occupational or professional degrees). An analysis of these features yielded a classification schema with seven institutional clusters—ranging from elite private colleges and universities to relatively nonselective, religiously affiliated baccalaureate-granting colleges (p. 235). Notably, Brint and colleagues found that these inductively derived clusters corresponded only loosely to the Carnegie Classification.

Organizational Forms as Resource Niches

In the 1980s, organizational theorists began to move away from the conception of organizational forms as internal structures and routines.[3] A number of methodological critiques had been raised with respect to earlier attempts at inductive taxonomy. Replications of the Aston studies raised questions about organizational sampling and the structural dimensions used to differentiate organizational forms. McKelvey (1975) argued, moreover, that the attributes selected in such studies tended to be too narrow—often deriving from a Weberian view of organizations as "closed" bureaucracies—and that the observers selected to report on those attributes tended to be top administrators. A more inclusive effort at organizational taxonomy would also need to consider attributes reported by low-ranked members of organizations and extend to the perspectives of external stakeholders, such as suppliers, customers, or clients (p. 517).

A shift in conceptualization was also evident in the ecological perspective that had provided much of the theoretical impetus for studying organizational forms as internal blueprints. Writing only a few years after Hannan and Freeman's initial statement on the population ecology of organizations, McPherson sought to describe organizational forms in terms of their niches, "location[s] in multidimensional space defined by the resources in the environment" (1983, p. 520). McPherson eschewed an emphasis on internal features of organizational forms—such as size and the structural dimensions (formalization, centralization, etc.) that had come to be associated with it in the literature. Instead, he suggested that the ecology of organizations be understood in terms of a duality between forms and their demographic niches (see Mohr & Guerra-Pearson, 2010, for an overview). This duality, in which "niches define forms and forms define niches," was soon picked up by Hannan and Freeman (1986, p. 57), who abandoned their earlier emphasis on internal organizational blueprints.

McPherson recognized that the boundaries of organizations were porous, noting that "individuals may be members of multiple organizations, or may enter or leave them repeatedly" (1983, p. 519). In the face of such fluidity, an emphasis on internal structures and routines made less sense in defining organizational forms than an emphasis on the demographic profile of members that different forms might draw from. Applied to the field of higher education, for instance, this conception might seek to identify categories of universities and colleges based on the gender, age, ethnic, geographic, and class composition of their student body or applicant pool.

The conception of niches in ecology has also been broadened beyond the demographic composition of organizational forms. By the mid-1990s, for instance, ecological theorists were defining resource niches in terms of the "social, economic, and political conditions that can sustain the functioning of organizations that embody a particular form" (Carroll & Hannan, 1995, p. 34). Other scholars, such as DiMaggio, noted that resource dependencies could be captured in the network relationships of organizations, and therefore analysts could rely on "an operational definition of niche and form as mutually defined by observable patterns of relations among sets of actors" (1986, p. 360).

In recent years, these insights have begun to be deployed in the educational field. Renzulli (2005) examines the emergence of the charter school form as a function of environmental conditions between 1991 and 1998. Analyzing the number of charter school applications across school districts in U.S.

states with charter school legislation, Renzulli finds that this organizational form has thrived in niches with high levels of urbanization, supportive state laws, a critical mass of nonreligious private schools, and a large proportion of nonwhite students. Extending such analyses of resource niches to higher education (with simultaneous consideration of multiple organizational forms) would represent a novel approach to classification.

Organizational Forms as Identities

Even as some scholars shifted the definition of organizational forms outside the organization during the 1980s, others continued to privilege an internal perspective but increasingly couched it in terms of culture and the subjective perceptions of members. In one widely cited article, Albert and Whetten (1985) proposed a view of organizational forms as identities, revolving around the sense of members as to "who 'we' are." In their formulation, such identities were rooted in features of the organization that were seen as central, enduring, and distinctive. Despite the durability of organizational identities, they were conceptualized as subject to claims-making and contestation. In the realm of higher education, for instance, some stakeholders characterize the mission of the university in reverent terms as a "church" of knowledge, while others view it more mundanely, as a "business" or system of vocational training (Frank & Gabler, 2006).

At first glance, the claims of uniqueness that are implicit in organizational identities may appear to clash with efforts at classification, especially when those efforts are directed toward the identification of relatively homogeneous classes of organizations. But empirical investigations of organizational culture have found that assertions of uniqueness tend to be paradoxical, as notions of identity draw on standardized cultural templates or narratives that are widely rehearsed in society. For instance, an early study of narratives by J. Martin and colleagues (1983) found that seven stories used to highlight organizational uniqueness could be found in a large variety of contexts. Scholars of organizational identity now readily acknowledge that identities are hierarchical, with higher-order categories and organizational forms that are more central, more enduring, and more constraining than lower-order identities, which may offer greater uniqueness (Whetten, 2006). The higher-order identities (e.g., Notre Dame's mission as a Catholic university) impose the greatest switching costs and thus offer a suitable basis for organizational classification (Whetten, 2006, p. 226).

A recent application of this perspective to education again focuses on charter schools, considering the emergence of this organizational form in Arizona between 1996 and 2001. Drawing on annual school report cards, King and colleagues (2011) analyze how newly founded schools construct their identities in this novel category. They note that "administrators craft the report cards to create public identities for their schools, broadcasting the schools' defining practices and policies and distinguishing the schools from their peers" (p. 557). A textual analysis of these mission statements reveals that schools commonly highlight social values, learning processes, aspects of curricular structure, and resources; they tend to downplay the demographics of their student body, including issues of ethnic identity. Based on the co-occurrence of these elements, King and colleagues found that the Arizona schools could be differentiated into two clusters. One cluster corresponds to an emerging organizational form that emphasizes vocational and social service programs; the other cluster emphasizes creative and artistic learning that represents an alternative to conventional public school curricula. Like the early Aston Group studies, the focus on the administrator statements in the report cards thus highlighted internal features of these organizations, but because the statements were defined by the administrators themselves (rather than being elicited by social scientists), they offer a link between subjective identity and organizational form.

Organizational Forms as Cultural Codes

A final perspective on organizational forms continues to privilege the understandings of participants in the field but moves the locus of perception from organizational insiders to include broader audiences. In a major revision of earlier theories of organizational forms, Hannan and colleagues (2007) highlight the role of "audience segments," particularly where these segments achieve some consensus on *cultural codes* that allow them to classify organizations and sanction deviance from categorical schema. The description of audience segments in the theory includes "insiders—the actual and potential members or employees of producer organizations—as well as various kinds of outsiders: buyers and suppliers, investors, critics, regulators" (p. 36). While the range of observers treated by the theory is thus quite encompassing, empirical analyses following this approach have tended to focus on external audiences of organizations, who are in the strongest position to evaluate and critique organizational behaviors that may not conform to their expectations.

An important aspect of the research on cultural codes involves the recognition that organizational membership in categories may be partial. Rather than examining classification systems with crisp boundaries, organizational theorists "usually study worlds in flux, with categories that emerge, transmute, and decay" (Hannan, 2010, p. 160). As Hannan has emphasized, the field of higher education is a relevant example of a domain where categories are evolving and the mapping of universities and colleges to those categories ought to involve considerations of partiality. For instance, we might conceptualize the category of "university" itself as containing full-fledged, prototypical members, such as Stanford University and the University of North Carolina, but also consider other organizations that do not match the dominant conception of the category, such as Britain's Open University, which only offers distance learning (Hannan, 2010). Audiences in higher education are especially likely to assign partial membership to newer forms of broad-access education, such as for-profit universities or "no frills" colleges, though that seems likely to change as perceptions and folk categories evolve.

The implications of partial category membership for organizations are well documented in recent empirical scholarship. One consistent finding is that many audiences sanction organizations that do not conform to cultural codes. For instance, firms that do not fall within standard industry categories and, therefore, are not followed consistently by a homogenous set of analysts suffer an "illegitimacy" discount (Zuckerman, 1999). Exceptions to this rule tend to apply in contexts where categories have yet to be institutionalized, as reflected in a lack of trained observers, taken-for-granted systems of classification, and/or organizational routines and infrastructure for assigning organizations to categories (Ruef & Patterson, 2009). Partiality may also be beneficial to newly emerging forms, which must simultaneously signal some differentiation from existing organizational arrangements—or risk being subsumed by them—while also drawing on the legitimacy of established categories (Ruef, 2000).

Another insight in the literature on cultural codes is that audience segments may include other organizations in a field: "producers themselves are [an] audience to each other" (Hannan, Pólos, & Carroll, 2007, p. 36). Brint and colleagues (2006) deploy this intuition to map the perceived structure of the field of higher education, drawing on the reference sets of universities that college presidents either believe to be similar to their own ("current reference set") or aspire to become ("aspiration reference set"). In the aggregate, the first set of comparisons thus allow us to view the cultural codes and boundaries that structure subjective categories formed by leaders in higher education, while the second set of comparisons address how well the aspirational identities of their institutions map onto those categories. Comparing the classifications that result from the current reference set of college presidents with other schemata, the correspondence to institutions identified inductively through a cluster analysis of "objective" features in the IDA survey is high—for example, 85 percent of presidential choices in a cluster of large research universities reference other universities within the same objective category. This statistic falls, however, for more peripheral categories in the field of higher education. For instance, 56 percent of presidential choices in a cluster of nonselective baccalaureate-granting colleges reference other colleges within that category. Moreover, the ability of a priori typologies, such as the Carnegie Classification, to capture the cultural boundaries drawn by university presidents seems to be modest. When Brint and colleagues (2006, Table 2) apply the 2000 Carnegie codes to 270 institutions in their sample, they find that only 54 percent of the reference choices fall within the Carnegie categories on average. The fit is especially poor for less prototypical schools, such as the institutions in the MA II (Master's Colleges and Universities) category (a mere 8 percent match with reference choices).

Summary

Our review of the literature on organizational forms suggests a rich array of perspectives and inductive tools for classifying organizations into categories, many of which have been applied in educational contexts. It also reveals dissatisfaction with a previous generation of a priori typologies, such as the Carnegie Classification, which sorted organizations into mutually exclusive categories based on heuristic rules, rather than statistical criteria or theoretical considerations.

Nevertheless, our understanding of classification in higher education remains incomplete. Partially, this is a problem of data. Surveys of institutions of higher education are often limited to four-year colleges and universities, excluding two-year colleges, for-profit schools, and many specialized institutions (e.g., Brint et al., 2006). This inevitably leads to the exclusion of many newer organizational forms in the field, especially those devoted to broad-access education. Moreover, the attributes chosen to guide any particular classification schema tend to be small in number, often limited to one audience of organizational observers or otherwise constrained by one of the perspectives shown in Table 4.1. Following McKelvey (1975), we argue instead that the data used to inform organizational classification ought to (a) sample from the broadest possible population of colleges and universities, (b) analyze institutional attributes and identity claims as inclusively as possible, and (c) address the viewpoints of multiple observers, including those internal to university and college administrations, as well as external stakeholders, such as prospective students and third-party evaluators (e.g., *U.S. News and World Report* rankings, *Princeton Review*, the American Association for Higher Education and Accreditation [AAHE], and the Council for Higher Education Accreditation [CHEA]).

The other problem with existing inductive approaches to organizational classification is one of modeling. We expect that the categories applied to institutions of higher learning will be relatively homogeneous, with a firm empirical foundation for the boundaries drawn between them. Early efforts at inducing taxonomies of organizations, such as those of the Aston Group, continued to rely on rules of thumb (e.g., means of dimensions in a factor analysis), rather than statistical criteria for distinguishing among categories (McKelvey, 1975). As noted previously, the recent literature has also recognized that category membership may be partial, with hybrid organizations that may be mapped to multiple categories (Albert & Whetten, 1985; Hannan, 2010). Traditional models of organizational classification, which emphasize discrete, mutually exclusive categories, are ill-suited to represent such hybridity. Finally, the existing inductive models tend to fit categories closely to the clusters of organizational features that are observed in specific data sets, leading to problems of "overfitting" and a poor ability to extrapolate classification to new organizations. Given the rapid evolution of the field of higher education, it seems critical that any existing system of classification be able to accommodate new colleges and universities without redrawing category boundaries in an ad hoc fashion.

These considerations lead to three additional criteria for classification, wherein inductive models ought to (d) identify relatively homogeneous categories of organizations on a statistical basis, (e) allow some organizations to exhibit partial membership in multiple categories, and (f) permit analysts to systematically infer the classification of new kinds of organizations, even when the data on those entities were not available when the original system of classification was developed. We now turn to the preliminary development of some tools for organizational classification, with these criteria in mind.

Data and Model

Data

Our sample of colleges and universities is drawn from the U.S. Department of Education's Integrated Postsecondary Education Data System (IPEDS), which is also employed by the Carnegie Foundation. IPEDS has a number of desirable attributes for purposes of developing systems of classification in higher education. On an annual basis, it collects data from every U.S. university, college, and vocational school that participates in federal student financial aid programs, as well as a smaller number of schools that do not. While IPEDS does emphasize degree-granting institutions, the sample is extremely broad, covering organizations that range from research universities and state colleges to technical schools, for-profit universities, tribal colleges, and schools of cosmetology. Under Title IV of the Higher Education Act (1965), data reporting is mandatory for any institution where students may receive federal funding.

The set of school attributes reported for the IPEDS surveys is also broad, covering institutional characteristics, demographics of enrolled students, faculty and staff composition and compensation, student financial aid, admission and test scores, graduation rates, and, in some years, mission statements. For purposes of exploratory analysis, we emphasize three clusters of variables that map closely onto the theoretical distinctions shown in Table 4.1. With respect to internal, institutional characteristics, we consider (1) institutional control (public, for-profit, secular nonprofit, religious nonprofit), degrees offered, forms of instruction (e.g., occupational, academic, continuing professional), special learning opportunities (distance learning, Reserve Officer Training Corps [ROTC], study abroad, etc.), and whether a school accepts various forms of transfer credits. With respect to the resource niche of each school, we consider (2) the gender, race, age, international, and in-state demographics of the student body (fall enrollment), with each dimension differentiated by percentage quintiles across the IPEDS sample. Finally, for subjective claims of identity, we consider (3) the mission statements that were issued by each school, as reflected in statements either provided directly to IPEDS (up to two thousand characters) or in school web pages. Table 4.2 illustrates these characteristics for a typical broad-access institution.

We impose some limitations on the scope of attributes used for organizational classification in the exploratory analyses. First, we do not consider any of the numerous performance metrics reported in IPEDS (especially student

TABLE 4.2 Reported characteristics for sample college in IPEDS database

Name:	**Shelton State Community College** (2007)
Location:	**Tuscaloosa, AL**
Carnegie Classification:	Associates College
Institutional control:	Public
Degrees awarded:	Certificates (up to two years), associate degrees
Educational offerings:	Academic, occupational, recreational, adult basic
Special learning opportunities:	Distance learning, ROTC, weekend/evening classes
Transfer credits:	Dual credits, AP credits
Other institutional characteristics:	Has library, historically black college
Gender composition:	54.3% female
Racial composition:	64.7% white, 29.1% black, 1.1% Hispanic, 5.2% other
Age composition:	47.5% under age 22; 36.3% age 22–29; 16.2% over age 29
International students:	0.1%
In-state students:	99.5%
Mission statement:	Shelton State Community College is a public *open-admission* comprehensive community college whose primary mission is to provide *accessible* postsecondary education, training, and community educational opportunities.

⟹ Internal structures and routines

⟹ Demographic niche

⟹ Organizational identity

test scores and completion rates), since we seek to separate the classification of institutions involved in higher education from efforts to evaluate them. Second, we do not consider subjective, external classifications of schools and universities by third parties. While various observers within a school may be asked to respond to IPEDS surveys, this data collection effort does not ask for external attributions from third parties.[4]

The following analyses focus on IPEDS data for schools in 2007, the most recent year when surveys collected mission statements from school administrators. For schools where mission data were not provided directly, mission statements were retrieved via a Google query that searched for "mission" or "about" in an institution's web pages. Harvesting data from the Internet was done using a web-crawling program for 1,100 schools. For data obtained from sites outside IPEDS, data cleaning was required to remove HTML code and as much header, footer, and navigation text as possible to focus data entries on mission statements themselves. Data cleaning was performed both in an automated fashion and by hand.[5]

Model

We model the assignment of organizations to categories using a suite of algorithms termed *probabilistic topic models*, focusing in particular on latent Dirichlet allocation (LDA), the simplest kind of topic model (Blei et al., 2003). To motivate this approach, we begin by assuming that the categories in a classification schema are defined as a probability distribution over a set of attributes or words used to describe organizations. For example, a category of "medical schools" in higher education might be associated with objective features, such as having a hospital, and identity claims regarding professional competence, each with a high probability. The same category might also have a very low probability of being linked to other attributes, such as remedial adult education or identity claims regarding environmental stewardship.

Following the intuition of Blei (2012), we then assume that a description of a specific organization sampled from a population is produced in a three-stage process: (1) the organization itself is characterized as being distributed over categories (which may involve exclusive membership in a single category or partial membership in multiple categories); (2) for each attribute or identity claim involving the organization, a relevant membership category is chosen at random (subject to the distribution in [1]), and then (3) a specific feature is chosen at random from the category's vocabulary of attributes (subject to the category selected in [2] and the preexisting distribution of attributes or words linked to the classification schema). So if the Southwest College of Naturopathic Medicine has a partial membership in the category of medical schools (e.g., 0.9) and a (much smaller) partial membership in the category of environmental and naturopathic programs (0.1), then there is a 0.9 probability that an identity claim in the college's mission statement will be selected from those that are typical of other medical schools.

The methodological challenge for LDA is that only the attributes or identity claims linked to organizations are observed in any given sample, while the underlying categories are latent (i.e., hidden) and must be inferred from those associations. To formalize the model, we let $\beta_{1:K}$ correspond to the K latent categories (where β_k is the distribution over a vocabulary in a category), $\theta_{1:M}$ correspond to the category memberships for the M organizations in a sample (where θ_m identifies the category membership for the mth organization), $z_{1:M}$ enumerate the categories assigned to individual attributes used to describe the organizations (where $z_{m,n}$ is the category for the nth attribute and the mth organization), and $w_{1:M}$ enumerate the words that are actually observed in the descriptions of the organizations (where $w_{m,n}$ is the word given to the nth attribute and the mth organization). With this notation, Blei (2012) notes that the generative process for LDA is given by the following joint distribution:

$$p(\beta_{1:K},\theta_{1:M},z_{1:M},w_{1:M})=\prod_{k=1}^{K}p(\beta_k)\prod_{m=1}^{M}p(\theta_m)\left(\prod_{n=1}^{N}p(z_{m,n}\,|\,\theta_m)p(w_{m,n}\,|\,\beta_{1:K},z_{m,n})\right)$$

The LDA procedure relies on hierarchical Bayesian modeling to fit categories to the observed attributes or identity claims of organizations. Bayesian modeling attempts to calculate a *posterior distribution* of the parameters that might generate the data observed. In LDA, the two key parameters are *Dirichlet* distributions (an extension of the beta distribution often used as priors in lower dimensional Bayesian models). The first key Dirichlet distribution is θ, the distribution of categories over organizations, which is sampled to assign how much of an organizational description is devoted to a certain category. The second Dirichlet distribution is β, which is sampled to assign the likelihood that an attribute or identity claim is devoted to a certain category. The interaction of these two parameters with the other multinomial distributions (z and w) shown in the equation results in the assignment of each attribute in an organizational description to a single category. The assignment of each attribute to a category still allows for organizations to be assigned to multiple categories. It also allows for polysemy—multiple instances of the same attribute in an organizational description that are assigned to different categories when distinct meanings are expressed.

Calculating posterior distributions in Bayesian modeling involves calculating integrals. However, the high-dimension integrals involved in hierarchical models like LDA are not directly calculable and must instead be approximated. The use of Markov chain Monte Carlo (MCMC), and especially the Gibbs sampler, has provided a necessary tool for the proliferation of Bayesian methods. In MCMC methods, repeated samples are taken from a given complex distribution, and the values of a previous sample draw determine subsequent sample draws, with the process continuing until convergence is found.

What LDA provides in terms of tangible data are *category attribute assignments*. In essence every attribute in an organizational description is assigned to a category at a given probability. This category assignment helps determine the *categorical membership* for each organization. From category attribute assignments, terms (unique attributes) can be scored in regard to their relevance to a category. From this scoring, term lists can be analyzed by researchers to analyze whether a category is meaningful. The following discussion of the application of LDA to the IPEDS data set offers examples of the output produced by the method.

Results

For the sake of comparison, we set the number of categories (K) to eighteen forms of organizations involved in postsecondary education, equal to that used in the 2000 Carnegie Classification system.[6] Tables 4.3, 4.4, and 4.5 summarize the preliminary results of categories derived through probabilistic topic modeling, focusing on internal institutional characteristics, student demographics, and mission statements, respectively.

Considering the classification of schools by internal institutional characteristics (Table 4.3), we find that there is considerable homogeneity among the elite research universities, coupled with great diversity among lower-tier, broad-access institutions. In contrast to the Carnegie Classification, which draws fine-grained distinctions among research universities (extensive and intensive), the LDA-derived schema places these institutions in a single category. Among the next tier of institutions, the LDA schema employs approximately as many distinctions as the Carnegie system. For instance, comprehensive colleges and universities are divided into two categories, with another category for religious liberal arts colleges. The LDA schema adds a new category of "professional schools," which subsumes a variety of specialized institutions emphasizing graduate-level education in the Carnegie classification (schools of law, graduate schools of business and management, etc.). At the baccalaureate level, the LDA schema distinguishes three categories, like the Carnegie Classification, albeit with a stronger emphasis on technical schools (Technical and Art Institutes I and II, Liberal Arts Schools).[7]

TABLE 4.3 LDA categories inferred from the internal structure and routines of U.S. postsecondary institutions

Category	Attributes	Institutional examples
Associate Colleges	Public, Associate Degree, Transfer Credits, Distance Learning	Eastern Arizona College, Sacramento City College
Community Colleges I	Public, Adult Basic and Recreational Instruction, No Bachelor's, Transfer Credits, Distance Learning	Glendale Community College, Asnuntuck Community College, Community College of Aurora
Community Colleges II	Public, Adult Basic and Recreational Instruction, No Bachelor's, Transfer Credits, Distance Learning	Rich Mountain Community College, Los Angeles Pierce College, Housatonic Community College
Comprehensives I (Career-Focused)	Bachelor's or Master's Degree, Teacher Certification, Study Abroad, Transfers	Saint Joseph College, University of Miami
Comprehensives II (Liberal Arts)	Bachelor's or Master's Degree, Teacher Certification, Study Abroad, Transfers	Husson College; Concordia University, St. Paul
Cosmetology and Med Tech Schools	Private For-Profit, No Bachelor's or Advanced Degrees, No Transfer Credits	Arkansas Beauty College, First Institute
Cosmetology Schools II	Private For-Profit, No Bachelor's or Advanced Degrees, No Transfer Credits	New Tyler Barber College, Elegance International
District and System Offices	Not applicable	City Colleges of Chicago, U-Hawaii System Office
Liberal Arts Schools	Bachelor's Degree, Teacher Certification, Transfer Credits, Study Abroad	Knox College, Lycoming College
Professional Schools	Private Nonprofit, Master's/Professional Degree, No SLOs, No Transfer Credits	Southwestern Law School, Fielding Graduate University
Religious Liberal Arts Schools	Private Nonprofit–Religious, Bachelor's or Master's Degree, Teacher Certification, Transfer Credits	Campbellsville University, College of the Holy Cross, Gordon College
Research Universities	Bachelor's, Master's, and Doctoral Degrees; Teacher Certification, AP Credit	University of Idaho, Drake University
Technical and Art Institutes I	Bachelor's Degree, No Advanced Degrees, Transfer Credits, Distance Learning	ITT Technical Institute, DeVry University
Technical and Art Institutes II	Private For-Profit, Associate or Bachelor's Degree, AP Credits	Indiana Business College, New England Institute of Art
Trade Schools I	Private For-Profit, Two-Year Certificates, No SLOs, No Transfer Credits	Refrigeration School, Taylor Business Institute

TABLE 4.3 (*continued*)

Category	Attributes	Institutional examples
Trade Schools II	No Bachelor's or Advanced Degrees, No SLOs, No Transfer Credits	Bridgerland Applied Tech, Everest College–Reseda
Trade Schools III	Private For-Profit, No Bachelor's or Advanced Degrees, No SLOs, No Transfer Credits	South Coast College, Stenotype Institute
Vocational Schools	No Bachelor's or Advanced Degrees, No SLOs, No Transfer Credits	Lincoln Technical Institute, Marinello School of Beauty

SOURCE: IPEDS module on institutional characteristics, 2007.
NOTE: "SLOs" refers to special learning opportunities, including distance learning, ROTC, study abroad, teacher certification, and weekend/evening classes.

TABLE 4.4 LDA categories inferred from the demographic niches of U.S. postsecondary institutions

Category	Attributes	Institutional examples
Career Colleges I	Medium Size, More Women, Older Students	Stautzenberger College, Career Technical College
Career Colleges II	Small Size, More Women, Oldest Students, Many Asian Students	Brown Mackie College, Indiana Business College
Career Colleges III	Medium Size, More Women, Older, Many Black and Hispanic Students	Concorde Career College, St. Louis College of Health Careers
Community Colleges I	Very Large Size, Many International, Part-Time Students	Riverside Community College, Butler Community College
Community Colleges II	Large Size, Part-Time Students, Few Asian Students	Appalachian Technical College, Edison State Community
Community Colleges III	Very Large Size, Part-Time, International Students	Cumberland County College, Neumann College
Community-Oriented Colleges	Large Size, Part-Time, International Students	North Florida Community, Buena Vista University
Continuing Ed Colleges I	Very Small Size, Oldest Students, Part-Time Students	Southeastern Business College, South Texas Barber College
Continuing Ed Colleges II	Small Size, Oldest Students	Antioch University, California Career College
Liberal Arts Colleges	Large Size, Young Students, Few In-State Students	Occidental College, Colorado College
Men's Military Schools	Medium Size, More Men, Young Students	Massachusetts Maritime Academy
Men's Vocational I	Small Size, More Men, Many Hispanic and Asian Students	Golf Academy of the Carolinas, Tennessee Technology Center

(*continued*)

TABLE 4.4 (*continued*)

Category	Attributes	Institutional examples
Men's Vocational II	Medium Size, More Men, Older Students	American Film Institute, Pennco Tech
Universities I	Very Large Size, Many International Students	University of South Alabama, CSU-Sacramento
Universities II	Very Large Size, Many International, Some Part-Time Students	Indiana State University, SUNY at Albany
Women's Vocational I	Very Small Size, Mostly Women, Many Hispanic and Asian Students	Professional Choice Hair, Dayton School of Hair
Women's Vocational II	Very Small Size, Mostly Women, Many Hispanic and Asian Students	Associated Technical College, Artistic Beauty College
Women's Vocational III	Very Small Size, Mostly Women, Many Minority Students	Toni and Guy Hairdressing, California Hair Design

SOURCE: IPEDS module on fall enrollments, 2007.

TABLE 4.5 LDA categories inferred from mission statements of U.S. postsecondary institutions

Category	Identity Claims	Institutional Examples
Art and Music Schools	School, Design, Music, Department, Art, College, Accrediting, Association	Hussian School of Art, Conservatory of Recording Arts
Career Colleges	Career, Skills, Training, Technical, Employment, Provide, Business, Job	College America, Medina County Career Center
Christian Colleges	Christian, God, Church, Seminary, Theological, Ministry, Jesus, Faith	Boise Bible College, Lutheran Theological Seminary
Community Colleges I	College, Community, Programs, Technical, Services, Associate, Transfer	Estrella Mountain Community, Wilkes Community
Community Colleges II	College, Community, Services, Quality, Needs, Support, Accessible, System	Coffeyville Community, South Piedmont Community College
Cosmetology Schools	Cosmetology, Beauty, State, Field, School, Pass, Training, Hair, Industry	Fayetteville Beauty College, Award Beauty School
Globally-Oriented Colleges	Global, Community, World, Values, Knowledge, Develop, Society, Diversity	Salem International University, Lafayette College
Liberal Arts Schools I	College, Arts, Liberal, Professional, Learning, Student, Personal, Diverse	Wheaton College, James Madison University

TABLE 4.5 *(continued)*

Category	Identity Claims	Institutional Examples
Liberal Arts Schools II	College, Human, Arts, Women, Justice, Commitment, Liberal, Intellectual	Siena College, Albright College
Massage Schools	Massage, Therapy, Providing, Quality, Dedicated, Highest, Institute, Graduates	New York Institute of Massage, E. Grady School of Esthetics and Massage Therapy
Medical Schools	Healthcare, Medical, Program, Research, Professional, Clinical, Practice	Jefferson College of Health, Academy of Oriental Medicine
Medical Tech Schools	Center, Medical, Engineering, Computer, State, Science, Student	Cleveland Institute of Dental-Medical Assistants, McLeod Regional Medical Center School
Nursing Schools	Nursing, Healthcare, Practice, Promote, Needs, Demonstrate, Competent, Skills	Episcopal School of Nursing, Medcenter 1 College of Nursing
Research-Oriented Universities	University, Research, State, Graduate, Undergraduate, Public, Programs	University of Mississippi, Eastern Kentucky University
Student-Oriented Universities	Community, Learning, University, Excellence, Values, Student, Diversity	Berkeley City College, Cameron University
Talmudic Seminaries	Understanding, Jewish, Seek, Moral, Ethical, Help, World, Means, Build	Telshe Yeshiva, Yeshiva Toras Chaim Talmudical Seminary
Technical Schools	Provide, Quality, Technology, Care, Employees, Services, Health, Focused	Chubb Institute, High-Tech Institute
Trade Schools	School, Training, Law, Industry, Career, Skills, Hands, World, Program, Classes	Tulsa Welding School, New England Culinary Institute

SOURCE: IPEDS module on mission statements, 2007.
NOTE: Excludes seven residual categories with low mission statement proportions or highly heterogeneous vocabulary.

The more striking divergence between the two classification systems occurs among institutions that do not offer at least a bachelor's degree. The 2000 Carnegie Classification applies a single category ("Associate's Colleges") to a diverse range of community, junior, and technical colleges, as well as other schools offering postsecondary vocational training. Yet in 2007, these organizations composed nearly one quarter of the entire population of schools in American higher education. On the basis of internal variation in school structure and pedagogical routines, the LDA model breaks this group into nine categories. For instance, community colleges are distinguished as public institutions that offer basic adult (e.g., GED) and recreational education.[8] In the interest of brevity, we do not discuss the differentiating features of other categories in the LDA classification here. But the general inference is clear: *the statistical variation in internal structure and pedagogy among non-baccalaureate-granting institutions requires a more nuanced classification than that presumed by the older Carnegie Classifications.*

An LDA analysis of the demographics of student populations across U.S. campuses reveals some similarities and some differences from the classifications induced from institutional characteristics alone (see Table 4.4). The research and state universities are placed into two categories, both of which are characterized by their large size and relatively high enrollments of international students. A distinguishing feature between them is the extent to which they encourage the enrollment of part-time students. The classic liberal arts colleges have student bodies that are slightly smaller, younger, and less likely to originate from the same state as their schools. Along with men's military schools, these categories capture a good deal of the variation in the demographic niches among higher-tier institutions.

As was the case for institutional characteristics, the LDA model proposes a large number of categories to accommodate the heterogeneity in student demography among broad-access institutions. For instance, in a set of categories that we label as "career colleges," the students are older, more likely to be female, and, often, more likely to be minorities than the students found in traditional institutions of higher education. Many of these colleges prepare their graduates for careers in health care, information technology, nursing, paralegal work, and the like. Another set of categories that we label as "men's vocational schools" are oriented toward male students, but also feature more minorities (category I) or older students (category II) than those found on traditional college campuses. The training in these institutions varies from esoteric pursuits—such as golf course management and cinematography—to automotive technology, computer-aided drafting, and HVAC repair.

Our inductive analysis of mission statements (Table 4.5) yields the greatest number of categorical distinctions among traditional institutions of higher learning and the lowest number of categories for broad-access institutions. The mission statements of universities differentiate between a category of institutions that emphasize research and those that highlight the diversity and values of their students. The identity claims of liberal arts colleges fall into three categories: those that embrace a global mission, those that highlight a classic liberal arts curriculum, and those that advocate progressivism in spheres such as social justice or the advancement of women. Baccalaureate and postgraduate schools with a religious identity (particularly Christian colleges and Talmudic seminaries) also stand out in analyzing mission statements.

The broad-access institutions, by contrast, tend to emphasize more mundane and practical concerns in describing themselves, with a focus on careers, technology, and training. On the basis of the LDA analysis, these institutions fall into ten categories: art schools, career colleges, cosmetology programs, institutes for massage therapy, medical technology programs, nursing schools, technical schools, trade schools, and (two forms of) community colleges. Compared to the inductive analyses of institutional characteristics and demographics, the mission statements tend to differentiate broad-access institutions by career tracks rather than institutional control, pedagogy, or student diversity.

Discussion

In the interest of stimulating new approaches to the classification of educational institutions, this chapter has provided an overview of frameworks that address categorization in organizational theory, as well as a probabilistic model (LDA) that allows these frameworks to be applied to empirical data on trade schools, colleges, and universities. Preliminary results suggest that the inductive LDA model may be well suited to categorize a variety of postsecondary institutions. Nevertheless, optimism must be tempered by the exploratory nature of this research. Far more work needs to be done to assess the reliability of categories derived using probabilistic topic modeling, assessing category consistency in the face of changing sets of attributes, samples of educational institutions, and organizational observers. With respect to the latter, our analyses have relied exclusively on attributes reported by university and college administrators, as well as members of the student population. An important supplement to the IPEDS database would consist of external (particularly, qualitative) assessments of postsecondary institutions, such as those offered by "college guides" and other third-party observers.

The construct validity of inductively derived classifications must also be examined in greater detail. In comparing these approaches to a priori schema for the classification of institutions in higher education, the implicit claims are that LDA models will create more "meaningful" categories for purposes of peer comparison and more "explanatory" categories for purposes of analyzing educational outcomes. The first claim can be investigated by interrogating the folk taxonomies used by administrators themselves (i.e., whom they identify as their peer institutions). The second claim can be assessed by considering the ability of the inductive classifications to explain student admissions, completions, financial aid, and job placements, as well as organizational outcomes such as research productivity, graduation rates, fiscal integrity, and reputation. If inductive approaches tend to explain more variance in such outcomes and prove more meaningful to university and college administrators, it may be time to jettison the Carnegie Classification in favor of alternative perspectives on organizational classification.

Notes

1. Meanwhile, more specialized classifications—such as those limited to for-profit institutions of higher learning—have been issued by other organizations (e.g., Institute for Higher Education Policy, 2012).

2. In referring to such features as "internal," it is perhaps important to acknowledge that they may nevertheless be transferred from one organization to another. Indeed, an early critique of analogies between biological species and organizational populations was that the blueprints used to define the latter lacked the property of heritability (Betton & Dess, 1985). A rich literature has subsequently developed to tackle the question of how personnel flows may transfer formal structure and routines from older to newer organizations (e.g., Phillips, 2002).

3. One telling marker, in this respect, was the title of a 1979 article in *Administrative Science Quarterly*, which called for the *resurrection* of taxonomic approaches to organizational analysis (Pinder & Moore, 1979), as pioneered in the 1960s by the Aston Group and Haas and colleagues (1966).

4. One alternative source of external categorization, however, may be the peer groups that are constructed by college administrators and submitted annually to the U.S. Department of Education (see Fuller, 2012).

5. Following listwise deletion, we have data on the institutional characteristics of 6,902 schools, on the fall enrollment demographics of 6,761 schools, and on the mission statements of 4,359 schools (including identity claims retrieved from school web pages).

6. Although the number of categories in an LDA classification is essentially arbitrary, calibrating it with an existing classification of colleges and universities offers two methodological advantages. First, it allows analysts to evaluate whether an inductively derived system of categories explains more variance in some outcome than an a priori

system, such as the Carnegie Classification, without adjusting model fit for the number of categories. Second, it allows differences between an inductively derived set of categories and a priori system to be evaluated directly, based on either the "meaning" attached to categories or the mapping of colleges and universities to them.

7. One distinction between the two technical school categories appears to hinge on the fact that the first group tends to highlight distance and online learning opportunities.

8. Of course, these broad-access institutions are known for their vocational programs as well. But this feature does not differentiate them very clearly from the other schools offering associate degrees and postsecondary certificates.

PART II

COLLEGE AND THE LIFE COURSE

5

THE NEW LANDSCAPE
OF EARLY ADULTHOOD

Implications for Broad-Access Higher Education

Richard A. Settersten, Jr.

The aim of this chapter is to situate the task of "remaking college" within the context of the radically altered landscape of early adult life: the ages from about eighteen to thirty-four.[1] Understanding this new landscape is important for mapping broad-access higher education because many of the challenges and opportunities in higher education today are tied to it.

A big part of the story about what is happening with young people today is also enmeshed with what is happening in higher education. How higher education plays out for young people is a major driver of inequality as individuals move through their twenties and as resulting advantages and disadvantages accumulate in the decades of life that follow. This story is not just about credentials and access to good jobs, better salaries, or greater job stability. It is also about a larger bundle of positive noneconomic outcomes that come with higher education. The significance of higher education in fueling these effects only heightens the need for immediate and revolutionary approaches to redesigning college.

The chapter begins by highlighting some key shifts in traditional markers of adulthood, and some problematic ways that researchers, educators, and the public think about the early adult years. It then turns to two hallmarks of this period of life today: the need to manage uncertainty, which is both something created by higher education and something to which higher education responds, and the need for *interdependence with* others, rather than complete *independence from* others, which is a traditionally cherished American ideal. The need for interdependence is reinforced by the sizable family support, both emotional and financial, now necessary for the success of young people—especially in navigating and financing higher education. Colleges and universities are unquestionably the most important institutions in which rising numbers of young adults spend time after they finish high school. Strengthening pathways into and through higher education, particularly broad-access schools, is central to strengthening the transition to adulthood. The chapter concludes with a discussion of the purpose and design of higher education, not only for launching young people into adulthood but also for lifelong learning and the organization of the entire life course.

Major Demographic Shifts in Early Adulthood and Their Implications for Higher Education

The last fifty years brought major demographic shifts in what we might call the "big five" social markers traditionally associated with becoming adult: leaving home, finishing school, finding work, getting married, and having children. From my perspective, the most profound changes are as follows, and all have important implications for higher education today.

Independent Living

Becoming an adult today involves a period of living independently before marriage. The media often paints a different picture, with its attention to the growing shares of young people who stay at home longer or return home later. But in the middle of the last century, young people were quick to leave home but quick to marry. What is perhaps the most remarkable shift in the early adult years is that they now entail a significant period of living without a spouse.

Of the many different living arrangements of young adults, only a subset involves parents (see also Rosenthal, 2007). The media would have us believe that living at home has become the "new normal." But living with parents in early adulthood is not new—these numbers have been growing for a few decades, even in better economic times. The recent economic downturn has simply heightened trends that have been growing since the 1980s. This signals to me a more fundamental change in the nature of parent-child relationships, as new kinds of parents have also actively cultivated new kinds of relationships with their children; the closeness and connection they feel make it more possible to live together. Interestingly, rates of coresidence with parents and extended family members today are actually lower than they were in the first few decades of the 1900s.

The proportions of young people living with parents are also not big enough to shoulder the claim that it has become normal and expectable for everyone or that it occurs for an extended period of time. Proportions are indeed sizable between ages eighteen and twenty-four because these are years that entail the most dramatic change in the lives of young people. In 2011, the percentage of young adults age eighteen to twenty-four who were classified as living with their parents was 59 percent for men and 50 percent for women, though this is inflated by college-going (that is, college students who depend on parents but live away are nonetheless classified as living at home) (U.S. Census Bureau, 2011). But for young adults age twenty-five to thirty-four, only 19 percent of men and 10 percent of women were classified as living with their parents. Coresidence with parents virtually disappears after age thirty-five. When it happens after age thirty-five, coresidence may have as much to do with the circumstances of parents and other family members as it does with the circumstances of children, if not more.

The shares of young people who live with parents are always higher for men than women, and for minority and most immigrant groups (particularly second-generation immigrant youth) than native-born whites. The cultures of many of these groups not only make it permissible for young people to stay at home but even carry the expectation that young people do so to contribute to the household or to conserve family resources (Rumbaut & Komaie, 2010).

In the United States, there is so much attention to living at home because leaving home has traditionally been the surest sign of independence—and independence has, in turn, traditionally been the surest sign of adulthood. As those links dissolve, it is no surprise that public concern increases. But as the prevalence of coresidence with parents grows, young people and their parents may begin to see living together as a more viable option and feel less shame. This is true in countries where there is a cultural expectation that young people remain at home until they marry or where the high cost or limited availability of housing makes multigenerational living a necessity (for international evidence, see Newman & Aptekar, 2007; Yelowitz, 2007).

In the United States, this cultural assumption—that youth should leave home early and not return—must be reconsidered. Evidence suggests that living with parents is not necessarily bad, even if it brings strain or challenges convention. For some youth and their parents, living at home can be a smart, and often mutual, choice and strategy for getting ahead (Settersten & Ray, 2010). This is particularly true if young people are working on degrees and gaining experiences that will help them in the job market, or are building a nest egg for a stronger launch and to pay off college debt. It is also true if parents have limited financial resources to help their children with higher education, and the provision of housing and other in-kind support makes higher education possible or frees up resources for other purposes. One striking fact that is seldom part of public discourse is that living at home keeps many young adults, even on the older end, out of poverty. For example, the official percentage of people age twenty-five to thirty-four in poverty in 2009 was 15 percent; without living at home, the poverty rate would have been an estimated 43 percent (Rich, 2010; U.S. Census Bureau, 2011). A common justification for requiring students to live on campus is that it leads some students to build relationships and access institutional resources that facilitate their success; yet for other students, these same requirements may create unnecessary financial hardship and may extract them from the more immediate support of families in ensuring success.

The Widespread Pursuit of Higher Education

The early adult years now involve the widespread pursuit of higher education, as a decent standard of living today generally requires college. This is the change most directly related to the task of remaking college. Higher education is central to the aspirations of most high school students: by their senior year, about two thirds of students today have definite plans to graduate from a four-year college, and one fourth plan on graduating from a two-year college (Aud et al., 2012; Schneider, Judy, Mazuca, & Broda, 2014). Only a fraction (12 percent) plans on entering vocational school or joining the military. These aspirations differ little by gender and race and ethnicity alone. What matters most is social class, where over 75 percent of students with parents who have college or professional degrees plan to graduate from college.

Over the past four decades, the costs of higher education have grown in tandem with the relentless demand for it, leading many young people and parents to wonder whether a bachelor's degree, in particular, is still "worth it" financially. The evidence suggests that it is: economic returns to education have increased in recent years, even after taking into account the greater costs of obtaining an education (Barrow & Rouse, 2005; Beach, 2009). But there is also growing cause for concern that the wages of college graduates are beginning to stagnate. In addition, a college education mainly "pays" if students actually finish; a partial degree does not bring the same benefits in salary or leverage on the job market.

Yet the evidence also suggests that choices about higher education must be strategic. Questions about whether or how much college "pays" must be understood in conjunction with debt. Debt taken must be judged against later potential earnings. This makes choices about majors or professions a crucial part of determining risk. Students also fare best when they are well matched (neither under- or overmatched) to the institutions they attend because their chances for completion are greater (Bowen, Chingos, & McPherson, 2009). Despite rampant concerns about student debt loads, some economists worry that students may underinvest in their futures, especially in hard economic times (e.g., Avery & Turner, 2012). As is also noted later, employment and pay alone are narrow indicators of the value of a college degree, which is associated with many positive life outcomes besides income (Hout, 2012).

Consistent with widespread aspirations for higher education, the bulk of high school graduates (70 percent) enroll in some type of postsecondary institution immediately after high school. At greatest risk are students who are sorely unprepared for college but have absorbed the mantra that college is for everyone. Although young adults today are more educated than any previous generation, many are floundering badly. Despite great advances in access to college on the front end, degree completion on the back end is very low (see also Brock, 2010). Graduation rates for full-time, first-time students at four-year universities seeking a bachelor's degree are 59 percent within six years and 60 percent within eight (Aud et al., 2010; Goldrick-Rab & Roksa, 2008). Only 37 percent of full-time students are graduating within the traditional four years (Knapp, Kelly-Reid, & Ginder, 2012). Graduation rates of African American and American Indian students are even more alarming. Only 40 percent of students in those two racial/ethnic categories graduate within six years, compared to Asians, whites, and Hispanics, who have rates of 70 percent, 62 percent, and 51 percent, respectively (Knapp et al., 2012).

Students in four-year institutions, then, are rarely finishing four-year degrees, and after six years, a student's chances of finishing are slim to nonexistent. In addition to a range of factors related to readiness, direction, and cost, the longer time to degree completion today is also produced by growing numbers of students who are combining school, work, and/or family (Fitz-patrick & Turner, 2007). This is especially true in broad-access environments. The bottom line is that the odds of finishing college are much lower than the public or politicians would like to admit, and young people and their families must more critically assess the chances of finishing as they make college choices. This is not easy.

While "college for all" is a salient cultural message, it is important to realize that only 32 percent of young adults between ages twenty-five and twenty-nine have a bachelor's degree today, and only 7 percent have graduate degrees (Aud et al., 2012). What is more, these basic figures have not changed significantly since the 1970s. This fact should shock the common assumption that acquiring a college degree has become normative for the masses. The fact that so many students start but do not finish today leads one to wonder whether college graduation will ever become normative, even with the more deliberate design and intentional support of broad-access institutions. And yet it is clear we must try: college completion sharply divides the well-being of individuals on many indicators throughout the subsequent life course.

Long Route to Financial Security

Regardless of whether young people enter college, it takes longer today to secure a full-time job that pays enough to support a family, and young people now have a greater range of employment experiences on their way to financial security. A greater share of young adults (age eighteen to thirty-four) in 2010 was living in poverty than the national average (18 percent versus 15 percent), and was particularly high for eighteen- to twenty-four-year olds (21 percent) (DeNavas-Walt, Proctor, & Smith, 2011). In the last three decades, those without college degrees have seen their wages and benefits erode. But even a college degree does not always guarantee stable wages and benefits. College graduates have made gains in earnings, but the strongest gains have come to men who completed some graduate school (Danziger, 2004; Danziger & Ratner, 2010). The earnings of women have improved and grown at greater rates than those for men, but their starting points were much lower and their average earnings remain below men's (Danziger, 2004; Danziger & Ratner, 2010). Of course, for men and women alike, even small gains in income because of college translate into sizable effects on lifetime earnings. As we will see, these factors are crucial to evaluating the relative costs and benefits of higher education.

The Timing of Partnering and Parenting

As a consequence of the aforementioned changes, marriage and parenting, in aggregate, now come much later in the life course. Whereas once couples partnered early and became adults together, young adults today build their own lives and then marry (Cherlin, 2005; Furstenberg, 2010). In 2010, the median age at first marriage exceeded twenty-eight for men and twenty-six for women (U.S. Census Bureau, 2010). For those attempting to pursue higher education and committed to finishing, marriage and especially parenting are often strategically delayed to gain educational credentials and work experience. These goals are linked to having enough money (or the potential to do so) on which to build a financially secure partnership or adequately provide for children. These considerations have become an important part of the calculus for young people from middle-class families. In addition, the pathway to marriage today is often punctuated by cohabitation, in both the expectations and the actual experiences of young people (e.g., Manning, Longmore, & Giordano, 2005; see also Giordano, Manning, Longmore, & Flanigan, 2012). However, for young adults from middle-class families, cohabitation is more likely to be a prelude to marriage and not involve children, while for young adults from working-class and low-income families, cohabitation is less likely to result in marriage and more likely to involve children.

Early partnership and childbearing separate the destinies of young people. For young adults with fewer prospects ahead of them—those with the least education and lowest incomes—children come much sooner, and often before marriage or outside partnerships altogether (Edin & Kefalas, 2005; Edin & Tach, 2012; Furstenberg, 2007). For those in school, or who have the hope of higher education, these statuses are major impediments to finishing a degree or to training that can help in the labor market (see also Roksa, 2009). It may also be that having limited prospects in education and work may lead young people, especially women, to parent earlier, as children may be viewed as an alternative source of accomplishment.

Experiences in early adult life—and in higher education—look very different depending on whether and when people become parents. In mapping populations served by the broad-access sector, it is important to understand dynamics related to both partnership and parenthood. A quick pace to parenthood similarly affects the "return" to education if it cuts short time in the labor market during a formative period of career development.

The Significance of Family Resources

Young adults often have starkly different sets of options and experiences depending on family backgrounds and resources. In the United States, the support and resources of parents play crucial roles in determining how young people fare through their twenties and in generating significant inequalities. Recent data suggest that parents now spend about 10 percent of their annual household income on their young adult children, regardless of income level (Wightman, Schoeni, & Robinson, 2010; see also Schoeni & Ross, 2005). The fact that families at all income levels are tithing for their young adult children is important because it reveals that parents' prolonged support is no longer restricted to the middle class and above; low-income parents see this need too. However, it also reveals how different the *amounts* of support are—10 percent of $40,000, for example, is considerably different from 10 percent of $200,000. The higher transfers in financially well-positioned families give a further boost to children who are already much better off going into adulthood, while the support extended in less well-positioned families, however helpful, is surely a strain. The media's focus on coddled young adults neglects the reality that those from disadvantaged families are getting less financial assistance, and those from fragile or troubled families may be getting no help at all.

The stark inequalities among young people, depending on what parents can provide at this juncture or what they provided in the two prior decades, makes what happens in broad-access higher education all the more important. Families with limited means are hard-pressed to find ways to support children, especially in a course of extended education for which they have little knowledge or funds. It also leads to some of the heaviness that those working in higher education feel in addressing the challenges that come with serving students who have decades of disadvantage behind them. These young people must be front and center in the design of broad-access higher education.

The significance of family support in ensuring the success of young Americans, and the "arms race" of parenting (Settersten & Ray, 2010, p. 5) that comes with it, has raised the presence of parents in higher education today. Any vision of broad-access institutions must, as at more elite institutions, include parents and other family members—whether in harnessing involved others to help ensure student success (rather than keeping parents at bay) or in figuring out how to compensate for limited or absent family involvement in other students. Educators must be mindful of the inaccurate assumptions they may make about the presence and levels of parental support for children's pursuit of higher education.

Racial Diversity and the Crisis of Men

Young people today are now more racially diverse than other adults in the United States. They are more likely to be black, Hispanic, immigrant, and multiethnic (U.S. Census Bureau, 2010). They are also more likely to be foreign-born, a characteristic that in past generations was truer of families' oldest members.

These shifts have prompted new inequalities in the opportunities and experiences of young people. There are good reasons to be concerned about the limited or tenuous connections that many members of these groups have to mainstream social institutions—including higher education. For example, in 2010, 15 percent of young adults age eighteen to twenty-four were "disconnected"—not enrolled in school or the military, not working, and had no more than a high school diploma or equivalent—a 3 percent increase since 2000 (Wight, Chau, Aratani, Schwarz, & Thampi, 2010). Black, Native American, and Hispanic young adults are more likely to fall into this category than their white and Asian counterparts, with rates of 24 percent, 29 percent, and 20 percent respectively for the first three and 12 percent and 7 percent for the latter two. These percentages are all carried by men, not women.

Even more concerning is the fact that men from these backgrounds are far more likely to experience spells of imprisonment, especially in their early adult years. The most conservative estimates, which come from the U.S. Department of Justice, are that about 1 in 3 black men and 1 in 6 Latino men are expected to go to prison during their lifetime—compared to 1 in 17 white men—if current incarceration rates remain unchanged (West & Sabol, 2009; see also Pettit & Western, 2004; Raphael, 2007; Western & Pettit, 2010). Among all twenty-something American males in 2008, 2 percent of whites, 4 percent of Latinos, and 10 percent of blacks were incarcerated (West & Sabol, 2009). These data highlight just how difficult the early adult experiences and circumstances of young black and Latino men are in the United States.

In every racial group, including whites, it is men who carry most of the crisis story lines of early adulthood: low achievement, being a high school dropout, college unpreparedness, unemployment, high-risk sexual and social behavior, anger and difficulty regulating emotion, alcohol and substance abuse, family estrangement, being a victim of violence (except sexual abuse), and suicide (Settersten, 2013).

These examples make clear that the new diversity of young people and the problems of men are crucial to understand in remaking college. These examples also suggest that there are serious challenges to expanding the reach and effectiveness of broad-access institutions.

Two Other Hallmarks of Early Adulthood and Their Implications for Higher Education

The Need to Manage Uncertainty

Perhaps the most important hallmark of early adulthood today is the uncertainty young adults face because of changing opportunities, limited support of the welfare state, and relative absence of social controls and clear pathways into the future. The transition into adulthood has in the span of a few decades moved from being highly standardized to being highly individualized. Individualization brings new freedom to live in ways that are aligned with one's interests and wishes, but it also brings a host of new risks, many of which are not known in advance. When individuals choose or find themselves on pathways not widely shared by others, or that are not reinforced and protected in institutions or policies, they may lose important sources of support and find their pathways prone to breakdown (see also Beck, 2000; Giddens, 2002).

These dynamics seem particularly acute in the realm of higher education, especially broad-access institutions. The trend toward individualization means that personal characteristics and resources have become increasingly important in determining how young people fare (Settersten, 2012), thereby exacerbating the risks faced by those from disadvantaged backgrounds. This makes the wide array of student services and resources offered in higher education all the more important to successful outcomes for "at-risk" students.

Beyond grades and test scores, several "soft" skills are crucial in navigating institutions of higher education and having success in them: the capacity to be planful but simultaneously flexible, for self-regulation and self-efficacy, for close relationships, and to relate to others from diverse backgrounds (for a discussion, see Settersten, 2012). In higher education, these skills are important for communicating and building supportive relationships with teachers, administrators, and peers; for accessing resources; and to be self-directed, meet expectations, handle disappointments, and persist in the face of setbacks.

These skills therefore help ensure the success of students as they enter higher education, but they are also skills that should result from higher education. These are the skills that disadvantaged students and those in broad-access institutions often lack upon entry. In seeking to improve experiences in higher education, it seems crucial to foster these skills in primary and secondary school students. The model of learning in higher education assumes that these skills are present; success in higher education depends on them. These skills are arguably even more important for success in online platforms, without the press of the formal classroom and the physical presence of professors and peers.

The Need for Interdependence

Achieving "independence" is often expressed as the ultimate marker of adulthood, but a more relevant milestone today might be the achievement of *inter*dependence. That is, to ensure success, young people need to build wide and strong webs of relationships with other adults, supportive ties that can be activated as needed to access opportunities and resources. This is in line with Granovetter's (1973) classic argument about the "strength of weak ties." But our notion of interdependence runs deeper than that: it is not about relying on others for your own welfare, but instead about making and maintaining positive and mutually supportive relationships. A mentoring relationship is a good example.

Here again, students from more privileged backgrounds have wider and stronger networks of social relationships. Some of what a degree from a more elite institution buys is a rich alumni network, which extends these connections further. Middle-class parents are more likely to activate their networks to help find opportunities and resources for their children—and to have people in their networks who are well positioned to help. In addition, middle-class parents expect to support their children through college and beyond, and middle-class students expect to have that support. This is not as true in working-class and low-income families, where there is a stronger emphasis on "independence" and encouragement to achieve it faster. Being an "adult" in these environments means making it without the help of others. This runs directly counter to the scenario that advantaged young people take for granted, and it is a strategy that is potentially detrimental today (Settersten & Ray, 2010). These are the kinds of students who are more likely to be found in broad-access institutions.

The need for interdependence is apparent in the United States, where the government and public place a high premium on personal responsibility and self-reliance (Hacker, 2006). It is up to young people and their families to take advantage of the opportunities they encounter or actively create, and to shoulder responsibility for problems that ensue as they navigate markets for education, jobs, and partners using whatever knowledge and resources they have acquired. The launching of children into adulthood is taken to be a "private trouble," to use C. Wright Mills's (1959) famous phrase, that requires private solutions, rather than a "public issue" that requires collective investment. Interestingly, this framing closely parallels the funding debate in higher education and the historic shift in who pays, from the public to students and families.

Four Common Misperceptions of Early Adulthood and Their Implications for Higher Education

Four common public misperceptions interfere with understanding what is happening with young adults today. These misconceptions must be shed if institutions of higher education are to be redesigned in innovative ways. They are as follows.

Years of Exploration and Growth

The first common misperception is the pervasive message—in the media, the public, and the psychology of this life period—that these are years of personal exploration, growth experiences, and plentiful choices. Experiences like these may characterize the lives of young people in relatively privileged positions. But many of the trends described earlier should make it apparent that this is not the case for most young people, including many young people from middle-class families.

This is a major challenge for broad-access higher education, in that many young people simply do not have the resources, ability, or support to engage in exploration. In addition, the relationship between exploration and later outcomes does not seem perfectly linear—that is, having too little exploration before locking into major decisions would seem a bad thing, but so too would having undirected and unlimited exploration. Intentional and time-bound exploration may be ideal as young people are sorting out why they are in school and what they want to be and do when they finish. Some of the services and policies of institutions may permit exploration, and others may limit it (e.g., rules about finalizing decisions about majors or metrics for judging "timely" progress). There are also pressing matters of financial cost—and even demands from families that institutions graduate students in four years. For traditional students (young and in school full time), these costs are shouldered by parents and by students themselves. For "nontraditional" students, these costs are likely to spill over to spouses and children, both in reducing immediate resources and in bringing "opportunity costs" of stepping out of work, which also affect future resources.

The Economy Is the Culprit

This second misconception somewhat contradicts the first but is nonetheless strong. Since late 2008, the economic recession has become the primary lens through which many phenomena are understood. The early-adult years are no exception. The recession has brought much-needed attention to the circumstances of young adults, but the recession has not suddenly produced these circumstances. It has exacerbated a set of patterns that were already in place. The economic downturn, however, has become a safe way for young people and their parents to explain delays in their progress—there is comfort in pointing to factors in the world "out there" rather than in oneself. Others understand that hard economic times alter individuals' circumstances and resources. These effects are real. But recent economic decline cannot become the primary explanation for patterns that have been growing for decades.

And yet for higher education and particularly broad-access institutions, the recession clearly is a serious force to be reckoned with as young people and their families question whether a college degree is worth the investment; as they may get even more instrumental in their decision making (e.g., what a degree will get them; where a particular major will take them); and as they desire and demand that degrees get completed faster and hold institutions accountable for it. The recession has brought new kinds of students into college classrooms, and some institutions, particularly broad-access ones, are wrestling with how to respond. Broad-access institutions were filled with swelling numbers of older students who lost jobs and traditional-age students with few employment options. The recession has crippled budgets and left programs and services vulnerable to cuts. The kinds of decisions that happen in times of retrenchment seem crucial for the fate of broad-access higher education, especially if they are not strategic or are not focused on vulnerable students.

The Middle of the Last Century Is "Normal"

The third misconception has to do with how much the middle of the twentieth century has clouded thinking about what it means to be "adult." One of the biggest problems both in the research literature and in public judgments about young people is that the "delay" in adulthood is often measured against the 1950s. The strong post–World War II script for life is so indelible that it often remains the benchmark against which individuals judge themselves and others, even today. Yet in the larger historical picture, that postwar period is an aberration, in both social expectations and economic opportunities. When a longer view is taken, even back to the early decades of the 1900s, it is clear that young people then, much as now, experienced a long period of "semiautonomy" and stuttered routes into adult life.

Young people are disserved when an historical anomaly is used as the standard for assessing how much and what has changed. In evaluating and responding to the transition to adulthood today, it would be more effective to stop focusing on what was "normal" for previous generations and instead focus on how to create institutions that are responsive to contemporary social and economic realities. Educators and other professionals must rethink their assumptions about this period of life, which is different from what they knew, as well as the people in it. It is not just "institutions" that resist change but the people who lead and work in them.

The People Rather than the Period

The final misconception relates to the problem of focusing too much on the people who are now young adults rather than the period itself. It is true that new kinds of young people now occupy this period of life and play important roles in reshaping it. But the more important point is that this period of life has been ruptured in fundamental ways. In focusing on the particular cohort of people now in their early adult years, it is easy to lose sight of larger social, economic, and demographic forces that have reconfigured this period of life. Those changes are not likely to go away as the next few cohorts file into early adulthood. In addition, the early adult years are being rewritten alongside other periods of life. For example, what it means to be "middle aged" or "old" today are dramatically different from what they were a few decades ago. It is important to keep an eye on what changes in early adulthood mean for other periods of life, as well as what changes in other periods of life mean for early adulthood.

Although it is natural to focus on young people in redesigning higher education, people in middle and later life must also be in view. This is especially important in broad-access institutions. Returning to school in midlife, for example, poses unique challenges and demands and different institutional and policy solutions relative to young adulthood (e.g., the need for insurance, rules related to pensions and Social Security, dynamics related to educational and occupational tracking, age biases against and social responses to older students, and the "midlife squeeze" in work, parenting, and parent care; see Settersten & Lovegreen, 1998; Jovic & McMullin, 2011).

Strengthening Pathways Through Higher Education

What sociologists call "structural lag" is this simple but enduring dynamic: behaviors change more rapidly than institutions. Given the reconfiguration of young adulthood today, it is no wonder that institutions of higher education are struggling to respond. The disruptive technological shifts of today—including the massive evolution of online education—have only heightened the sense that higher education is in flux if not crisis. The other chapters of this book take up in depth the remaking of higher education today.

Community colleges are a large part of broad-access sector and seem ideal institutions for investment. They touch large numbers and a wide variety of young people, serve many purposes, are flexible, and offer connections to a range of potential career paths. Yet community colleges have been undernourished and are in need of support and reform. Four-year residential colleges and universities, in contrast, are by design in loco parentis institutions that provide extensive wraparound services—shelter, directed activities, adult and peer support, health care, and entertainment. They are explicitly designed to bridge the family and the wider society and tailored to provide the sort of semiautonomy that characterizes early adulthood.

Why not better resource community colleges—and other broad-access institutions—so that they, too, can provide a similar range of protective services? As also noted by Brock (2010), it is both an irony and a tragedy that already-advantaged students in the most selective institutions are further wrapped in support, while those in the least selective institutions are provided little support and experience deeper cuts. At the same time, it is important to rethink the organization of four-year institutions—especially in addressing the gap between access to college, which has grown dramatically, and degree completion, which has not. This gap sounds an important alarm about the viability of college for many young people, at least within institutions as they are now organized and with the characteristics of students as they now are. Of course, it also is important to remember that success in higher education depends on programs and policies that affect student achievement in secondary and primary schools (for illustrations, see Bloom, 2010). Institutions of higher education cannot suddenly or fully correct for deficits or problems of the past.

Four-year institutions are not exempt from having to rethink their mission and impact in a new era. Even more, they should not be held as the "gold standard" against which other types of higher educational institutions are to be judged. Four-year institutions are just one category of a wide range of schools, and efforts to remake college must not be blinded by "traditional" curricula and modes of learning. Much can be learned from and done to strengthen the experiences of students at struggling branches of public universities and at land-grant institutions. These students are central to the broad-access sector too.

Four-year institutions are also not the only route to a successful adulthood. Other routes must be made more visible and more valued, for in the United States anything less is interpreted as failure. Youth with bachelor's degrees have traditionally enjoyed multiple advantages in the life course. But the "college for all" mentality—if it is used exclusively to mean a bachelor's degree from a four-year school—does a disservice to many youth who simply do not have the intellectual, motivational, or economic resources to get one, just as it does a disservice to broad-access institutions that might better serve these students. The turn toward online platforms as a mode for broadening access does not solve these problems and may even exacerbate them, especially as students with limited resources attempt to create DIY ("do-it-yourself") degrees.

New institutions and policies are needed to reflect the new experiences of young people—or to offer new direction to their lives, as may be the case. For example, policies that make financial aid and scholarships dependent on full-time study seem likely to be questioned in the future as growing numbers of students combine work and school in various full- or part-time statuses, fluctuating over time in response to family, economic, and other concerns. The extraordinary growth in online programs—now in the mainstream and even led by elite institutions like MIT and Stanford—similarly reflects the need to reach students of "nontraditional" ages and circumstances, as well as to reach students of all ages who need training other than traditional four-year degrees.

Higher Education and the Life Course: The Future

An outdated model of the life course continues to underlie the organization of higher education. It assumes that education is heavily front-loaded, and that once individuals have it they are good for the long haul and have little need to return later on. This "inoculation" approach to higher education may have worked in an earlier time, but it seems ill-suited to the world and to lives today. The rigid clockwork of the life course that once existed has loosened. In its place, great variability has emerged in the timing and organization of work, family, and retirement transitions, leaving the life course highly individualized. The disparate pathways into and through higher education are typical of many experiences throughout the life course.

Even more, broad-access higher education has a special role to play in responding to the discontinuity in lives today, whether in providing opportunities for adults of any age to deepen training or freshen skills related to current positions, pursue second or third careers in midlife or beyond, or continue learning when family and other responsibilities take priority, or serving people who for one reason or another bypassed higher education earlier in life or simply seek self-enrichment. Lives today have irregular rhythms, but they are longer. There is time. Dramatic increases in human longevity in the last century have made it possible to reconfigure the life course and to allocate experiences in new ways—not only permitting the rapid extension of education on the front end, but also an intermittent space for education and other activities throughout adult life.

Despite these possibilities, educational institutions nonetheless continue to define what it means to be "adult"—at least in four-year institutions, which remain largely populated by traditional-age students and are seen as places to get ready for adulthood (Settersten, Ottusch, & Schneider, forthcoming). Those who are young and in school (even in graduate and professional schools) are viewed as being in a role that sets them apart and even protects them from adulthood. To be fully adult is to be out of school.

Broad-access schools serve a wider range of students, including students of nontraditional ages. And yet institutions of higher education routinely require that parents' income be used to determine financial aid, and they assume that parents are providers (it is extraordinarily difficult for students to become legally "emancipated" from parents when they are in college). Institutions of higher education make the problematic assumptions that parents are both present and involved in supporting their students and that parents play healthy and helpful roles in fostering the development of students. These are not always accurate assumptions, and when institutions act on the basis of these assumptions, they can jeopardize the success of students. For many students, especially in the broad-access sector, parents may not be a relevant part of the picture. At the same time, for traditional-age students, higher education today cannot be transformed without engaging parents, many of whom may not have the skills or knowledge to help young people navigate college even if they are involved. The latter is particularly true in the broad-access sector and for parents of first-generation college students.

Institutions of higher education treat students as if they are autonomous, but students of all ages are embedded in larger matrices of family and social ties that can help them along or hold them back. Rather than design processes and policies that place a premium on autonomy, institutions must begin to better recognize the interdependencies that students carry with them. Again, this seems especially true of older students and of those in broad-access environments. Human beings are rarely autonomous, and relationships are part of "choice sets." How students relate—or are able to relate—to institutions of higher education depends on the relationships they have with other people and the other roles they are juggling.

Strategic exploration is important for students—in finding institutions, majors, degrees, and jobs that are a good match to who they are, how they learn, and where they want to go in the future. Many policies, however, actively discourage and penalize exploration (e.g., time limits in locking into majors, completing degrees, and transferring credits). There are significant and understandable tensions related to having time to explore and being timely. Students often do not know in advance what it is they want to do, and they have been told that higher education is precisely for figuring that out, especially in the first few years. When majors are declared late, for example, students may not be able to complete degrees on time, whether because there is neither enough time nor adequate course offerings to meet requirements. Unbridled exploration comes at a financial cost to students and their families, and students and institutions alike are judged by timely degree completion.

What might be done to create structures that permit greater flexibility without penalty? This is important for students of any age. But for older students, these tensions are exacerbated—there is little time or money to "waste" in school, and there is a limited time horizon to reap the benefits of their investments. There is also the problem of information—whether information is available, helpful, and delivered in the right way or at the right time to help students make decisions. There is danger in assuming that students know what they want, that it can be applied in an unpredictable world, or that it can be applied in their own lives.

The problem of information also relates to the value of education. A common refrain among those who work in this sector is that higher education is meant to broadly improve the future outcomes of individuals. The focus, however, is rather immediately and narrowly focused on getting credentials that lead to better jobs and wages in the labor market. It is important for educators and students to think beyond jobs and earnings. Other kinds of noneconomic benefits come with higher education (e.g., health, civic engagement, parenting strategies, and parental investments in child development).

Educators must more critically examine their assumptions from a life course perspective: Are students really being equipped with skills and capacities that will have broad applicability and durability over time? Are their degrees or credentials truly gateways to long-term opportunity? What other long-term outcomes should students expect beyond jobs and wages? The effects of college may be less about what is learned there and more about where college takes students once they leave (e.g., certain types of jobs, workplaces, neighborhoods, networks). For this reason, higher education policy is social, economic, and health policy too—and must be thought about in this way. These kinds of questions demand new thinking about what is learned in higher education, how it is learned, and how to measure the success of students, instructors, and institutions.

In addition, it is important to rethink the assumption that students will—or should—finish college where they start it. Particular attention must be paid to a group of students we might call "swirlers." More than one third of students attend more than one college, and over one fifth of students who eventually complete a degree do so at a college other than the one in which they started (National Student Clearinghouse Research Center, 2012). How can institutions best serve students when they may intersect with only a portion of students' pathways? Institutions must be willing to invest in the well-being of students who will not ultimately stay and may even be better served by another institution. It means that something like "learning progress" might need to be advanced as an alternative and appropriate goal for students and broad-access schools, rather than focus so exclusively on completion.

Attempts to remake higher education must both respond to the kinds of people who are moving through them and somehow capitalize on (and not penalize people for) the constraints they face. Broad-access institutions seem in their very nature to be designed to help people work with the messiness of their lives and manage future risks. That makes the task of architecting broad-access institutions a messy business of its own, one that responds not only to the deficits of the people served but also to their strengths. It also serves as a reminder that the solution to student success is not wholly found within schools. Others, students chiefly among them, are accountable too.

Finally, the transformation of the early adult years is a window into how the whole life course is being reworked. These changes should lead to demand for and interest in higher education in all periods of life, if educators and institutions can get creative about how to design and deliver it. Higher education is not and need not be just about young people and early adulthood but about opportunities for learning throughout adult life. The success of students and institutions has shifted from being about "access" to being about "completion." But success in college is surely more than getting in or finishing. How might higher education be assessed in more meaningful ways? Even more important, how might higher education be made more meaningful throughout people's lives? The last hundred years brought revolutionary changes to the human life course. The future of higher education—and the human condition—now rests on remaking college in equally revolutionary ways.

Note

1. Following the MacArthur Research Network on Transitions to Adulthood (e.g., Settersten, Furstenberg, & Rumbaut, 2005), "adulthood" is often construed to begin at the common legal age of eighteen or twenty-one, but the transition to adulthood occurs throughout the twenties and even into the early thirties, given that movement into traditional adult roles, and the social, psychological, and economic autonomy of young people, now occurs at the upper end of this band.

6

THE "TRADITIONAL" COLLEGE STUDENT

A Smaller and Smaller Minority and Its Implications

for Diversity and Access Institutions

Regina Deil-Amen

What happens when a norm of behavior becomes the exception numerically yet the social construction of that norm remains prominent? In such a situation, those who do not conform to that norm tend to be marginalized despite their existence as the collective majority. They become, in essence, a marginalized majority. This is exactly what has occurred for most postsecondary students in the United States.

The Other Half

Our conceptions of the typical college student are based on traditional notions and an imagined norm of someone who begins college immediately after high school, enrolls full time, lives on campus, and is ready to begin college-level classes. Yet such an assumed norm does not reflect the diversity of today's college students. As Cox notes, "Although the community college sector is often treated as an adjunct to U.S. higher education, it . . . constitutes the first stop for roughly half of today's college students" (2009, p. 2). In contrast to popular images of who a college student is, enrollment data reveal a different picture. Over the past half century, the greatest increase in access to higher education has occurred through the doorways of community colleges, which have grown far faster than the four-year sector. Since the mid-1960s undergraduate four-year institutions have doubled their enrollments, yet two-year colleges have expanded at more than twice that rate, and now their enrollment is approaching half of all undergraduates (Cox, 2009; Rosenbaum, Deil-Amen, & Person, 2006).

In fact, as Table 6.1 displays, there are just as many undergraduates in community colleges (42.8 percent) as in four-year public and four-year private not-for-profit institutions combined (42.6 percent). And the rapidly growing for-profit sector now enrolls the next largest proportion (almost 14 percent) of students (U.S. Department of Education, National Center for Education Statistics, 2012a, Table 3). Apparent from this table, focusing attention on the traditional four-year sector as the norm is quite dismissive of a clear majority of our nation's students and the institutions that serve them. They are the relatively neglected other half of U.S. higher education, with nearly 60 percent of all undergraduates enrolled in for-profit and less than four-year colleges.

When only first-year students are considered, the freshman class is even more distributed away from traditional four-year contexts, as Table 6.2 shows. Using the most recent data available for first-year students only, the majority (57 percent) are enrolled in community colleges while only slightly over a quarter (26 percent) are enrolled in four-year nonprofit or public colleges and universities. And the growing popularity of for-profit colleges is reflected in their 15 percent share of all first-year student enrollments (U.S. Department

TABLE 6.1 Headcount of students enrolled as a percentage of the total undergraduate enrollment in U.S. Institutions, 2010–2011 academic year (25,646,077 students)

Four-year institutions (50.9%)	Two-year institutions (46.4%)	One-year institutions (2.7%)
Four-year public (30.4%)	Two-year public (42.8%)	One-year public (0.4%)
Four-year nonprofit (12.2%)	Two-year nonprofit (0.3%)	One-year nonprofit (0.1%)
Four-year for-profit (8.3%)	Two-year for-profit (3.3%)	One-year for-profit (2.2%)

SOURCE: U.S. Department of Education, National Center for Education Statistics, 2012a, Table 3.

TABLE 6.2 Percentage of first-year undergraduates in each type of U.S. postsecondary institution, 2007–2008 academic year

Type	Four-year institutions	Two-year institutions	One-year institutions
Public	17.8%	57.0%	0.9%
Nonprofit	8.6%	0.6%	0.6%
For-profit	10.6%	10.6%	4.5%

SOURCE: U.S. Department of Education, National Center for Education Statistics, 2010, Table 241.

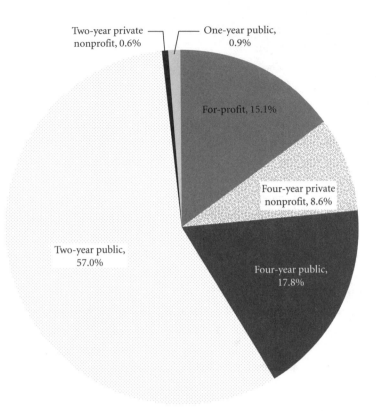

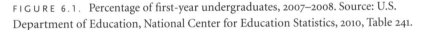

FIGURE 6.1. Percentage of first-year undergraduates, 2007–2008. Source: U.S. Department of Education, National Center for Education Statistics, 2010, Table 241.

of Education, National Center for Education Statistics, 2010, Table 241). Figure 6.1 graphically illustrates this same distribution across institution types.

Clearly, the dominance of community colleges and for-profit colleges as entry points for almost three quarters of our nation's students is out of line with the attention that traditional four-year sector institutions receive as bastions of opportunity. Even among students beginning in four-year colleges, only half of those entrants maintain continued enrollment in a single institution, with many swirling between the four-year and two-year sector (Goldrick-Rab, 2006). Realizing that the other half noted previously is actually more the *other three quarters* of undergraduates entering higher education makes the marginalization of this majority especially troubling. Perhaps such marginalization contributes to marginalizing policy actions, such as the recent movement of the funding allocated to community colleges from the Department of Education to the Department of Labor as workforce development funds. This shift occurred despite the fact that, for decades, an overwhelming majority of community college students have desired and continue to desire bachelor's degrees (Dougherty, 1994).

"In short, the traditional college student is no longer the typical college student," says Cox (2009, p. 7). The "ideal" student model is certainly no longer typical, and in fact, many nontraditional characteristics are now more prevalent than traditional ones. Further considering incoming first-year students in college credit classes, Figure 6.2 shows that well over a third (38 percent) are now age twenty-four or older. More than half (53 percent) are *not* enrolled exclusively full time. Instead, they attend part time or part of the year. Almost half (47 percent) are financially independent, and half of those (25 percent) have financial dependents of their own. A mere 13 percent of beginning students live on campus, while about half commute from off campus, and close to a third live with parents or family (U.S. Department of Education, National Center for Education Statistics, 2010, Table 240).

The degree to which students are prepared for college-level coursework is another nontraditional characteristic, arguably the most critical.

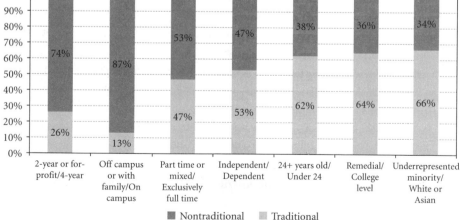

FIGURE 6.2. First-year undergraduate students, 2007–2008. Source: U.S. Department of Education, National Center for Education Statistics, 2010, Table 240.

More than a third (36 percent) of beginning college students take remedial/developmental courses in college. Interestingly, although most remedial students are enrolled at public two-year colleges, the percentage of first-year students at public four-year nondoctorate institutions who take remedial classes (39 percent) is almost as high as the percentage of first-year remedial students in public two-year colleges (42 percent) (U.S. Department of Education, National Center for Education Statistics, 2010, Table 241). And these percentages are relatively low, since they exclude those referred into remedial-level classes who chose to forgo those classes. At many community colleges, more than 80 percent of students test into remedial/developmental level, as is the case in the City University of New York (CUNY) community college system (Jaggars & Hodara, 2011).

The Norm of Multidimensional Diversity

Diversity in higher education is too often framed narrowly as the inclusion of nonwhite students into America's elite private and public colleges and universities to create a more "multicultural" student body. The framing of this pursuit implies the scarcity of such "diverse" students. However, in many broad-access public universities and less selective colleges, a diverse and multicultural student body is present and growing. In fact, currently, in the other half of higher education, especially in community colleges, such diversity abounds, and this abundance occurs along multiple dimensions, not just race/ethnicity and socioeconomic status (SES). In this sense, diversity is the norm, not the exception.

In addition to SES, gender, and race/ethnicity, parameters of nontraditional diversity that need to be seriously considered include the type of institutions students are accessing; on- or off-campus residence and commuting choices; patterns of full-time, part-time, and part-year attendance; age; financial status as dependent, independent, or independent with dependents; and level of college preparedness. In fact, each of these dimensions of diversity reflects greater proportions of nontraditional status than does race/ethnicity (Figure 6.2), which makes attention to them even more compelling. Furthermore, underrepresented minority students are disproportionately underprepared, which makes these dimensions of their college experience inextricably linked. Latina/o and low-SES students are concentrated disproportionately in community colleges and broad-access universities, so any discussions of these subgroups should contend with these conditions. Patterns of work and parenting while enrolled inevitably affect students of different ages differently. Which students are more likely to commute, live with family, or be financially independent? Are older students more likely female with children? Any given dimension of each student's college experience cannot be extracted. Should institutions respond in ways that better address these multiple dimensions of diversity? Several decades ago, feminist scholars of color discussed their insights on how race, class, and gender cannot be disentangled because each is simultaneously relevant in lived experience. Similarly, scholars should be unwilling to continue to ignore the fact that diversity is so common as to be considered a norm in all but a minority of higher education contexts. It is the water in which open- and broad-access institutions swim. And this diversity extends far beyond race, class, and gender, and so should our frameworks and the scope of our research efforts.

Unfortunately, the discussion of diversity in terms of scarcity at the top reifies the notion that larger systems of inequity can be addressed by focusing on inclusion into the more elite four-year sectors. Such a focus overshadows the ways in which access to college is inherently structured to exclude the broader majority, which masks the inequities inherent in the stratification of higher education institutions and opportunities. Discussions of diversity and equity need to be broadened to address who has access to what institutions and resources, and how elite institutions and their students benefit from this structured inequality (Labaree, 1997c). Limiting the "diversity agenda" to a narrow focus on letting underrepresented minorities "in" to the top tiers of higher education excludes and renders invisible the realities of most nontraditional students with nontraditional pathways who are worthy of inclusion in the diversity agenda—the other three quarters flooding the gates of entry into our postsecondary institutions every year.

Who Counts?

A conceptual overemphasis on a student "ideal" that predominates while marginalizing open- and broad-access institutions can operate surreptitiously to exclude and deprioritize. There are ways in which our professional behaviors (our speaking and writing) entirely exclude, or section off, the broadest-access postsecondary contexts and their students, sending a signal connoting that they "don't really count." In reality, community colleges, private two-year colleges, for-profit colleges, and four-year commuter institutions and their students, staff, faculty, and administrators do count in the larger equation of postsecondary access, funding, instructional labor pools, the wider economy, and the societal mission of opportunity higher education fulfills. Our parameters for considering issues of diversity need to expand to recognize postsecondary institutional diversity, along with the diverse college-going behaviors among the other half of postsecondary students. It is important for scholars to be self-conscious enough to understand how our own language and framing contribute to marginalization and the continued reification of the traditional college student and traditional college-going patterns.

To exemplify what tends to "count" in our conceptual popular imagination and what does not, I draw from a recent widely discussed and important book on U.S. colleges, *Academically Adrift* (Arum & Roksa, 2011). The book focuses on traditional-age students beginning at four-year colleges and universities. Despite the narrow specificity of this sample, this book begins in the first nineteen pages with commentary on "U.S. higher education," "colleges and universities," "undergraduate learning," "undergraduate education," "student cultures," "the college professoriate," and "the higher education system" that excludes community colleges (and other nontraditional institutions) altogether. And it frames "college culture" as the culture of residential college life for traditional-age students engaging in peer cultures dominated by social activities, fraternities, and sororities. The authors find that professors do not expect undergraduates to work very hard to earn good grades and that undergraduates are focused more on social experiences than academic achievement.

The entire discussion of these topics revolves only around public and private four-year colleges and research universities, without an apology or acknowledgment that half of all institutions and well over half of today's undergraduates are excluded from the discussion. Yet because of our prioritizing of four-year traditional notions and normalized marginalization of other college-going patterns, it seems entirely appropriate to a reader to begin reading a book about "college" without a single mention of any two-year or for-profit institutions. It also seems entirely reasonable that esteemed scholar James Rosenbaum would suggest, in a review blurb for the book, that this book "might be the most important book on higher education in a decade." However, it would rarely if ever be deemed appropriate to write a book about community colleges and discuss their history, student culture, faculty composition, and system of funding for more than the first tenth of the book as if the content represented all of higher education. In fact, most commonly, qualification about a specific institutional focus on community colleges appears in the title or abstract (see the work of Thomas Bailey, Debra Bragg, Kevin Dougherty, Frankie Santos Laanan, and Dolores Perin).

To further emphasize my point, when the sampling for *Academically Adrift* is detailed on page 20, the authors state that they carefully considered the representativeness of their student sample generated from the twenty-four colleges included by comparing it to "U.S. Higher Education more broadly." Yet their comparison extends only to traditional-age students in four-year institutions nationwide, as if this were an adequate representation of the entire population of students and institutions in the United States. Despite this narrowing of who "counts" as college students, the remainder of the book continues to frame the discussion as relevant to "college student life" generally (e.g., p. 81) and the experiences of the "typical college student" (e.g., p. 88). The methodological and statistical rigor of the sampling and analysis is sound, yet the book suffers from an ailment common to most of us— prioritizing a traditional college student minority and inappropriately extending that minority experience to the majority. This, marginalizes, and sometimes renders invisible from the conversation, the functions and circumstances of the other half of our postsecondary system. Multiple studies have shown that students commuting to two- and four-year colleges and nontraditional-aged students do not prioritize the social aspects of campus life and in fact often actively avoid them to preserve time to focus on their academic obligations and other work, family, and community obligations. Where do these students, and the instructors and faculty who teach them, fit into this framework?

Another example of scholarship marginalizing the diversity of institutional types while prioritizing one sector is the research on one of our most compelling issues of diversity—the experiences and challenges of underrepresented racial/ethnic minority males. This is possibly the most at-risk subgroup in U.S. higher education, with males constituting only slightly more than a third of all African American and Latina/o undergraduates, according to Integrated Postsecondary Education Data System (IPEDS) 2009 enrollment data.

Over the last decade, research on experiences, pathways, and attainment among African American and Latino males in four-year colleges has grown considerably. Some studies address enrollment, persistence, and attainment gaps (Arbona & Nora, 2007; Bowen, Chingos, & McPherson, 2009; Fry, 2002; Hagedorn, Chi, Cepeda, & McLain, 2007; Ryu, 2010; Saenz & Ponjuan, 2008). Others examine institutional policies and practices (Cuyjet, 2006; Harper, 2008; Strayhorn, 2010; Zell 2009) and qualitative student narratives regarding identity, racism, and organizational experiences (Baber, 2010; Harper, 2009; Harper & Davis, 2012; Harris & Harper, 2008; Schwartz, Donovan, & Guido-DiBrito, 2009). All of this research, however, focuses on students attending four-year institutions, despite the reality that according to 2009 IPEDS data, 43 percent of African American male college students and over half of Latino male college students are enrolled at community colleges. In fact, 60 percent of Latinos begin their postsecondary education at community colleges (Gándara & Contreras, 2009; Padilla, 2007).

Studies of minority males not attending four-year institutions are less prevalent (Harris & Harper, 2008) yet extremely valuable in providing some empirical evidence that African American and Latino males at community colleges behave in ways distinct from their four-year counterparts and from females of the same race/ethnicity. For example, in contrast to African American males attending four-year institutions, those at community colleges are less likely to talk with faculty outside class time, meet with an academic advisor, or participate in cocurricular activities (Flowers, 2006; Pope, 2006). In community colleges, Latino males are less likely than Latinas to engage "help-seeking" behaviors, utilize academic services, or participate in learning communities (Saenz et al. 2010). Also, net of other factors, African American and Latino males who perceive a supportive campus environment are more likely to persist to degree completion (Hagedorn, Maxwell, & Hampton, 2002), and more diverse institutions, such as Hispanic-serving community colleges, are positively associated with Latinos' perceptions of support (Núñez, Sparks, & Hernández, 2011; Perrakis & Hagedorn, 2010). Similarly, Perrakis (2008) finds that African American and white male students attending racially diverse community colleges in Los Angeles feel more positively about campus climate and their ability to complete coursework and degree requirements than males in less diverse colleges. Finally, qualitative research by Zell (2009) provides an interesting twist, revealing Latinas in community colleges who credit their partners (husbands, fiancés, and boyfriends) for their successful persistence through college. The women describe partners who themselves do not have a college degree and in some cases put their own college goals aside to support their female partners.

Reconceptualizing the Perceived Norm

What problems emerge when we draw from traditional theories to understand this collective majority of students? One major consequence is that those who do not fit the mold are framed as deficient. When students are measured against a traditional norm of college-going that is no longer an actual behavioral norm, nontraditional students are found wanting. Our centering of the traditional norm turns attention to remedying the deficiencies of the deficient students rather than remedying the deficiencies of institutions inadequately serving the collective majority. By deconstructing this fictional ideal student norm, we can refocus attention to the aspects of postsecondary education structured in ways that perpetuate inequities.

Traditional theories of college student persistence illustrate the limitations of operating under the perceived norm. These theories were based on norms of college-going for predominantly white eighteen- to twenty-three-year-olds, enrolled full time, residing on campus, and for the most part beginning with college-level classes (Astin, 1984; Tinto, 1993). Critics rightly criticize Tinto's framework in particular for assuming that a disconnection from a home community must occur before integration into a college community can happen, which discounts the experiences of students whose racial/ethnic community of origin remains salient (Guiffrida, 2006; Hurtado & Carter, 1997; Tierney, 1992, 1999). Furthermore, frameworks centered on traditional residential students discount the experiences of more than half of the undergraduate population—two-year college and four-year commuting students who enroll in college while remaining in their communities of origin. This has left a void in our understanding of how integration—a sense of connection, belonging, and congruence with the college community—happens for commuting students who do not break former connections to forge new connections in some semi-isolated residential college social world.

However, this does not render such traditional theories completely useless, and they should not be dismissed altogether. As Deil-Amen (2011a) and Karp and colleagues (2010) contend, aspects of these frameworks, such as the concept of integration, can be expanded to include realities of students traditionally marginalized by such theories. Research shows that commuting two-year college students challenge the dichotomous notion of integration occurring along purely academic or social lines. They experience "socio-academic integrative moments," or events, activities, interactions, and relationships in which academic and social elements combine simultaneously to enhance learning, information acquisition, procedural knowledge, feelings of college belonging, college identity, connectedness, and intellectual competence (Deil-Amen, 2011b). Often these moments occur within and just beyond the classroom, the most common place where commuting students meet other students and faculty, develop a sense of belonging, become involved in opportunities for engagement, and learn success strategies (Hughes, Karp, & O'Gara, 2009).

Unlike expectations of more "traditional" students, purely social relationships are often devalued by two-year commuters and even described as unwanted obstacles or distractions (Deil-Amen, 2011b). Rather than connecting through social ties with college peers, nontraditional college-goers view the social aspects of college life as distracting, and instead reinforce their motivation and commitment to goals through a clear sense of purpose (Zell, 2009). Subjective college experiences that cultivate development of a "college-going identity" and validate pursuing college goals are also important for nontraditional groups in ways that may not be as salient for students originating from social-class communities with strong college-going norms (Collatos, Morell, Nuno, & Lara, 2004; Saunders & Serna, 2004). These findings are consistent with what other researchers have found regarding the importance of feelings of community and belonging for community college, commuter, and Latina/o students in particular (Braxton, Hirschy, & McClendon, 2004; Deil-Amen & Rios-Aguilar, 2012; Karp & Hughes, 2009; Rendón, 1994; Rendón, Jalomo, & Nora, 2000; Torres, 2006).

Reframing our views of diversity in higher education exposes how the conceptual practice of confining the diversity agenda to a discussion of "getting in" to selective institutions is limited at best and absurd at worst. No, we do not want to render the diversity concept useless by including too many subpopulations, and this fear often leads to confining diversity to particular vulnerable (often legally defined) subpopulations. However, is this practice of drawing boxes around a targeted set of diversity characteristics the most effective approach? What if we took the definition of diversity to its logical extreme and attempted to map it and its interrelationships more carefully? What if we made the study of these interrelationships and their impact on opportunity the focus of a research agenda centered on equity? This exercise might effectively make visible the invisible majority. It might reveal with more clarity exactly which institutions "need" to increase diversity and which do not. The uneven playing field is not only about SES and underrepresented minority student status. By limiting diversity to only particular student characteristics without acknowledging other dimensions of diversity—including diversity in institutional type—we are shortchanging the equity agenda.

There is no doubt that diversifying the student body and faculty and administration of our most elite colleges and universities is valuable and necessary. However, the diversity agenda needs to expand to recognize that privilege is structured, and equity needs shift as the institutional context shifts. For instance, there is almost no discussion of how nonselective, nonprestigious four-year colleges and universities have increased their racial/ethnic minority enrollments drastically. We assume this spells opportunity, but one study reveals how such an institution's career center responds to pressures to preserve its reputation and legitimacy with employers: by mitigating inequality for some while reproducing inequality for others—namely, African American and Latina/o students—regardless of their qualifications (Damaske, 2009).

Where Subjectivity Meets Objective Diversity

Some of the most meaningful aspects of students' diverse backgrounds are difficult to quantify and categorize. For example, the ways in which students give meaning to their college pursuits in the context of their family relationships can vary substantially, and more elite institutions tend to reward students who fit only one particular mold in this regard. For instance, in my study of low-income university students, many of them (mainly Latina/o) consider interdependence and mutual obligation between family members to be of high moral value. This is not unlike prior ethnographies detailing the interdependent systems of families surviving and functioning in contexts of poverty (Stack, 1997). Students who separate from their families to attend college on campus experience the psychological and emotional stress and anxiety of removing themselves from interdependent systems within their family and extended family. They feel guilty about any additional financial burdens their absence might cause. Rather than feeling entitled to the financial support of their families, hardworking, committed, high-achieving students are concerned and uncomfortable about their "selfish" pursuit of college for individual gain while their families are struggling (Deil-Amen, Rios-Aguilar, Irwin, & Gonzalez Canche, 2010).

Students with this perspective differ sharply from our notions about millennial-generation students and their "helicopter parents," which are based on middle- and upper-class norms. Rather than welcoming and educating parents who are not as familiar with college life and helping students deal with the pressures of feeling obligated to continue helping their families, university staff instead keep parents at arm's length, encouraging separation from presumed "overly involved" parents. Consequently, lower-income or Latino students are left to deal alone with the pressures of trying to straddle school while helping and remaining present with their families and of informing their parents of the expectations of college work. Between 2007 and 2011, my graduate students and I conducted interviews of 194 students at a large university in the southwestern United States (Deil-Amen & Rios-Aguilar, 2012; Deil-Amen, Rios-Aguilar, Irwin, & Gonzalez Canche, 2010; Everett-Haynes & Deil-Amen, 2011; and Martinez & Deil-Amen, in press). One low-income white female student told us:

> My family has a lot of financial problems, so that's another stress that I'm constantly dealing with. I have to call them like, "Mom, are you gonna be able to pay rent this month?" . . . I've actually used some of my loans to help them pay their rent this year.

A commuting Latino who lives with family was asked if they are supportive. He explained:

> I think they try to be, but a lot of the time, because they were so used to me being there all the time and always helping out . . . it's sort of hard for them to deal with the fact that I have ten papers to write, three books to read . . . that I have all these teachers and all these things that I have to do. . . . Sometimes it's with help, like, moving a lot of stuff, since we're downgrading since we can't afford anything, so we're selling a lot of stuff, so it's . . . just little things like going to the store for them. Just simple things, because they're busy too.

Another Latino who talks to his mom twice a day by phone revealed:

> I'm the first person to go to college in my family, so they don't really understand the time and dedication I have to put into this. Sometimes they get upset when they invite me somewhere and I have to say no. But they get over it, and they're kind of adjusting to my schedule too. Like, I'm usually at school. If I have any time left over, that's when I go visit them.

A Latina whose father left school after third grade and whose mother completed secretarial school after high school described her "frustrating" predicament "because I'm over here, and they're over there . . . and I just kind of had to deal with it until they learned." Her parents who "just didn't like" the idea of her living away at an in-state college rather than commuting to one close to home would say, "Why are you doing this? You really don't need to do this." She elaborated:

> I had homework to do and . . . other stuff to do. For them, it wasn't that important. They just couldn't believe that it would take me a whole weekend to do homework. Then it's just also the financial situation. . . . Coming here I kind of had to ask for more money, and they were just like, "Why do you need all this money?" And I'm like, "Well, it all adds up—textbooks, food, and everything." So it's just little stuff like that became a big deal in our family.

Another Latina expressed guilt about living on campus and not being available to help her parents and nine-year-old brother, who is now alone through the evening after school while her parents work multiple jobs:

> It's horrible. I used to cry myself to sleep just saying, "I'm not there, and I'm not being good to my parents. They've given me so much, and they've always been there, and now I'm not home." Especially my little brother [*tears up*]. . . . I'm his big sister, and it makes me so sad not being there for him.

Another example of a more subjective, yet very meaningful aspect, of diversity difficult to quantify involves a study by Naffziger and Rosenbaum (2011), which shows how expectations for the purpose of college vary by socioeconomic status. Poorer and working-class students view college as a means to acquire the skills they need to avoid an undesirable job, while middle- to upper-class students define college as a space for personal exploration. Brint and Rotondi (2008) similarly report that middle-class undergraduates extend the meaning of college beyond the value of the degree to the chance to participate in "the full college experience," which includes "a style of life in which opportunities to spend time with friends, participate in campus activities, and 'enjoy life' were abundant" (p. 15).

Perceptions of the "college experience" may be the same as they were thirty or fifty years ago, particularly among middle-and upper-middle-class college students. However, as nontraditional students become a numerical majority, is this old model of college as a separate space to explore identity and possible career interests giving way to a new model of college as a tool, an instrumental pathway, to a better job or career future?

Unexpected Diversification

In a somewhat bizarre, yet logical shift, community colleges across the nation are currently diversifying their campuses by adding on-campus housing. In colleges where most students commute, students who live on campus are now a small but growing minority. When viewed from this perspective, diversity is turned on its head. The relative absence of the "ideal" traditional student makes their intentional "inclusion" a mechanism for diversifying the clientele community colleges serve. In the wake of the recent recession, student groups who had traditionally attended four-year campuses are now turning to the more affordable community college as an option—one that is becoming particularly popular in rural communities.

Along with several other State University of New York (SUNY) community colleges, Onondaga Community College in central New York is a good example. On their website, the admissions page boasts, "Over the past five years, we have invested over $50 million in improvements including three new residence halls" and includes an attractive photo of the residence buildings and the heading "Living on Campus" plus the subtitle "the total college experience" (see Onondaga Community College, "Admission," n.d.). The "residence halls" link leads to another page that claims, "Onondaga is a residential campus! Our state-of-the-art residence halls offer students the opportunity to affordably experience the benefits of on-campus living. Students live in a single, double, or triple room in a traditional or suite style setting." Under the heading "The Benefits of Living on Campus," the page includes, among other benefits, "Greater Academic Success" and explains, "Studies have shown that resident students have consistently achieved higher grades than their nonresident counterparts" (see Onondaga Community College, "Residence Halls," n.d.). The number of community colleges incorporating or expanding on-campus living options is growing rapidly; there are now more than three hundred nationwide.

Multidimensional Diversity

The studies mentioned previously have much to contribute to discussions of diversity. For example, interrelationships of gender, nontraditional family dynamics, perceptions of support, frameworks of understanding, and college behaviors are clearly relevant and prevalent once the full diversity of postsecondary contexts are considered. Figure 6.3 compiles the dimensions of diversity discussed in this paper and a few more obvious components that have not been discussed.

The dimensions are configured as a system operating interactively as connected realities for students, not as disembodied characteristics. Researchers should make every effort to address how multiple dimensions of diversity operate simultaneously for individuals, and their relevance varies across different college contexts. Dimensions pictured include type of institution; on- or off-campus residence choices and commuting patterns (residence); full-time, part-time, and part-year attendance patterns; age; financial status as dependent, independent, or independent with dependents; level of college preparedness; college knowledge; college-going identity; networks of support; SES; parent education; race/ethnicity; disability status; sexuality; gender;

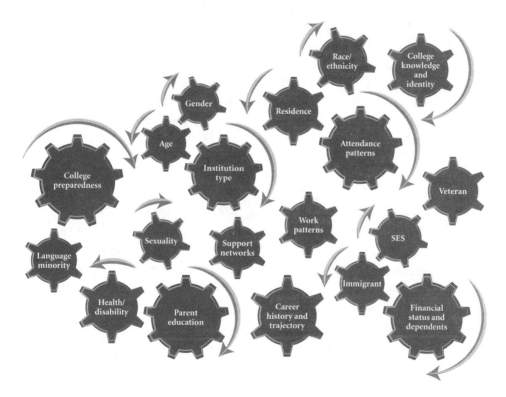

FIGURE 6.3. Interactive multiple dimensions of diversity.

patterns of work; career history; career trajectory; veteran status; immigration status; and language minority status.

A multidimensional accounting of diversity must also consider the reality that student mobility patterns (discussed in detail in a later section) result in student enrollment in multiple institutions and/or institution types, sometimes simultaneously. How we envision the architecture of organizational fields in constant fluid motion, intersecting via individual student experiences, is critical to moving forward with our theorizing of diversity in higher education, and in our conceptions of higher education generally.

Broader Societal Impact

Understanding how each dimension in Figure 6.3 can operate in concert with other dimensions can help broaden our theorizing of student pathways, especially as they relate to intersections with other organizational fields. For instance, the inclusion of work patterns and career trajectories matters not only for understanding how they shape individuals' pathways through college, but also for understanding the larger labor market context in which higher education operates. Saenz and Ponjuan (2009), for example, discuss Latino male workforce patterns, including participation of Latino males in alternative (noncollege) career pathways, the military, and prison to understand their college participation patterns. Deil-Amen and DeLuca (2010) describe the relevance of majors/programs as elements of diverse pathways by suggesting how two-year colleges may provide trajectories through particular selective programs into career fields that lead to greater market rewards for students.

Another broad societal impact involves changing societal norms in higher education and college-going. Given the low rates of retention in two-year and for-profit colleges, the overwhelming predominance of first-year students in these institutions is troubling. Consider (a) the disproportionate enrollments of low-income and underrepresented minority students in two-year and for-profit institutions, (b) the social and residential segregation of neighborhoods by race/ethnicity and social class, and (c) the high rates of stopout and dropout among lower-income, first-generation, and underrepresented minority students, where more than two thirds do not complete degrees. These three realities combine to form, I hypothesize, a dominant norm across whole communities where those who go to college usually leave without completing a degree. Existence of such a pervasive cultural norm in which the idea of going to college is so coupled with the reality of not finishing can have serious repercussions for how nontraditional students make decisions about going or not going to college, where to go, and how to finance it. In essence, the idea of attempting college and not finishing becomes normalized. Such subjective understandings inevitably factor into students' decisions about how to manage the financial and other risks of going to or staying in college (Deil-Amen & Goldrick-Rab, 2009).

Taking Affirmative Action

There is much to learn from theories of cultural wealth and cultural integrity, funds of knowledge, and alternative forms of capital (Moll, Amanti, Neff, & González, 1992; Villalpando & Solorzano, 2005; Yosso, 2005). These frameworks shift attention from student deficits to strengths inherent in underrepresented racial/ethnic minority students' homes and communities and the skills and dispositions they develop to survive and thrive in those contexts. Sedlacek (2004) offers systematic ways to assess the noncognitive characteristics students possess that lead to college success—better than what the SAT and other standardized measures alone can predict. These approaches provide frameworks for validating and legitimately rewarding the positive attributes of traditionally underrepresented populations in the absence of overt affirmative action policies. Using these frameworks to shape research agendas can provide evidence to better affirm what works for students who have traditionally not been as successful in higher education relative to more privileged groups.

Such reorientation of frameworks of meritocracy can subvert attacks on affirmative action. This reorientation is one part of a two-part method to acknowledge diversity in ways that increase opportunity. The other half involves changing structures directly. True opportunity will not result from funding structures that starve both community colleges and broad-access four-year public universities. True opportunity will not result from the underfunding and the teacher and administrative turnover inherent in underresourced K–12 schools. True opportunity will not result when health needs and labor market realities are excluded from efforts to improve education and job outcomes. True opportunity will not result if the enterprise of educating our poor is not innovative, with successful efforts supported and rewarded.

Lack of fundamental structural change may be linked to the failure of colleges to teach teachers, administrators, and local and state policy makers how to (structurally and instructionally) improve the success of students who are multiple grade levels behind. Our entire teacher education and educational leadership curricula are void of such content. Yes, teachers learn cultural sensitivity, behavior management, and content-based knowledge. However they do not learn specifically how to improve a student's skills within a particular time frame when the student is behind a grade level or more. They do not learn how to enter an underresourced context and create change that will actually enhance student learning to generate this type of improvement in achievement for the students who demonstrate a need for it. Such approaches need to be essential components of teacher education and educational leadership curricula.

A national network of research faculty and equivalent research personnel based in our education schools and related centers needs to be funded in coordinated state-level and national-level efforts to observe and share what works in such K–12 school contexts to improve student achievement and improve and support student transition into a variety of college contexts. Researchers and faculty waste valuable resources operating as silos to advance the interests of our professions, our careers, and our institutions by competitively seeking funding, writing academic and other publications. Yet the important work of partnering with educational practitioners (call it outreach or service) to work with students in the P–20 pipeline too often rests as a third priority at best.

Who are these school practitioners to be centrally involved in this coordinated effort? K–12 teachers and school leaders; school counselors; community college instructors, administrators, and district leaders; school boards and community college district boards; local government officials; and college administrators and decision makers. We also need to recognize and incorporate the ground-level organizational knowledge about how institutions are experienced by students in their day-to-day negotiation of postsecondary educational contexts. There is a range of postsecondary "managerial professionals" (Rhoades & Slaughter, 1997; Rhoades, 1998) who advise and coordinate students' transitions into college as well as all outreach and recruitment efforts. These positions have grown prevalent as universities attempt to improve student retention and graduation and now constitute about a third of all professionals at four-year public universities (Rhoades & Sporn, 2002).

Managerial professionals are higher education employees who are neither faculty nor administrators but professional staff performing many functions for which faculty used to be responsible, including undergraduate academic advising and teaching unit-bearing classes. Managerial professionals "share many characteristics of traditional liberal professions—a technical body of knowledge, advanced education (and in some cases certification), professional associations and journals, and codes of ethics. Yet they also mark a break with the liberal profession of faculty, being more closely linked and subordinate to managers, and indeed being very much managers themselves" (Rhoades & Slaughter, 1997, p. 22). Too often research efforts examine students, faculty, or administrators while neglecting these important players who are highly educated and manage and enforce organizational policies and procedures directly with students. They therefore witness firsthand the impact of particular policies on student experiences, decisions, and behaviors. They witness firsthand the diversity of circumstances and challenges students face and the differential impact organizational policies and procedures have on different students.

A missing piece in our efforts as researchers and thought leaders is lack of an incentive structure to work in a coordinated multistage fashion that incorporates the realities of the school and college/university practitioners noted previously. This coordinated effort, outlined here and illustrated in Figure 6.4, is compatible with four themes noted in Stanford University's goal to build new frameworks for research on broad access higher education.

1. Observe successful educational practices that work for particular populations of students.

2. Share such observations across a broad network of researchers and scholars.

3. Implement policies and practices that forward these observations of what works and for whom.

4. Develop a shared knowledge bank that can be easily accessed by practitioners, researchers, policy makers, and evaluators involved in implementing change or improving existing practices.

5. Continue to do observational research and assessment to improve change efforts.

6. Report on successes and challenges that surface based on this continual research and evaluation to adjust and replenish the knowledge bank.

These coordinated efforts form a loop of activities that come full circle to affect change in a way that involves scholars as leaders, experts, and resources

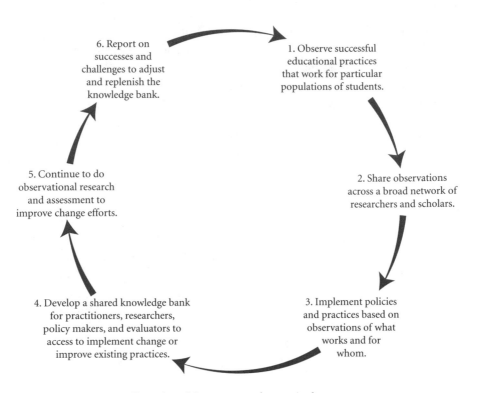

FIGURE 6.4. Coordinated, multistage, research-practice loop.

in the enterprise. This loop of linked knowledge and implementation can be entered at any point by any participant. Many individual departments, colleges, or research centers may be engaging in something similar on a smaller scale. For instance, the Community College Research Center (CCRC), in their research on developmental education and dual enrollment, provides a working attempt at such a loop. They have noted and documented what programs and efforts are happening within institutions and the degree to which they have been empirically assessed. They have performed their own assessments and also incorporated a sense of the organizational and administrative roadblocks, the resistance, and the financial limitations preventing more effective or wider implementation.

For the knowledge bank to operate effectively, intentional efforts to participate in national dialogue and decision making to build consensus about what works would need to occur. This intentional effort could not be realized simply by the uploading and sharing of papers generated from multiple players. The success of the loop would need to involve designated staff and professionals to work with a national network of scholars to devise knowledge bank content tailored to practitioners for implementation and appropriate evaluation of practice and policy efforts.

Furthermore, the "for whom" component is relevant to the issue of diversity. For too long, it has been assumed that what works for dominant and more elite groups can work in underresourced contexts with differing challenges. This is a hypothesis that thus far has not been borne out in reality. Resource-rich schools with great pools of upper-middle-class parental capital and assistance function very well for those students. The same structure has not been shown to function very well in the absence of such parental support. In fact, I would argue that our public schools are structured to succeed dependent on parental resources. It makes little sense to expect the same school structures to operate effectively for low-SES communities. Perhaps examples of schools over the past several decades that have experienced some success can be assessed and used for the knowledge bank. The work of Bud Mehan and other reform efforts would be ideal candidates for inclusion (Hubbard, Mehan, & Stein, 2006). There are a multitude of large and small success stories in states and cities across the nation. We know what does not work, but there is a dearth of shared information about what has worked.

Reprioritizing

Similarly in higher education, we need to shift our thinking from a framework of hierarchy based on selectivity to a horizontal view treating access as a positive value. As Arum and Roksa (2011) reveal, we need to give teaching and learning more serious priority. Likely, it is in open- and broad-access institutions that intentional efforts to improve teaching and learning are being applied. What works in this regard? Rather than accountability systems that prioritize degree completion, we need to move toward prioritizing learning and other measures of progress and success.

Priorities That Account for the Influence of the Policy Field

The history of the expansion of community colleges and state universities prioritized the goal of increasing access, while today's agenda prioritizes completion. As Bragg reminds us, "The community college saga served an important purpose in an era when open access was of paramount importance, but today, when college completion is so highly prized, it underscores the complexity of achieving the nation's college completion agenda" (2012, p. 109). Recent agendas pushed by the Lumina Foundation, the Bill & Melinda Gates Foundation, state boards of trustees, legislatures, and governors focus on increasing output and efficiency in public colleges and universities, like the National Governors Association's (2010) Complete to Compete initiative.

However, measuring success solely in this way leads to the deprioritizing of the learning that takes place in broad-access institutions, and it will always increase pressure for broad-access schools to do one of two things—increase selectivity or shortchange access (and high academic standards) in the interest of higher completion. Why? The strongest predictors of completion are precollege academic preparation and SES, so those open-access institutions enrolling the poorest and the least academically prepared students will always be at risk of the lowest completion rates in a higher education context in which only about half of full-time college students finish a credential within six years and only 20 percent of full-time students pursuing an associate degree receive one within three years (Bragg, 2012). Such statistics do not bode well for open- and broad-access schools that enroll the most part-time students, who have much lower completion rates than their full-time counterparts (Jones, 2011). The quickest and easiest way to increase completion is to increase selectivity at admission or to create other barriers to access for those least likely to complete.

Priorities That Account for the Influence of the Field of Higher Education

Engaging in the loop detailed here puts scholars and researchers in a better position to improve completion without sacrificing access. It would allow us to lobby for an agenda based on what works in real practice for more underprepared and part-time lower-SES students, with a contextualized sense of what is feasible in terms of scale and within particular resource parameters, and with a better sense of where to allocate resources. Paying closer attention to context also necessitates recognition of the field level—the extent to which the dynamics of the labor market, of K–12 schools, and of the more elite sectors of higher education affect what broad-access colleges and their students do with regard to enrollment and completion. In so many ways, the closer to open access an institution is, the more it operates at the mercy of policy and performance in the K–12 education sector, the economic sector, and the higher-status/higher-selectivity institutions in the higher education sector.

Winston's (1999) economic perspective on what he describes as the complicated and unusual industry of higher education may be informative to understand the nuanced ramifications that selectivity within the field of higher education has on broad-access colleges. He argues, that in this industry "the production of education depends to some extent on peer effects generated" (Winston, 1999, p. 14). He posits that elite colleges benefit from the peer interaction that occurs between the student-consumers themselves because these institutions are able to control their selection of students. In other words, elite colleges depend on their own customers to supply an important input to production. Elite institutions strive for a reputation of academic excellence as a measure of instructional quality, yet such institutions can cut corners instructionally because part of the quality of the college experience that elite colleges can offer involves interaction with other "quality" students. Therefore, they are not compelled to offer small classes or instructional techniques that prioritize learning outcomes because students interact with other high-quality peers on campus, and that aspect of their education creates valuable learning and engagement opportunities. This is consistent with various ethnographic and historical studies of elite colleges (Karabel, 2005; Soares, 2007; Stevens, 2007).

Borrowing Winston's framework, I suggest that broad-access four-year institutions and community colleges have considerably less control over student quality, so the benefits of peer interaction with "quality" peers are not part of the educational goods and services such institutions can offer. The economics of how selectivity operates to subsidize higher achieving and more desirable students who gain admission to more elite institutions needs to be addressed. Could we not recognize access and diversity as metrics of value just as we do selectivity? Furthermore, the ways in which more broad-access institutions invest in and achieve measured learning gains, particularly for more diverse and lower-achieving students, should be rewarded in ways that translate into organizational subsidies to further such efforts (in the same way donors subsidize the education of students in elite colleges). A singular focus on completion does not consider the differences in student populations that different institutions serve and neglects the goal of ensuring that community colleges have adequate resources to serve learners who need more academic and social supports to be successful (Bragg, 2012, p. 113).

To progress with such an agenda, data collection on measurable learning gains would need to be prioritized at the classroom, program, and institutional level. Researchers would need to contextualize each instructional approach, intervention, or academic-support effort. Research would also need to focus on the value students see in particular instructional approaches and peer interactions in broad-access institutions. Students may highly value socio-academically integrative opportunities within and outside the classroom, with other students, with instructors, and with managerial professionals in ways that do not mirror the integrative preferences and behaviors of more traditional students (Deil-Amen, 2011b). What students in more selective institutions perceive as valuable may not be as relevant to students enrolled at broad-access schools. The integrative moments valued by commuting, older, and lower-achieving students situated in local communities may differ drastically based on their learning needs and expectations about what college life should entail (Deil-Amen, 2011b). How "selective" or how involved in campus life their peers are may not be as important as how helpful they can be. The sheer magnitude of available peers may not be as useful as finding a few key matches with whom to connect and mutually benefit in meaningful socio-academic ways, especially given the more transient nature of commuting students (Deil-Amen, 2011b).

Additionally, the increasing tendency for students to enroll at multiple institutions needs to be seriously considered, especially as it relates to the gathering and tracking of accurate data. More than half of all undergraduate students now attend more than one college, engaging in various mobility patterns. One mobility pattern involves traditional transfer from community college to a four-year institution, and another is reverse transfer from a four-year to a two-year college. Interestingly, more than one third of lower-income students at four-year institutions reverse transfer to a community college while only about 10 percent of low-income students ever transfer from community colleges to four-year institutions (Goldrick-Rab & Pfeffer, 2009). Lateral transfer between four-year colleges or universities is most common among higher-SES students. Less-talked-about mobility patterns are consistent (usually part-time) simultaneous enrollment at multiple institutions, as well as "dipping," which is remaining mainly full-time in one institution while taking classes in other colleges here and there (McCormick, 2003).

Taken together, these two patterns are experienced by more than a quarter of undergraduates. It is no longer the norm that students will finish a degree in their institution of first enrollment; nor should it be assumed that any one institution should be considered fully responsible for an individual student's completion. In fact, any given college may intersect only briefly with one part of a student's pathway through higher education. However, despite this, federal data systems do not adequately track (and sometimes omit) a substantial number of these students. Furthermore, IPEDS limits data collection to first-time, full-time degree- or credential-seeking students. Such data systems leave the burden on individual states or on the lowest-resourced broad-access sector to fill the gaps.

Finally, vast changes in the field of higher education continue to be driven by the surge in online education. Once the purview of the now rapidly growing for-profit higher education sector, the expansion of online education is happening faster than our theories have accommodated the shift. Beyond learning and completion outcomes, colleges must now begin to think about how to embed student support and other student-affairs-relevant components—from advising to academic support services to financial aid assistance to social engagement efforts—into online enrollment experiences. Perhaps nothing short of the architecture of the entire organizational field of higher education must change to accommodate such shifts in the delivery of higher education.

Priorities That Account for the Influence of the Labor Market Field

Another issue applies to how the labor market influences the field of higher education at the open- and broad-access end of the spectrum of institutions. Interestingly, while the available scholarship estimating the returns to obtaining a college education reaffirms that there are strong positive earnings gains from just attending community college classes as well as completing a degree (Belfield & Bailey, 2011; Kane & Rouse, 1995, 1999; Grubb, 1996; Jacobson & Mokher, 2009), there is virtually no research that analyzes how job market information, benefits, and opportunities are linked to students' decision-making processes regarding completion. At two-year and online colleges in particular, serving the bulk of returning adults, and with more than 80 percent of all community college students nationally working either full- or part-time (Mullin, 2012), the movement of students between college and jobs is fluid and constant, and in most cases simultaneous, unlike more traditional and selective four-year institutions in which college precedes job and career.

Two different labor markets exist for college students. One, the baccalaureate market, places great emphasis on credentials, and the other, the sub-baccalaureate market, values experience more than credentials (Belfield & Bailey, 2011; Grubb, 1993, 1996, 2002). Students who enroll in broad-access institutions experience this and are, in a sense, constantly navigating both markets to make their decisions about continuing in college or not. How do our models of success consider this, especially in light of the reality that persisting in college often involves decisions about incurring further costs rather than reaping more labor market benefits? This is an important dynamic to consider, especially given two realities. First, the labor market is demanding more highly trained workers, which has increased the enrollment of part-time, nontraditional-age learners, who are flocking to attend broad-access colleges, particularly those offering more flexible, online options (Carnevale, Smith, & Strohl, 2010). Second, those who choose broad-access institutions are more likely to modify their choices about their enrollment and investment in college dependent on labor market opportunities. What role does learning about and/or attaining better career options while at a community college, for instance, play in defining success?

Priorities That Account for the Diversity of Racial/Ethnic Diversity Issues

The issue of racial/ethnic diversity is salient here as well. Unlike underrepresented racial-minority students who live on four-year campuses and tend to seek commonality along racial/ethnic lines, racial-minority commuting students may not view campus as the ideal place to interact with same-race peers. Many come from already segregated high schools and neighborhoods, and while enrolled in college, their primary social/cultural life remains off campus, where they engage in same-race, same-ethnicity community interactions through friendships, churches, and other community involvements. They therefore may likely expect their time on campus to be an opportunity to interact *across* racial lines (Deil-Amen, 2011b). In this respect, they are ironically like white students who come from highly segregated predominantly white schools and neighborhoods who seek a level of diversity in their campus experience. However, commuting students differ in that the dominant purpose of such interactions is more likely to be academic than social (Deil-Amen, 2011b).

Again, this subjectivity of students and how they value, understand, and negotiate their broad-access college contexts are understudied areas of inquiry. Most have some common understandings about what more traditional students seek and value in a "college experience." Less understood is how *most* students experience and find value in college-going that involves commuting to campus and incorporating college into their work and family lives. Less understood is how students who struggle academically interpret their pursuit of college. All of this is about the sociology at the heart of Tinto's persistence framework—how students perceive a normative congruence between their own expectations and what their college offers (Deil-Amen, 2011b). Without drawing from persistence frameworks directly, Cox (2009) superbly elaborates these dynamics by describing how the fears of community college remedial students shape their actions, interpretations of, and responses to remedial instruction.

Studying student subjectivity in context is also valuable for understanding how students from similar demographic backgrounds may respond to challenges in different ways. Recent research shows that students may frame and interpret the same challenges quite differently, which thereby influences how they differentially respond (Deil-Amen & Goldrick-Rab, 2009; Martinez & Deil-Amen, in press). The classic sociological exploration of how agency and structure intersect is relevant in this regard, and more developed theories of resiliency in higher education are needed (Everett-Haynes & Deil-Amen, 2011).

From Margin to Center

I will discuss remediation (developmental education) further as a final example of this idea of the marginalizing of the majority. Our conceptual categories tend to measure, categorize, label, and therefore frame remedial students as deviant exceptions to the rule while "college-ready" students are framed as the norm. In other words, being underprepared for college is marginalized while college readiness is normalized. This greatly delegitimizes two-year colleges, for which serving remedial/developmental students is now a central function, with approximately 60 percent of community college students demonstrating a need for at least one developmental course (Adelman, 1996; Attewell, Lavin, Domina, & Levey, 2006). Some community colleges serving mainly low-income and minority students have upwards of three quarters needing re-mediation (McClenney, 2009).

Normalizing college readiness while treating remedial students as a dis-tinctly different group creates a nonremedial/remedial dichotomy that downplays the tremendous lack of college readiness throughout postsecond-ary education, not just on the borderlines of remedial testing and placement (Deil-Amen, 2011a). When we consider more broadly the vast number of two-year and four-year students who are not referred to or enrolled in remedial classes, yet are, for the most part, equally unprepared for the rigors of their college classes, the underprepared student group swells to a majority in higher education overall. The nonremedial/remedial dichotomy masks an important reality—underpreparedness for college is now a norm in our higher educa-tion system.

This dichotomizing also marginalizes the study of underpreparedness to narrow comparisons of the outcomes of remedial students with comparable samples of nonremedial students within the same types of institutions. Many studies have analyzed the relative benefits or disadvantages of participation in remedial coursework by using complex and precise statistical tools and quasi-experimental approaches to account for selection bias and differences in the placement of students into remedial coursework (Attewell & Lavin, 2007; Attewell, Lavin, Domina, & Levey, 2006; Bailey, 2009; Bettinger & Long, 2009; Calcagno & Long, 2008). Their purpose is to compare similarly prepared stu-dents exposed to different remedial "treatments." These studies have shown mixed effects and some modest positive benefits from exposure to remedial coursework but no strong evidence that access to remediation in community college substantially facilitates or hinders credit or degree completion. The most striking finding from these and similar studies is that nearly all under-prepared students—both those who are enrolled in remedial/developmental classes and those who are not—struggle to persist, are at risk of noncomple-tion, and are significantly delayed in their acquisition of a college credential. As a whole, underprepared students are more similar to each other than they are to college-ready students, yet our research tends to focus on differences among the underprepared.

In addition, marginalizing remediation locates discussion of it in the community college sector, which has several consequences. First, this makes community college remedial students doubly marginalized, sectioned off in our conceptual realities as different from the rest of postsecondary students.

Second, it renders invisible the experiences of four-year college and university students who face the challenges of remediation and underpreparedness (more broadly defined) within different, yet similarly challenging, institutional contexts. Those beginning in the four-year public sector, for instance, may be just as vulnerable as those in community colleges, especially given the contexts they face—huge lecture classes with hundreds of students and workloads and grading standards often strikingly different from those of their high schools. While those students—especially lower-income, racial-minority, and first-generation college students—who gain access to universities are often viewed as success stories relative to those who enroll in community colleges, my research reveals that these students are similarly vulnerable to failure. Many find themselves underprepared to succeed at the university, and their attempts to cope intersect with other relevant components of diversity. They struggle with GPAs low enough to lose their financial aid, stereotype threat (Steele & Aronson, 1995), doubts about their ability to succeed academically, fears of being stigmatized, and reluctance to ask for help (Deil-Amen, 2011a; Martinez & Deil-Amen, in press). The words, in our interview, of one underprepared (nonremedial) African American male university freshman sum up this combination of fears, particularly fear of being the example of the low-achieving minority student that his peers and instructors expect:

A lot of time I feel pressure to be a successful black man, seeing as a lot of black men are in jail, dead, at my age, especially where I grew up. . . . You think about it like, man, I don't want to be the dumb black kid in the class. "Just because he's black, he's not smart enough." I want to prove to them we can do it too. . . . All the time I wonder if I got this grade because they were like, "Oh, he can't think at this level, so all his papers can only be a B, or all his papers can only be a C," or "Oh, this is the black kid's paper. Looks like he tried, but he's not as smart as the white kid." I think about that all the time. I want to prove everything that people hold against black people wrong. Like, they're like, "Oh, the black person always needs help. Oh, he's not smart; they're not smart enough." To an extent, I am kind of afraid to ask for help, and all the time I think to myself, "Man, am I smart enough? . . . Am I not smart enough as a person?" . . . Or would it be, "Oh, he's black. It's okay. He's just not that smart." You know what I'm saying? Man, that's just annoying [*pressing his hands to his forehead*]. Got to get it by yourself. Got to understand this. . . . I feel ostracized a lot.

Conceptually dismantling remedial/nonremedial dichotomies can motivate a broader approach that centers on common challenges faced by all underprepared students, regardless of their institutional label/designation, and in light of the different institutional contexts. Adelman (1999, 2006) supports this idea, as he highlights the prominence of high school academic rigor over remedial placement and institution type in influencing bachelor's degree completion. Bailey also moves in this direction by emphasizing underpreparedness rather than remedial designation, describing how students enter college "with academic skills weak enough in at least one major subject area to threaten their ability to succeed in college-level courses" (2009, p. 13).

Future Directions

Future scholarship should consider the extent to which conceptual frameworks are driven by the marginalization of the majority and the prioritization of the minority noted previously. Analyses should also consider how flows of money and resources are guided or supported by this prioritization and marginalization. Attention should be focused on how policy and practice decisions are made within the context of this framework of prioritization and marginalization.

With regard to models of policy making, three initiatives—Achieving the Dream, the Equity Scorecard, and Pathways to Results—are highlighted by Bragg (2012) as excellent examples of how efforts to increase college completion need not sacrifice college access in the process. Focusing on what developmental-level students need to be successful and on what facilitates and impedes equity in access and completion across racial/ethnic subgroups is a first step that these initiatives take in foregrounding access in the quest for improved success. Measures of success are determined from the ground up, in context of what the colleges understand to be markers, or milestones, of progress toward reasonable goals. For instance, success in Achieving the Dream is measured in terms of student progression to and through developmental and gatekeeper courses (with a C grade or better), persistence from term to term, and the completion of certificates and degrees. The Equity Scorecard expands definitions of success by measuring inequities between different student groups in four areas:

- access (e.g., enrollment, curriculum, financial aid)
- retention (e.g., persistence, course-taking patterns, completion)

- completion (e.g., transfer eligibility, certificate or degree completion)
- excellence (e.g., course grades, grade point averages, honors or awards)

Pathways to Results breaks from the norm of operationalizing student success at the level of institutional accountability by infusing an alternative means of identifying gaps and successes—by structuring of the assessment of opportunities and success as a pipeline issue. They create practitioner groups made up of community college educators, K–12 educators, university partners, employers, and community-based organizations (as well as other important stakeholders) to map specific curricular pathways from high school to and through higher education and into employment. These practitioners form inquiry teams that examine curriculum alignment and program quality to identify areas of strength, weakness, and inequities in which student subgroups access, use, and benefit from differing pathways.

Each initiative also goes a step further to engage in continuous improvement through data collection at the institutional level (with state-level support) to evaluate efforts and practice on an ongoing basis. In this way, these initiatives are informative with respect to their strategies for coordinating efforts between community colleges and state policy actors to work together, with practitioners, organizational leaders, policy makers, foundations, and researchers collaborating over the long term to enhance student completion in the context of open-access institutions and to incentivize existing and pilot programs that show evidence of success. Further steps to consider additional aspects of organizational fields, such as the impact of intersections with labor market demands and opportunities, would be an added asset to such approaches.

PART III

ASSESSMENT AND GOVERNANCE
IN THE CHANGING ECOLOGY

7

MEASURING COLLEGE PERFORMANCE

Richard Arum and Josipa Roksa

Public and private investment in higher education, the significance of post-secondary attainment for individual life-course outcomes, and the presumed importance of human capital formation for economic competitiveness have contributed to a burgeoning interest in measuring college quality. It is thus not surprising that while metrics of institutional quality in higher education have shaped organizational orientations and practices for decades, higher education practices and outcomes are facing increasing scrutiny and demands for accountability.

Although accountability has been a part of the higher education discourse for a long time, it was brought to the forefront and became the centerpiece of national policy discussions with the Spellings Commission report *A Test of Leadership: Charting the Future of Higher Education*. In the report, the commission noted "that students, parents, and policymakers are often left scratching their heads over the answers to basic questions" given the "lack of clear, reliable information about the cost and quality of postsecondary institutions, along with a remarkable absence of accountability mechanisms to ensure that colleges succeed in educating students" (U.S. Department of Education, 2006, pp. vii, x). Since the commission's report, various external assessments and accountability measures have been proposed or advanced at all levels of the system.

For example, the Association of Public and Land-grant Universities (APLU) and the American Association of State Colleges and Universities

(AASCU) launched the Voluntary System of Accountability (VSA) in 2007, urging institutions to report publicly information on their practices and outcomes, including learning outcomes assessments. VSA also conducted a pilot project in which a subset of institutions agreed to assess and report information on standardized measures of general collegiate skills, such as critical thinking, complex reasoning, and writing. Public colleges and universities in Texas have been required to make public a range of information, from course syllabi and faculty research grants to teaching loads and course evaluations—the latter of which were used to measure and financially reward faculty members' presumed commitment to teaching. The federal government has also continued to move in this direction, from releasing the College Scorecard[1] in early 2013 to recently announcing a plan to develop a rating system of colleges and universities and subsequently to link that rating system to federal financial aid (White House, 2013).

In multiple public forums, we have vehemently argued against the desirability of an externally imposed accountability schema. We are deeply skeptical of increased centralized regulation of this character—fearing that the unintended consequences would far outweigh any benefits—and have instead called for institutions themselves to assume enhanced responsibility for monitoring and improving student outcomes. Moreover, most of the institutional measures previously used to measure college quality were generally not designed for accountability purposes. Nevertheless, given current policy attention, social scientists would be remiss not to think carefully about and engage in discussions about assessment and accountability.

In this chapter, we aim to contribute to the broader policy discourse and public understanding of the subject by highlighting two different aspects of the accountability dilemma: normative and technical. Deciding what to measure is a political decision, one that is informed by specific values and understandings of the purposes of higher education. Highlighting assumptions and values underlying the debates about accountability is important for providing clarity and deeper understanding of proposed measures. The second issue is technical and involves considering the strengths and limitations of various proposed accountability metrics. This aspect of the accountability debate is very much amenable to social science inquiry, as the methodological soundness of proposed measures can be empirically investigated. Exploring the values and measurement properties of specific accountability metrics is not only a useful academic exercise but one that may have substantial consequences given that different outcomes and measurement strategies may disadvantage some types of institutions over others—this might particularly be the case for broad-access institutions that educate most of the students yet operate under considerable constraints.

Accountability Pressures in Context

Although concerns about accountability are not new, the current context of higher education as well as growing evidence regarding limited learning place accountability in a new light and provide proponents with a stronger rationale for its implementation. Recent years have witnessed reductions in state government support for higher education, tuition increases much above the rate of inflation, and students and parents taking on increasing shares of college financing, often through borrowing. This combination of events places higher education in the spotlight, giving strength to an increasing chorus of voices asking whether higher education is worth the costs and, in particular, what students are getting for their money.

The answer provided by recent studies suggests that students are not getting sufficient academic value, relative to their investment, beyond the credential—and that is for those who manage to cross the finish line and leave with a degree in hand. The Spellings Commission's *A Test of Leadership* was one of the most visible indictments of higher education, placing the issue of learning on the national agenda. Using data from the National Assessment of Adult Literacy, the commission argued that "the quality of student learning at U.S. colleges and universities is inadequate, and in some cases, declining" (U.S. Department of Education, 2006). In the same year, former president of Harvard University Derek Bok lamented in an aptly titled book, *Our Underachieving Colleges*, that many students today are graduating from college "without being able to write well enough to satisfy their employers . . . reason clearly or perform competently in analyzing complex, non-technical problems" (2006, p. 8). Recent studies of collegiate learning provide further evidence for this claim.

In *Academically Adrift* (Arum & Roksa, 2011), we followed over two thousand students through a diverse set of four-year institutions and found that large numbers of students demonstrated limited or no growth on the Collegiate Learning Assessment (CLA), an objective measure of critical thinking, complex reasoning, and written communication, during their first two years of college. Subsequent data analyses considering all four years of college revealed similarly disturbing patterns: if the CLA was scored from 0 to 100, 36 percent of students failed to demonstrate even one point improvement on the measure over the whole four years of college (Arum & Roksa, 2014, p. 38). Moreover, a recent replication study, using data from the Wabash National Study of Liberal Arts Education, relying on a different measure of learning— the Collegiate Assessment of Academic Proficiency—reported equally limited improvement in critical thinking among students attending four-year institutions (Pascarella, Blaich, Martin, & Hanson, 2011). The consistency of findings across data sets and measures reduces the likelihood that the results are simply an artifact of the unique properties of assessment tools or samples studied.

While previous studies reveal some variation in student learning across institutions, the need for improvement is widespread. Descriptive results in *Academically Adrift*, for example, distinguished among highly selective, selective, and less selective colleges. Less selective colleges were defined as those with incoming freshmen at the 25th percentile scoring lower than 950 on their combined SAT. Seven of the twenty-four colleges and universities examined in the reported study were included in this category. The student acceptance rates at these schools averaged 64 percent, qualifying them as "broad access" by most definitions. Academic rigor at these institutions was slightly lower than elsewhere, but the problem of a lack of academic rigor and limited improvement on the CLA measure was prevalent across institutional types.

Findings of this kind have led to an increasing focus on university functioning, placing institutional spending as well as activities of faculty and administrators into the spotlight. Scholarly publications on these matters often help to add fuel to the accountability debate. Studies have questioned "the priorities of the professoriate" and shown increasing prioritization of research over teaching across a wide range of institutional types (Boyer, 1990). Commercialization of higher education following the Bayh-Dole Act of 1980 and the "output creep" through which faculty have gained increased discretionary time to pursue their professional goals have also been argued to have undermined undergraduate education (Powell & Owen-Smith, 2002, p. 115; Massy & Zemsky, 1994). Moreover, colleges and universities have increasingly turned toward part-time instructors for teaching, with the percentage of part-time faculty representing nearly half of all faculty and instructional staff in higher education today (U.S. Department of Education, National Center for Education Statistics, 2009).

It is not only the composition of faculty and the distribution of demands that have shifted. Perhaps a more profound, and related, shift reflects the change in the relationship between students and institutions over the course of the twentieth century. Students in higher education are increasingly defined as "consumers" and "clients." In this context, schools are expected not to provide quasi-parental guidance and social regulation but instead to meet client needs through the delivery of elaborate and ever-expanding services. Accordingly, colleges and universities have increasingly diverted resources toward nonacademic functions. Rhoades (2007) has documented that over the past three decades nonfaculty support professionals have become the fastest-growing category of professional employment in higher education, with the most significant increase occurring in the broad area of student services, including admissions, financial aid, career placement, counseling, and academic services such as advising and tutoring.

Broad-Access Institutions

Isomorphic pressures in the field of higher education have compelled most institutions to move in similar directions toward treating students as consumers, divesting from academic functions, and increasing demands on faculty that are not related to undergraduate learning and/or hiring non-tenure-track faculty to attend to teaching of undergraduates. However, some institutions are likely more susceptible to these pressures than others and operate in more difficult circumstances that limit their ability to respond effectively. Although our discussion here is largely suggestive given limited research on broad-access institutions, it highlights the importance of thinking carefully about how different institutional types may be disproportionately affected by changes in higher education.

The first factor that places broad-access four-year institutions in a challenging position is their greater dependence on meeting the expressed needs of non–academically oriented students. While highly selective institutions reject most of those who apply, broad-access colleges depend on everyone or almost everyone willing to come and able to pay. If students as consumers expect certain luxuries and services, combined with a credential for limited efforts, these institutions are in the weakest position to resist. Indeed, a recent study found that while most students have a preference for nonacademic spending, such as student activities, sports, and dormitories, only high-achieving students have a preference for academic quality (Jacob, McCall, & Stange, 2013). Given that broad-access institutions have limited control over whom they admit, they are likely to face higher pressures for accommodating student preferences. This applies only to residential broad-access institutions, as the same pressures would not be manifested in the same way in two-year colleges, which are overwhelmingly commuter institutions enrolling a disproportionate number of nontraditional-age students and in many states are facing a surplus demand.

The second factor creating difficulties for broad-access institutions is their chronically underresourced position. Limited resources often lead institutions to try to decrease labor costs by hiring part-time, non-tenure-track instructors. This increases institutional reliance on a group of faculty that are particularly sensitive to and dependent on students' course evaluations, which are often used as the only (or most important) metric of teaching quality. If students as consumers emphasized rigorous instruction, this could have positive consequences. However, students often adopt a market-based logic of education that encourages them to focus on the instrumental value of education—obtaining credentials—and on obtaining them with the lowest possible investment of time and energy (Labaree, 1997a). Consequently, students' curricular decisions are often related to the leniency of the course, and their course evaluations are related to the grades they believe they will receive at the end (Johnson, 2003). Faculty, particularly those whose lives are more closely tied to students' course evaluations, thus potentially have a greater incentive to offer easy classes accompanied by inflated grades, creating a downward spiral in academic rigor.

Finally, broad-access institutions enroll a higher proportion of students not prepared for college-level work and who require developmental coursework. They are thus faced with finding ways to compensate for poor academic preparation in addition to ensuring students' progress toward graduation and facilitating their learning. This is challenging, as academic preparation is a key predictor of postsecondary outcomes, including both graduation and learning (Adelman, 2006; Arum & Roksa, 2011). Moreover, recent government and public pressures to improve graduation rates, which are often low at broad-access institutions, introduce additional incentives to lower academic rigor in order to push more students through the pipeline to completion. Broad-access institutions are thus positioned at the intersection of many shifts, from changes in funding and faculty composition to changes in student-institutional relationships, producing a unique set of challenges.

The location of broad-access institutions in the ecology of higher education has consequences for thinking about accountability and measurement
of student outcomes. Any measure that relies mostly on inputs, which has
been the focus of evaluation regimes for higher education to date, will disadvantage and inappropriately assess the contributions of broad-access institutions. Similarly, any measure that focuses on outcomes without giving careful
attention to the characteristics of students enrolled will also disadvantage
these schools. And even measures that focus on understanding what is happening within higher education institutions—such as those that aim to assess
academic engagement—will underestimate the success of these institutions
unless the measures take into account the level of resource investment. The
accountability movement has made enough progress to make the question
of whether something will be measured moot. The more pressing questions
now are what will be measured and how. Higher education institutions, and
broad-access institutions in particular, have much at stake in joining the conversation about measurement and proposing alternative assessment strategies
aligned with their institutional characteristics.

Normative Dimensions of Assessments

Identification and use of college-quality metrics must always inherently rely on
normative assumptions—albeit often unstated—about what the purposes and
functions of higher education should be. Resistance to assessment measures is
often the result of underlying disagreements about the desirable aims of higher
education, rather than objections to the technical character of the measurements per se. We believe it is useful to highlight, rather than leave unstated, the
normative dimension of assessment and accountability efforts.

Social scientists and historians have emphasized the extent to which the
education sector as a whole has faced challenges in defining explicitly agreed-
on and measurable outcomes. "The history of higher education," according to
Labaree, "has been a tale of ambivalent goals and muddled outcomes" (1997b,
p. 41). Given this ambiguity, education systems have developed organizational
practices that are "loosely coupled," where institutional legitimacy is gained
not by measurement of efficient performance but through "ceremonial ritu-
als" and adoption of taken-for-granted "isomorphic practices" (Weick, 1976;
Meyer & Rowan, 1977; DiMaggio & Powell, 1983). It is also worth emphasizing here, as we have elsewhere, that it would be shortsighted to assume that

higher education is primarily focused on outcomes associated with enhancing undergraduate student learning. The higher education system as a whole has multiple functions, including generating scientific discoveries, potentially contributing to economic development, as well as producing general knowledge and local forms of cultural enrichment and entertainment (including, of course, athletic spectacles). Stevens and colleagues have highlighted "the plurality of institutional domains in which higher education is implicated," noting that higher education systems can be conceived of as hubs "connecting multiple social processes that often are regarded as distinct" as well as "sieves for regulating the mobility processes underlying the allocation of privileged positions in the society, incubators for the development of competent social actors, and temples for the legitimation of official knowledge" (2008, p. 128).

Focusing solely on the subset of higher education goals related to the development of students, Labaree has suggested that expectations of the normative functions of U.S. schools have varied historically. Specifically, Labaree highlights the extent to which, while educational objectives have always been contested, the emphasis has shifted from the state's interest in the preparation of democratic citizens, to taxpayers' interest in efficiently producing graduates for a stratified occupational structure, to a consumer orientation where students aspire solely to gain credentials that are useful for individual social mobility. According to Labaree, this latter orientation can lead to a type of "credentialism that is strikingly counterproductive for both education and society" (1997a, p. 73).

Labaree's conceptualization of historic variation in the normative orientation of higher education, while helpful and informative, underemphasizes the extent to which the moral development of students—not just their civic development—was historically a primary organizational goal. The explicitly moral dimensions of these institutions have been most clearly highlighted in Reuben's work. Reuben notes that prior to World War II, "university reformers continued to view piety and moral discipline as one of the aims of higher education, but wanted to replace older, authoritarian methods with new ones" (1996, p. 12). Universities saw as their mission helping "people live properly" and attempted to achieve these ends through curricular as well as extracurricular avenues (Reuben 1996, p. 8).

Recent policy initiatives have attempted to move past prior contested, contradictory, or ambiguous goals by working to define and articulate a normative consensus around student learning outcomes. The Association of

American Colleges and Universities (AAC&U), for example, engaged a broad set of institutions over multiple years to advance "a set of educational outcomes that all students need from higher learning" with competencies "keyed to work, life, and citizenship." The LEAP (Liberal Education and America's Promise) Initiative in particular advanced the following four broad domains as its "essential learning outcomes": knowledge of human cultures and the physical and natural world, intellectual and practical skills, personal and social responsibility, and integrative and applied learning (Association of American Colleges and Universities, n.d.). The AAC&U notes on the website that learning objectives defined in this LEAP Initiative are best developed by a "contemporary liberal education" but asserts in the formal report that "the recommended learning outcomes can and should be achieved through many different programs of study and in all collegiate institutions, including colleges, community colleges and technical institutes, and universities, both public and private" (Association of American Colleges and Universities, 2007).

In addition to historic variation in normative goals, of course, there is also significant institutional variation in higher education. The U.S. higher education system is notable for its institutional differentiation in comparison to other national contexts, with schools often focused on distinct types of goals for their students (Arum, Gamoran, & Shavit, 2007). The Lumina Degree Qualifications Profile attempts to build on the earlier LEAP Initiative to advance a normative framework for higher education that is coherent and shared but also recognizes distinctions through highlighting variation in competencies that should be assessed by different types of institutions. These differences would potentially have implications for the assessment of broad-access institutions. The Degree Qualifications Profile's identified domains for student learning, however, share much in common with the earlier LEAP Initiative, employing the following categories: specialized knowledge; broad, integrative knowledge; intellectual skills; applied learning; civic learning; and an undefined "institution specific areas" component (Lumina Foundation for Education, 2011, pp. 18–20).

Setting aside the Lumina Foundation, the AAC&U, and other efforts to forge a normative consensus around student learning outcomes, the current era is arguably distinct in another important way: today's discourse on higher education is impoverished for a diverse set of reasons. First, the dominance of a neoliberal market-based logic has marginalized practitioners' concerns that empowering students as consumers does not always lead to educational outcomes that are aligned with broader normative expectations. Second, the end of the Cold War has eliminated an underlying rationale for political and state support of these institutions. Third, possibly as a product of the organizational maturity of the sector, institutional leadership has typically been professionalized and bureaucratized. In spite of a few notable exceptions (Derek Bok, Michael Crow, Carol Geary Schneider, etc.), the changes in the functions of administrative leadership have led to a decline in the prominence of figures (such as Robert Hutchins or Clark Kerr) who saw their roles as including responsibility for defining and articulating an organizational vision for higher education (Greenberg, 1998). The currently used measures of college quality have thus often emerged from without as opposed to within higher education institutions.

Current Measures of College Quality

Popularized institutional ranking exercises, such as those undertaken by *U.S. News and World Report*, best represent the conception of college quality permeating academic and policy discourses throughout most of the twentieth century. The metrics used by *U.S. News and World Report* focus primarily on organizational resources, inputs, and reputation. The input measures have received a disproportionate amount of attention, given that many institutions are constrained in their ability to increase their financial resources and reputations are slow to change. Moreover, input measures are most visible, as every year a new cohort of high school graduates enters the anxiety-inducing chaos that characterizes access to the institutions at the top of the *U.S. News and World Report* rankings (Fallows, 2003). Input measures highlight characteristics of the incoming students, such as their SAT and ACT scores and high school class standing, as well as institutional acceptance rates. This encourages colleges and universities to focus on increasing the number of applications, rejection rates, yields, and entering students' test scores. And indeed, colleges and universities have paid close attention to these rankings and invested much energy in fashioning their recruitment and admission routines to improve (or at least maintain) their location in the status hierarchy (Stevens, 2007).

The underlying assumption of the *U.S. News and World Report* strategy is that abundant resources and highly selected student inputs produce better outcomes. The role of resources in producing desirable educational outcomes, however, has been questioned since systematic research on K–12 education in the 1960s challenged that conventional wisdom (Coleman et al., 1966). Peers, on the other hand, represent a significant component of school effects, and some of their characteristics are easily measurable. Focusing on characteristics of the incoming student body—although held in disdain by most academics—is thus not without merit. Regardless of whether these inputs track with institutional performance, they cannot serve as an adequate basis for an accountability framework because they do not measure institutional performance directly; nor are they capable of being perceived as legitimate for such purposes. Recruiting a talented pool of students says nothing directly about what those students have gained and how they have benefited from attending specific institutions.

At the end of the twentieth century, public and policy attention began to shift slowly from focusing on inputs to asking questions about outcomes, particularly graduation rates. The U.S. Department of Education began requesting information on graduation rates and reporting it publicly in the Graduation Rate Survey.[2] State departments of education similarly began collecting data on graduation rates, and policy makers expressed an increasing interest in tying state expenditures on higher education to institutional graduation rates. *U.S. News and World Report* responded too: it now includes indicators of the freshman retention rate (the percentage of first-year freshmen who returned to the same college or university the following fall) and the overall graduation rate (the percentage of entering freshmen who graduated within six years). These outcome measures now make a sizable contribution to the rankings, as they represent 22.5 percent of the total score (Morse, 2013).

The conceptual shift leading to a focus on outcomes as opposed to inputs is important, but the measurement is problematic. Graduation rates not adjusted for student backgrounds are misleading measures of institutional performance. Students' background characteristics, and particularly their academic preparation, account for much of the variation in the likelihood of graduation. While recent research suggests that institutions do have an impact on graduation rates, that impact fades in comparison to the effect of student characteristics (Bowen, Chingos, & McPherson, 2010). Raw graduation rates are very good proxies of student characteristics and thus inadvertently contribute to an emphasis on inputs. The easiest way to increase graduation rates is to select certain types of students.

Student characteristics can be controlled for, albeit imperfectly, but resulting outcomes are inconsistent and much less easily interpretable. The most recent rendition of *U.S. World and News Report* includes a "graduation rate performance," which reflects the difference between the actual six-year graduation rate and the graduation rate predicted by a regression model controlling for several characteristics of the entering class as well as the institution (Morse, 2013). An obvious question is what characteristics are included and whether they adequately control for students' backgrounds and relevant institutional resources (Porter, 2000). State data systems often have even less information about student backgrounds and thus even less ability to adjust graduation rates for student characteristics. Moreover, reported measures of institutional graduation rates often fail to adequately account for the fact that over half of the students in higher education attend more than one institution. Worse still, reliance on these metrics equates institutional performance with an outcome that implicitly encourages lowering standards and increasing organizational investment in social as opposed to academic functions, as social engagement has been promoted as an institutional strategy to reduce student attrition (Astin, 1993; Tinto, 1993).

When focusing on neither inputs nor graduation rate as an output provides a compelling indicator of institutional performance, an obvious next step is to consider what happens inside higher education institutions. This is also an empirically compelling shift because most of the variation in student outcomes, from persistence and graduation to learning, is within institutions, not across them (Arum & Roksa, 2011; Carey, 2004; National Survey of Student Engagement, 2008). The creation of the National Survey of Student Engagement (NSSE) in 2000 drew attention to students' activities within institutions (Confessore, 2003). NSSE was designed to measure student engagement in college and to capture what research suggested were good institutional practices. It was designed not as an accountability measure but as an institutional tool to provide colleges and universities with information about various student activities and institutional services. Using NSSE to make comparisons across institutions comes with some of the same challenges as using graduation rates—student engagement in particular activities likely has more to do with student characteristics and motivation than institutional practices. Not adjusting responses for student characteristics leaves open the possibility that institutions are getting credit for selecting individual students, not necessarily contributing to student development above and beyond those initial individual-level inputs.

More problematic from the accountability perspective is that NSSE asks students to self-report their learning during college. Students overall report that they learn a substantial amount and that they notably improve their general collegiate skills such as critical thinking, analytical reasoning, and writing. This provides false assurance to higher education institutions, suggesting that they do not have to worry about academic rigor or student learning outcomes. Little notice is paid to an obvious contradiction—NSSE (2007) survey responses also indicate that students spend a limited amount of time studying and are infrequently asked to do complex and deep thinking inside or outside the classroom.

So how exactly are students learning so much and developing their general collegiate skills? The NSSE answer implicitly is that they are learning outside the classroom, especially in interactions with their peers. This logic was used to justify increased spending on social integration and student services. It has thus helped to shift institutional attention increasingly away from academic and toward social realms of college. Keeping students engaged became synonymous with keeping students engaged socially, without much regard for academics. Social engagement has its place in college, but its contribution to developing students' academic skills and attitudes is questionable at best. Indeed, recent empirical analyses examining the relationship between a range of NSSE measures and gains on objective measures of critical thinking have raised questions about the association between student activities captured by NSSE and the development of students' general collegiate skills (Carini, Kuh, & Klein, 2006). The NSSE experience highlights the challenges and potential pitfalls of relying solely on student self-reports of the activities and outcomes, often examined in a cross-sectional framework, for accountability purposes.[3]

New Approaches to Measuring College Quality

Given increasing scrutiny of higher education and calls for accountability, the question of defining and measuring college quality is crucial. Current indicators, whether considering inputs and graduation rates or relying on cross-sectional student self-reports, are inadequate for the task. Moreover, the current choice of measures is a product more of historical coincidence and political expediency than serious consideration of what higher education should accomplish and how those goals can most effectively be assessed. Reaching consensus on the purposes of higher education is a difficult task, in part because of the autonomy of individual institutions (as well as departments and faculty within institutions). It seems clear, however, that an adequate system of accountability will have to take the goals of higher education seriously. The key question is thus: What are the goals of higher education, and in particular, what skills, attitudes, and dispositions should be expected from college graduates? Moreover, how well are institutions preparing college graduates in these different realms?

Graduate Wages

One widely agreed-on goal of higher education (even if contested by some academics) is to prepare students for the labor market. This has in recent years led to a proposal to use graduate wage data as a metric of institutional performance. Following the standard human capital framework, this approach does not measure the actual skills of college graduates or estimate a specific contribution institutions make to those skills; instead, it uses wages as a proxy for skills (i.e., students who have higher wages are assumed to have more valuable skills). Considering graduate wages as a measure of college quality gained national attention in recent discussions surrounding the introduction of gainful employment rules (U.S. Department of Education, 2011). While focusing on students' ability to repay debt, these discussions have closely tied program performance to students' short-term labor market outcomes. Institutions can use wage data from the Bureau of Labor Statistics until 2015, at which point they will have to use data from the Social Security Administration, which include information on individual students rather than averages for fields of study.

Although the gainful-employment regulation has focused on programs at for-profit colleges and on certificates and vocational programs at nonprofit institutions, it has stimulated a broader discussion about "valuable" versus "worthless" degrees. The National Governors Association's March 2011 report *Degrees for What Jobs?* is perhaps the most visible of recent endeavors to tie system and institutional performance to student labor market outcomes. The report narrowly defines the purpose of college in relation to labor market needs and urges governors to demand that their higher education institutions develop courses and programs to prepare students for "high-paying, high-demand" jobs. Moreover, according to the report, public higher education institutions should be required to collect and publicly report institutional impacts, assessed through indicators such as students' wages and employability (National Governors Association, 2011).

While paying attention to college graduates' labor market outcomes is potentially a useful enterprise, using graduate wage data as a measure to assess institutional quality presents many challenges. First, it is well known that school-to-work transitions in the United States are only weakly linked to educational institutions (Kerckhoff, 1995). Although colleges have placement offices and career services, relatively weak institutional linkages limit the ability of colleges and universities to shape students' labor market outcomes. Significant variation in outcomes is often associated with student background, local labor market conditions, and graduate geographic mobility. Research on institutional selectivity, for example, suggests that students' labor market outcomes have little if any relationship to institutions attended once individual-level background characteristics are properly taken into account (Gerber & Cheung, 2008). Moreover, none of the nationally representative large-scale data sets collected by federal agencies include measures of students' skills as well as wages. This makes it impossible to model empirically the extent to which variation in skill development (e.g., test score growth) occurs across institutions relative to the extent to which graduate wage variation occurs across institutions. Such analyses would serve to either empirically demonstrate or call into question the technical feasibility of using graduate wage data as a metric of college performance at the institutional level. Some preliminary indicators can be obtained from the data set collected for the *Academically Adrift* study, which shows limited evidence of systematic institutional differences in recent college graduates' income levels (Arum & Roksa, 2014), but a more extensive consideration of this issue would require a different national data collection effort.

Second, focusing on early labor market outcomes can be largely misleading. Students in professional programs, for example, tend to work in occupations with higher initial earnings but lower earning trajectories over time (Roksa & Levey, 2010). This in part reflects the advantage of liberal arts and science majors in the process of promotion, particularly in the middle of the occupational hierarchy (Ishida, Spilerman, & Su, 1997). Moreover, many students choose their major with the intention to enroll in graduate or professional schools. This "option value" of undergraduate education is greater for liberal arts and science fields, and students choose to major in those fields in part because of their expectations of continuing their education (Eide & Waehrer, 1998). If graduate school enrollment does not immediately follow undergraduate education, or if graduate education is combined with employment (i.e., students take part-time or other low-paying jobs while continuing their studies), early labor market outcomes of these graduates would reflect poorly on what in the long run may be an economically productive trajectory.

Similarly, recent descriptions of certificate programs have highlighted the shortsightedness of trading immediate returns for a longer-term perspective. While certificate programs are often able to place their students in jobs immediately after graduation, many of their graduates have little or limited ability to advance without additional education (and often more general education). Some institutions and states have considered addressing this issue through "stackable certificates or degrees"—that is, programs in which students acquire a lower-level certificate that can be used to enter the labor market immediately and is then tied to a degree, which students can pursue subsequently to advance their economic positions. Long-term outcomes of these students may be desirable, but it would be difficult to relate them to the institutional performance of their certificate-granting program. Judging school performance based on the outcomes of graduates from a decade earlier generates metrics that are not particularly useful for measuring current institutional performance and guiding ongoing reform efforts.

Learning Outcomes

Instead of presuming that wages represent a certain level of skills, one could directly measure college graduates' specific skills and competencies. Indeed, measuring college performance by focusing on learning outcomes with value-added test score growth has gained increasing attention. The Council for Aid to Education has promoted this strategy and facilitated its spread in hundreds of institutions using the Collegiate Learning Assessment (CLA) (see Council for Aid to Education, n.d.). Similarly, institutions participating in the pilot project on learning outcomes of the Voluntary System of Accountability, sponsored by APLU and AASCU, use a value-added strategy to assess student learning (see Voluntary System of Accountability, n.d.).

The value-added strategy has many advantages over other approaches. First, this strategy provides for more timely feedback and does not require postgraduate tracking of individuals. Second, measurement is focused on an outcome that colleges can directly control and have implicitly assumed institutional responsibility for achieving. Third, the value-added methodology provides a reasonably straightforward approach that is interpretable and aligned with normative values of equity and achievement: regardless of where individuals start in terms of performance levels, all students can learn and demonstrate growth, and that is the case regardless of whether they are enrolled in elite or broad-access institutions. By focusing on gains in performance, the value-added approach is able to partially self-adjust for individual-level differences; for example, if students are not motivated test takers or are subject to stereotype threat, their performance should be lower at each test administration, and schools should still be able to demonstrate gains in performance.

While a value-added approach to assessing learning outcomes has much to commend it, what specific competencies are to be measured? Gaining reasonable consensus on learning outcomes is challenging enough, but developing assessments, particularly those that could be used across institutions, presents an even bigger set of challenges. Although conceptualized in different ways, three broad domains inspire widespread agreement and potentially warrant assessment: general collegiate skills, subject-specific knowledge, and affective growth and personal development. For logistical and pedagogical reasons, the primary focus in recent years has been on general collegiate skills (e.g., critical thinking, complex reasoning, and written communication). These competencies have been equated with the "twenty-first-century skills" that are generally transferable across jobs, occupations, and industries as well as necessary for exercising responsible democratic citizenship. In addition, institutional mission statements and faculty surveys demonstrate organizational commitment to these competencies (Bok, 2006). Logistically, these competencies are empirically the easiest to measure in a value-added longitudinal design, as all students, regardless of curricular emphasis, are expected to improve on these measures and performance can thus be assessed at college entry and subsequent time points. Several widely used assessment indicators attempt to measure these general collegiate competencies, including the Collegiate Learning Assessment (CLA), the Collegiate Assessment of Academic Proficiency (CAAP), and the Proficiency Profile (formerly known as the Measurement of Academic Progress and Proficiency or MAPP).[4] While there are notable differences in the characteristics of these assessment tools, at the institutional level they generate similar results (Klein, Liu, & Sconing, 2009).

It is highly desirable that these assessments of general collegiate competencies are supplemented by measurement of subject-specific performance. This is technically more difficult to accomplish in a longitudinal value-added framework, as college students in the United States frequently drift in and out of majors throughout their collegiate enrollment. However, there are two ways to deal with this methodological challenge. First, short assessments could be given to all students taking introductory coursework in a particular subject area. For example, in the first weeks of an introductory course, all enrolled students could routinely be given a discipline-focused skills assessment regardless of planned major. These short assessments could serve as a pretest for measuring student learning in the course as well as provide a basis to identify value-added gains for students who subsequently went on to major in that subject area. This would require academic fields to articulate what competencies are being developed in particular majors—perhaps a useful exercise given the growth of relatively weakly defined curricular programs on many campuses. An alternative but less desirable methodological approach to measuring subject-specific competencies would be to adjust student exit exams in a particular curricular area by controlling for measured student characteristics (social background, prior SAT and ACT scores, high school coursework, etc.) and prior demonstrated generic skills.

The third domain reflects broader student development that is harder to measure effectively. This domain includes important components of affective growth and personal development. Researchers have tracked individual growth in civic engagement, moral development, leadership skills, multicultural tolerance, creativity, and other similar areas with only limited success. Nevertheless, this broad domain is normatively significant and could be acknowledged and recognized in assessment design. The Wabash National Study of Liberal Arts Education is one noteworthy recent endeavor that includes a number of indicators reflecting components of affective growth and personal development. The study includes, for example, well-known measures of moral reasoning (the Defining Issues Test, DIT-2); leadership (the Socially Responsible Leadership Scale, SRLS-R2); and attitudes, cognitions, and behaviors regarding diversity (Miville-Guzman Universality-Diversity Scale, M-GUDS) (see Wabash College, n.d.). By collecting longitudinal data on students from entry into college through their senior year, researchers using the Wabash data have been able to report value-added measures of these different indicators. One startling finding from the Wabash Study is that most of the affective and personal development indicators show smaller gains over time than do measures of general collegiate skills, such as critical thinking (Blaich & Wise, 2011). Given the low average gains for critical thinking, and the general assumption by students and colleges that students are developing in other areas, even if not in the academic sphere, these results deserve careful attention in future research.

Considering the challenges of assessing students' affective growth and personal development, one possibility may be to shift methodologically from an individual-level value-added framework to an aggregate cross-sectional identification strategy. Consider, for example, the innovative accountability system adopted in New York City public schools, where one component of a larger assessment regime that primarily focuses on value-added test score gains is based on student and teacher surveys measuring "learning environments" (see NYC Department of Education, n.d.). In higher education, one could use similar student (and perhaps faculty) surveys—adapting existing instruments such as the National Survey of Student Engagement (NSSE) or questionnaires developed by the Higher Education Research Institute at UCLA—to identify the presence or absence of particular behaviors and institutional practices in this area. Although inadequate on its own, this strategy, when combined with other assessments, could potentially provide some insights into the extent to which schools foster climates that contribute to this broader aspect of student development. To allow comparability across schools, a set of assessment experts could be convened—as was the case in the New York City accountability design phase—to provide input on a standardized set of questionnaire items that would be targeted to this domain.

Conclusion

As social scientists we can benefit from reminding ourselves of our professional responsibilities as well as the limitations of our ability to contribute effectively to policy discourse on assessment and accountability. Our expertise can be usefully applied to descriptively identifying the normative dimensions of assessments and the technical feasibility of proposed metrics for higher education as a whole and specifically for broad-access institutions. What we as social scientists are not in an appropriate position to do is advocate for what ought to be measured—although as educators and citizens we have an obligation to develop value judgments and articulate principles about which goals we personally hold as desirable. "The distinctive characteristic of a problem of social *policy* is indeed the fact that it cannot be resolved merely on the basis of purely technical considerations which assume already settled ends," Weber (1949, p. 56) wrote. Instead, "normative standards of value can and must be the objects of *dispute* in a discussion of a problem of social policy because the problem lies in the domain of general *cultural* values" (p. 56).

Social scientists could relatively easily and effectively design, evaluate, and improve technical instruments that could assess college performance, if there were in fact a normative agreement among institutional stakeholders about what ought to be measured and the political will to implement such a schema. "Goal setting is a political, and not a technical, problem," Labaree (1997b, p. 40) has suggested. "It is resolved through a process of making choices and not through a process of scientific investigation. The answer lies in values (what kind of schools we want) and interests (who supports which educational values) rather than apolitical logic" (p. 40). We believe that recent efforts to develop a consensus on such matters have been inadequate to the scope of these challenges. Academic professionals have a significant role to play in identifying and articulating as well as engaging stakeholders to rally support for rationales that provide a compelling case for specific functions of higher education today. Recent declines in state support for higher education suggest that existing institutional rationales have been inadequate to the task of maintaining particular resource streams. If higher education has come to be understood not as a moral imperative but rather simply as a system of allocating credentials for the labor market success of individual consumers, why should taxpayers and legislators feel compelled to invest scarce public resources in such an endeavor?

Focusing attention on the normative dimensions of college performance metrics highlights that although quantifiable evaluations and measurements in higher education are not new, what we value and measure emerges from political and institutional processes. In fact, we have been measuring features of college quality for decades, albeit with measures that arguably are not properly aligned with the normative commitments of many educators. The limitations of these existing measures and the problematic character of the organizational incentives they have promoted suggest the need for new metrics to guide institutional behavior. Rather than passively waiting for the dreaded imposition of externally imposed measures, educators at broad-access and elite institutions would do well to work proactively to make clear their normative commitments and support internal use of assessments aligned with cherished values.

Notes

1. See http://www.whitehouse.gov/issues/education/higher-education/college
-score-card.

2. The information is easily accessible online through two government websites (in addition to a range of nonprofit agencies): College Scorecard, at http://www.white house.gov/issues/education/higher-education/college-score-card, and College Naviga-tor, at http://nces.ed.gov/collegenavigator/.

3. For a recent evaluation of NSSE as an indicator of learning, see Porter, 2012.

4. Another test, the Critical Thinking Assessment Test (CAT), has been recently developed by researchers at Tennessee Tech and funded by the National Science Foun-dation (NSF). Being more of a research than a commercial enterprise (although in-stitutions can purchase it for their use), this test is less well known and has not been incorporated into national efforts, such as the Voluntary System of Accountability.

8

EXPLAINING POLICY CHANGE IN K–12
AND HIGHER EDUCATION

William R. Doyle and Michael W. Kirst

Education reform in the United States in the last half century has been overwhelmingly focused on K–12 education. Educators in primary and secondary schools have gone from a tradition of relative autonomy to the point where the impact of local, state, and federal policy initiatives can be observed in most every classroom in most every public school in the country. In contrast, while higher education has undergone policy reforms, the impact of these reforms has not been nearly so far-reaching. Most college and university administrators and faculty, in stark contrast to K–12 school administrators and teachers, still retain high levels of autonomy in their profession, without much awareness of or engagement in state and federal policy.

Why would this be so? How could it be that while K–12 has seen wave after wave of reform efforts, higher education has been relatively unscathed? We point to a few key issues that set the groundwork for policy reform in higher education and K–12 education.

Our goal in this chapter is to highlight the differences that we observe in the political sphere that have driven the differential development of policy for K–12 and higher education. We offer theoretical accounts from multiple perspectives on how policy is developed in each of these two realms. We then use this comparison to describe what might need to occur in the political arena in order for large-scale policy reforms to occur within higher education, as they have in K–12 education.

Our plan for this chapter is as follows: we begin by describing the impetus for reform in K–12 and higher education, showing the interests and motivations of major stakeholders in each field and how these have driven current policy. In this section we suggest that public pressure placed on politicians led directly to efforts first to reform the external operations of primary and secondary schools, such as finances, while continued dissatisfaction led to the current push for changes in what is taught, who teaches, and how content is taught. Higher education, by contrast, has been charged with responding to the changing nature of the workforce, with more and more workers needing at least some form of postsecondary education to be successful. In stark contrast to K–12, policy changes for higher education up until the recent moment have been concerned with increasing the size of the system or with increasing access to the system. For higher education, reforms intended to change the way the system operates have been virtually nonexistent.

We next turn to theoretical explanations of changes in policy, first in K–12 education and next in higher education. We consider multiple theories that might explain what has happened in the two fields, including Kingdon's agenda-setting theory, advocacy coalition and regime change theories, and rational choice theory. Since public opinion has been shown to be a driver of policy change in other areas, we review trends in public opinion regarding how the public views K–12 education and higher education. The evidence we review shows that the public has long been more critical of K–12 than higher education and has only recently begun to question the value of a college education. We conclude by discussing what the political science literature suggests might be the key changes in the external environment that would lead to major policy reform in higher education.

Our perspective in this chapter is primarily backward-looking, accounting for the differential development of politics and policy making in K–12 and higher education over the last half century. The events we catalog and the theories developed to explain them may not be a guide to the future development of policy making for higher education. The disruptive influence of new business models (described in Chapter 1) may remake higher education not only as a part of the economy but as social policy as well.

What Drives Policy Change in K–12 Education?

In broad terms, three change epochs in public policy influenced the development of K–12 policy making in the latter half of the twentieth century: civil rights, equitable financing of public services, and international economic competition. At the beginning of 1965 the influential concepts were civil rights,

192 DOYLE AND KIRST

equity, and minorities. In the 1980s, policy focus shifted to quality, productivity, and efficiency. The number of new policies created after 1965 is impressive, but interest groups composed of educators did not initiate most of these policy reforms (Wirt & Kirst, 2009).

The ideas, advocates, and first efforts for K–12 reform came from outside the K–12 formal school system. There was substantial resistance from professional educators, school boards, and other organized education interests to these reforms. A major question for this chapter is why these powerful internal forces were overwhelmed by many external forces in K–12 but not in postsecondary education.

Resistance to reform in K–12 education was strong and deeply rooted in professional and bureaucratic ideas, values, organizational culture, and the personal belief systems of policy makers, politicians, and K–12 school officials. Even though the 1983 "Nation at Risk" report (National Commission on Excellence in Education, 1983) received widespread attention, the reaction of K–12 lobbies was to intensify the existing system by adding more school time and resources. During the 1980s, K–12 educators contended that they taught the students, but the students did not learn. The entire system had scant connections to productivity or student outcomes.

As the pressure mounted in the twenty-first century, it included using student test scores for educator compensation and promotion. Most educators resisted this. They had never experienced a compensation system other than a civil service system using experience and college credits beyond the BA. Almost no incompetent teacher had ever been dismissed, and teacher unions were powerful in most states.

K–12 is now in an era where there are two main bottom lines: improving classroom instruction and increasing student achievement. The primary concern of K–12 policy has shifted from adults, who are employees of school systems, to outcomes for children. These types of interventionist policy frameworks have not penetrated as deeply into postsecondary education. Moreover, ever since the 1980s, K–12 education has used systemic standards-based reform to implement a complicated set of policies that require school system practices that are vertically and horizontally aligned to student outcomes. Federal and state policies now influence not only what is taught in classrooms but also how it is taught.

The latest step in this ongoing process has been the voluntary adoption in nearly all states of the Common Core State Standards. These standards are designed to change instruction and learning by pushing teachers to focus on fewer learning outcomes in much more depth. These standards are likely to force changes not only in what is being taught but also in assessment and accountability policies tied to student outcomes (Kirst, 2013).

What Drives Policy Change
in Higher Education?

The rapid increase in technological and knowledge-based industries since the middle part of the twentieth century changed American higher education's relationship with American society. First, the increased payoff to higher education meant that many more people attended college, shifting the system from a narrow one to a mass enterprise, now on its way to becoming a universal system of higher education. Second, the increased demand for technological advancement gave the federal government a strong incentive to use colleges and universities as a center for research and development (Goldin & Katz, 1999, 2008).

Higher education as an industry responded to both of these challenges well, providing much more access than previously and responding to government incentives by establishing the world's preeminent research universities. Public higher education in particular developed rapidly during the time period from 1945 to 1980, with institutions being built and expanded by state government. Most state policy makers assumed during this period that support for higher education's development would be sufficient to ensure that it would serve its societal role (Kerr, 1991, 2001). The challenges of this time meant that many states put in place the first systems of governance of higher education, meant to coordinate the efforts of the states' systems of higher education and ensure that institutions were meeting some public needs (Glenny, 1959).

We are now in the middle of a third transition in public policy for higher education. States are no longer in a financial or organizational sense able to maintain their roles as owner-operators of public higher education. Nor are states able to maintain historical financial or relationships with private institutions of higher education. State funding for higher education appears to be on a downward trend. The federal government finds itself in the same situation, unable to keep up with the rapidly increasing costs of higher education. Instead, policy makers find themselves in the paradoxical position of needing higher education more—because of the increased importance of a college degree—and being less able to directly control the system (Zumeta, Breneman, Callan, & Finney, 2012).

In the current moment, a need for high-quality higher education to satisfy workforce needs contends with rising frustration with increasing costs (and therefore prices) of higher education, which limit access and make efforts to provide student aid increasingly futile. These two converging trends are leading policy makers to question the internal operations of colleges and universities, including traditional modes of delivery and the organization and governance of institutions.

Some observers have suggested that widespread changes to higher education are under way and that ongoing efforts to hold faculty and administrators accountable for productivity are the beginnings of a wider set of changes that will be coming for the rest of higher education (June, 2011). Our view is that most of the action regarding accountability for higher education has been in the form of what Tyack and Cuban term "policy talk" (Tyack, 1991; Tyack & Cuban, 1995). While discussions of higher education accountability are widespread, we note that few faculty in higher education must directly take into account the policy direction set by state or federal leaders when leading their classrooms, while the same cannot be said for teachers in the K–12 system.

In the next two sections, we describe theoretical accounts of how policy is made in K–12 and higher education. We evaluate the applicability of various theories drawn from the political science literature to the major policy changes we observe in K–12 and higher education. We note from the outset that we do not believe that the same theories apply equally to K–12 and higher education—some theories apply only to K–12 education while others apply best to higher education. These accounts lead to our final two sections, in which we contrast how politics has driven major K–12 reform efforts with how politics might drive major higher education reform efforts.

Theoretical Explanations of Policy Making in K–12 Education

There are several descriptive/analytical approaches to political developments in K–12 and a few that focus on theoretical constructs (McDonnell, 2010). This work has implications for predicting postsecondary future changes.

We begin by observing that public opinion will play a key role in policy formation, as public demands for change need to be addressed by policy makers. Public concern about, and disapproval of, K–12 education is much greater than concern about postsecondary education. For decades, the annual K–12 Gallup poll has given schools in a state or nation a C–, while a 1999 poll demonstrated that the public gives higher education a B/B+ (Bushaw & Lopez 2011; Immerwahr, 1999a).[1] Without an aroused public, postsecondary education reforms did not attract much political momentum in the past twenty years. In contrast, public grades for K–12 were lowest just before President Bush proposed No Child Left Behind (NCLB) in 2001.

A crucial reason for a shift to enlarged state education control is the widespread loss of confidence in local K–12 educators and their communities. The federal government led in 1965 with the Elementary and Secondary Education Act (ESEA), which embodied a view that local educators could not be trusted to improve education for low-income and minority children. Increased state governance capacity improved education for children with disabilities, English learners, and other special categories. Then the key instrument of local control—the property tax—began to diminish through equity and tax limitation assaults (Reed, 2001).

By 1983, public and state policy makers believed that local communities could no longer adequately educate the typical student with no special needs. So systemic, standards-based reform began by influencing what and how teachers taught. No Child Left Behind was the capstone of accountability pressure on local schools and is administered through states. State policy makers now have the instruments to connect the capitol to what goes on weekly inside local classrooms. At the time, forty states passed charter school laws to allow more parental choice and create competition.

The loss of confidence in local education is palpable and well documented (Fusarelli & Cooper, 2009). It varies in form and intensity by state, but the trend is similar (McGuinn, 2006). However, we must be careful not to view the aggregate impact of state policy growth as strictly a zero-sum game whereby one level gains and another loses influence on policy and school administration. Rather, the result can be an increased volume of policy and control at all levels. For example, state academic standards policies can stimulate more curriculum activity at the district and principals' offices. State policies can be the local springboard for local authorities to devise new solutions.

Theoretical Concepts of K–12 Policy Change

To explain policy change in K–12, several theoretical frameworks have been developed. While none of these can provide a complete account of the antecedents of policy change, several partial theories have been prominent in the K–12 literature.

The first major framework comes from Kingdon (1995) and is known as the *converging policy stream model*. According to Kingdon, policy emerges from the coupling of three independent process streams: problems, proposals, and politics. Policy entrepreneurs play a crucial role in bringing the three streams together, and promising a policy window opens it at particular times. For example, the "Nation at Risk" report in 1985 came at a time of U.S. economic recession that was alleged to have been created by international education competition (Kingdon, 1995).

Another widely used theory is the *punctuated equilibrium model*. According to proponents of this model, policy change is incremental. These analysts characterize most policy domains as having long periods of stability interrupted by changes to the system. Stability is maintained by policy monopolies and supported by policy ideas linked to core values. Changes occur when those opposed to or excluded from policy monopolies redefine the dominant policy image and provide new understandings of policy problems and new ways of thinking about solutions (Baumgartner & Jones, 2002).

Three factors common to theories of agenda setting and policy change are (1) the content and appeal of an alternative policy, (2) structures that support current policy monopolies, and (3) interests supporting the status quo versus those mobilizing to change it.

Content and Appeal of Alternative Policies

There has been much more development of various "frames" with which to understand K–12 policy issues than there has been for postsecondary education. Rhetorical framing helps policy solutions resonate with widely accepted values, mobilizes support, and minimizes opposition. Successful framing embodies a theory that assumes a positive relationship between the policy and improved educational outcomes, is grounded in evidence, is universal and inclusive, and uses everyday language (Stone, 2011).

Structures That Support Current Policies

A major reason why policy ideas endure, become monopolies, and resist change is that they are embedded within institutions. Path dependence, the process in which policy choices create institutional arrangements that make it costly to reverse or change them, has been used to explain how policies became embedded (Pierson, 2000).

Interests

In determining the prospects for policy change, one needs to identify and mobilize groups who are dissatisfied with the status quo and are open to change. McDonnell (2010) suggests that there are four factors in assessing the interest environment for policies linking finance and student learning:

1. A crowded environment: The interest environment is dense and includes a wide range of stakeholders and groups.

2. Variation in stakeholder views: Positions of groups can vary from state to state, depending on historical and political factors.

3. Different policy arenas: Types of groups differ as issues move from one arena to another (i.e., from courts to legislative arenas). Each arena has different norms and rules with respect to decision making. In legislative arenas, broad-based coalitions and public opinion serve as factors.

4. Importance of national organizations: Prominent national organizations transmit new ideas to state and local affiliates and communicate information about operational models.

Policy Windows and Policy Entrepreneurs

The key to understanding why some problems make it onto the public agenda lies first in differentiating problems from underlying conditions. As Kingdon says, "Conditions become problems when we believe we can do something about them" (1995, p. 109). Problems can rise to the top of the public agenda in a number of ways, including changes in systematic indicators, focusing events, crises, and even the personal experiences of policy makers.

Kingdon suggests that policies exist in what he describes as the "policy primordial soup," an arena consisting of think tanks, academics, and policy entrepreneurs, all of whom share ideas and form a variety of combinations of policy solutions. These solutions may or may not be connected to specific problems.

Last, Kingdon posits that the politics of policy making are governed by several different factors. First among these are changes in the national mood—when constituents change their minds about a problem, policy makers are likely to follow. Second, turnover in control of the government can create political opportunities for changes in policies. Last, the process of bargaining for policy change can shift direction rapidly as more participants jump into the process (Kingdon, 1995).

Kingdon hypothesizes that policy entrepreneurs play a key role in the policy formation process. These individuals are committed to developing and implementing certain policies in a given realm. An example of policy entrepreneurs in the field of K–12 education are individuals who are committed to implementing charter school reforms in states and districts. Policy entrepreneurs have become a part of the policy development landscape in K–12 education, while they are still relatively rare in higher education (Mintrom, 1997). Next we describe the nature of these types of individuals and some of the keys to their success.

Punctuated Equilibrium and Charter School Advocacy Coalitions

Charter schools have been one of the more important policy innovations to take place in K–12 education over the last two decades. The spread of charters fits the political science theory of "punctuated equilibrium," in which a policy change takes place after a long period of control by a dominant coalition (e.g., traditional education interest groups). Charter schools were created initially by the state of Minnesota in 1991. After that, charters became a powerful new idea that spread across the country through advocacy by policy entrepreneurs who galvanized an interstate policy issue network (Kirst, Meister, & Rowley, 1984; Mintrom, 2000). Over forty states have passed charter laws enrolling over one million pupils in thirty-six hundred schools. As charters spread across the nation, an opposing coalition and policy issue network formed to restrict further charter expansion and impose more state and local regulations. These pro and con "advocacy coalitions" engage in major policy disputes and minor skirmishes across the United States (Sabatier & Jenkins-Smith, 1993).

Political Regime Change Theories

Regime change can be an alternative theory to the short-term perspectives used by both Kingdon and Baumgartner and Jones. A policy regime change unfolds over a long period of time, such as the evolution of federal policy from ESEA in 1965 to NCLB in 2002. A "policy regime" is the set of ideas, interests, and institutions that structures governmental activity in education and tends to be quite durable over time (McGuinn, 2006). "Major change" in the policy regime is not fine-tuning or incremental but rather is a fundamental reshaping of ends and means such as the passage of No Child Left Behind (2001) and Race to the Top (2009).

Building on several political analyses in fields like regulatory change and immigration reform, McGuinn claims NCLB is the final blow to the old K–12 equity regime created in 1965 (Milkis, 1996). The 1965 educational interest groups that featured more money and education process change (teachers, civil rights) were not overthrown in a single decisive assault. They were undermined gradually by a major shift in public opinion favoring accountability and pupil outcomes. The data system supporting K–12 reform is much more informative and transparent than postsecondary data. Education emerged as one of the top issues in the nation during the 1990s and galvanized a new policy debate and result. The "equity regime" was replaced by an "accountability regime," and the old coalition was largely ignored during the passage of NCLB in 2001.

The transformation of K–12 education, however, should not be overstated. Schools still look very similar to 1965, with a teacher in a classroom using minimal technology. The dominant model in K–12 education remains a course-and-class batch-processing learning model relying on seat time for credit. Assessments in K–12 are overwhelmingly multiple choice, with minimal attention to creativity.

Theoretical Explanations of Policy Making in Higher Education

In this section, we explore several theories regarding how policy making works in higher education as opposed to K–12.

Politics of Deference

Many have characterized the political attitude toward higher education as being one of deference: higher education is funded to the best ability of policy makers and more or less left alone. Compared with other areas of major state expenditure, such as K–12, transportation, and corrections, institutions of higher education and their leaders are not subject to scrutiny or micromanagement (Zumeta, 2001). Few believe that this mode of exchange is still the dominant one in higher education, yet lobbyists for the sector tend to frame their arguments not in terms of the interests of institutions but rather in the broad public interest, arguing that what is good for higher education will be good for the country. Lobbyists also emphasize that higher education is so complex that only institutional leaders can oversee their own affairs.

Higher Education as a "Subgovernment"

Most of the literature on federal policy for higher education has characterized higher education as a "subgovernment," following the classic literature on policy "iron triangles" first described by Cater (1964) and Freeman (1965). For instance, in one of the early major studies of higher education policy making at the federal level, Gladieux and Wolanin (1978) characterize the higher education subgovernment as being made up of three mutually reinforcing parts: the legislative subcommittees responsible for higher education, the bureaucracy responsible for implementing legislation, and the lobbying groups for higher education. The shape of policy making taking place in this subgovernment is characterized by mutual reinforcement and lack of conflict. Parsons (1997) and Hannah (1996) reinforce this view of higher education policy making as an insular subgovernment.

As part of the possible structure of higher education as a subgovernment, one aspect worth consideration is the role of lobbying and lobbyists in higher education policy making. Analysts disagree on the extent to which higher education lobbyists influence policy making at the federal level. The influence of the higher education lobby pales in comparison with the influence of lobbies such as those for energy companies or organized labor. In general, higher education lobbyists have not been proven to be effective at the federal level in accomplishing specific policy objectives of their constituent organizations, such as receiving direct federal funding for operations or reducing regulatory requirements. Higher education unions are much weaker than the dominant K–12 components of NEA and AFT. Lobbyists for higher education at the federal level have been effective at what is known as "negative agenda setting." An example of this is a provision in the most recent reauthorization of higher education funding that specifically forbids the federal government from collecting student unit record data.

Lobbying for higher education at the state level is a different matter. College presidents or other direct institutional representatives do most lobbying for institutions in state capitols. While the literature is still growing, it does appear that lobbyists for institutions of higher education are effective at accomplishing their policy goals at the state level (McLendon & Cohen-Vogel, 2008).

Partisanship and Higher Education Policy

Higher education does not have a clear association with one political party or another. Higher education is not a clearly partisan issue like gun control or abortion. However, this surface appearance has masked two trends: First, partisanship has characterized federal policy making for higher education for some time. Second, at the state level, partisanship does not appear to be nearly as prevalent as in other issues.

At the federal level, higher education has become an increasingly partisan issue. Both qualitative and quantitative studies have identified an important change, mostly occurring around the time of the Republican takeover of Congress in 1994. Both sides support Pell Grants, which masks sharp disagreements over student loan policies, policies related to for-profits, and efforts to change the efficiency and cost structures of higher education (Doyle, 2010b).

The evidence on the levels of partisanship at the state level is more mixed. Republican-led governments appear to be more likely to adopt performance funding and similar programs, but there have not been strong partisan effects found for policy adoption of things like merit aid or even governance reform (Doyle, 2010a; McLendon, Hearn, & Deaton, 2006; McLendon, Hearn, & Mokher, 2009).

At this point, there is not enough evidence to say whether partisan politics plays a large role in state policy making for higher education. The two factors that are likely to affect this are the differing nature of parties across the states. For instance, Republicans in Maine are likely to have policy views distinct from Republicans in Texas. Second, the historical development of higher education in each state may have resulted in partisan identification with differing policy options. The one warning sign is that analysts are suggesting an increasingly strong alignment between national politics and local politics, with more uniform policy views within parties and hardening differences between the parties (Levendusky, 2009).

Rational-Choice Theory and Higher Education Policy

Rational-choice theorists start with a basic set of assumptions. They assume that individuals have preferences, that these preferences can be ordered, that preferences are transitive, and that people will choose the option closest to their preference every time (Downs, 1957).

Fernandez and Rogerson (1995) extend this line of inquiry to education funding. They suggest that education funding, and particularly higher education funding, is unique in that it includes both government support in the form of subsidies and student or family payments in the form of tuition. This implies that the level of subsidies also rations the amount of the public good provided—people who cannot pay do not benefit. Even though the entire population is taxed to provide higher education, only those who are rich enough to afford it will go. Their model suggests that this dynamic will create coalitions between income groups. If upper- and middle-income groups band together, levels of subsidies will be sufficient so that the better-off can afford to go but not so low as to allow poorer people to attend. If lower- and middle-income groups band together, subsidies will be quite high, and prices will be low or close to zero. Doyle (2007) tests the Fernandez and Rogerson model in the context of state support for higher education and finds some evidence to support their hypothesis.

Changing Public Opinion Trends

The political science literature supports the idea that public policy generally follows public opinion in democracies (Wlezien, 2004). The public's values in a given policy area will determine the scope of action that policy makers are willing to undertake. As mentioned previously, the difference in public opinion between K–12 education and higher education is remarkable. This is one of the key contrasting points with K–12 education. Generally the public supports higher education and does not demand reform. Instead, the public seeks greater access and affordability to colleges and universities (Immerwahr, 1999b, 2000, 2004; Immerwahr & Johnson, 2007).

Immerwahr (1999a) highlights the key differences in public opinion regarding K–12 education and higher education. First, the public knows more about K–12 education, and relatively little about higher education. Second, the public tends to view the quality of K–12 education as problematic and higher education as being of very high quality. Third, the public generally understands that K–12 is paid for through tax dollars, while there does not appear to be broad public awareness that public colleges and universities also receive state support. Instead, most people think that higher education (even public higher education) is funded primarily by tuition (Immerwahr, 1999a). Given that most people do not know how these institutions of higher education work, there is unlikely to be consensus on policy changes for this sector.

One of the most important findings for the reform of higher education, particularly in the area of college success, has to do with the public's perceptions regarding responsibilities for educational success. Immerwahr (1999a) reported that 75 percent of Americans say that almost all K–12 students can learn and succeed in school given enough help and attention. But for higher education, the story is quite different:

> With virtual unanimity (91% to 7%) people think that the benefit of a college education depends on how much effort the student puts into it as opposed to the quality of the college the student is attending. . . . [W]hen it comes to college, the public blames the problems on the consumer, rather than on the producer. (Immerwahr, 1999a, p. 10)

Figure 8.1 shows the two key colliding trends in public opinion regarding higher education. A declining proportion of the population believes that any qualified and motivated student can go to college, while an increasing proportion of the population believes that a college education is necessary to succeed. Of all of the broad trends surveyed in this chapter, we believe that this is the one most likely to lead to a call for reform in higher education.

More recent data from the Pew Research Center (2011) details how public concerns about the internal operations of colleges and universities has grown. Similar to previous trends, only 22 percent of respondents in this survey agreed that most people can afford to pay for a college education. In contrast to the past, however, the Pew researchers find a growing skepticism among the public regarding the education that colleges and universities provide. Fifty-seven percent of respondents to this survey said that colleges provide only a fair or a poor value for the money spent. However, the same survey found that among college graduates, 86 percent said that college has been a good value for them personally (Pew Research Center, 2011).

The 2012 election provided a compelling window on the public's views of college costs. Both candidates publicly committed their support for the Pell Grant program, and the only areas of disagreement between the two major-party candidates were slight ones regarding the role of banks in student lending and the regulation of for-profit institutions. Neither the presidential candidates nor any gubernatorial candidate placed any emphasis on fundamentally reforming the way higher education does business. This again

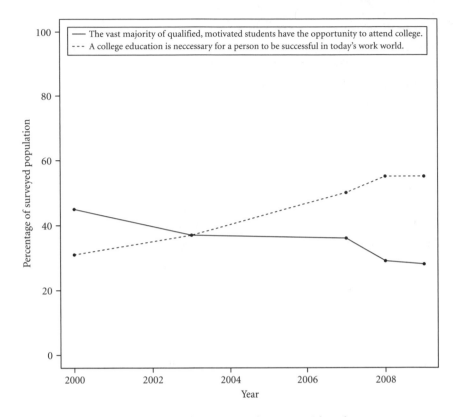

FIGURE 8.1. Percentage of population saying they agree with each statement.
Source: Immerwahr & Johnson, 2010.

contrasts with K–12 education, where reform has been a constant refrain among candidates in national and state elections.

Policy Windows for Higher Education

Kingdon (1995) details how policy windows for policy change can open when problems, policies, and politics come together. What could a policy window for higher education look like? We describe shortly a list of possible problems that may arise in the near term to create policy windows for major changes in higher education policy. This is not meant to be a predictive exercise so much as to illustrate some of the conditions that may combine to create an opportunity for major policy change.

Multiple possible events or changes might move the problem of access to and success in higher education to the top of the policy-making agenda. These could include the following:

- A state funding crisis leads to the denial of admission to large numbers of students, particularly students from middle- and upper-income families that have traditionally gone to college. When this occurs, there is likely to be an outpouring of public anger.

- A lack of funding from the state level may not lead to denial of admission but rather to widespread cancellation of classes at public universities and colleges, meaning that many students are unable to graduate. The average time to graduation at bachelor's degree–granting institutions could increase from six years to seven or eight, leading to anger from a broad swath of middle- and upper-income voters.

- The generational gap in educational attainment widens. As the baby boomers retire, the lack of educational capital among the younger generation becomes alarmingly clear and in many states rises to the level where it is considered a crisis. Pressure comes from the business community to "do something" about the lack of qualified candidates for jobs.

- The public could become aware of a drop in the quality of higher education. K–12 reform efforts have been driven primarily by public concern about the quality of education. Several authors have documented what appears to be alarmingly low levels of student gains in higher education, yet this problem has garnered little attention from policy makers (Arum & Roksa, 2011; Pascarella, Blaich, Martin, & Hanson, 2011).

Advocacy Coalitions and Higher Education Policy

As mentioned previously in this chapter, the advocacy coalition framework suggests that policy making typically takes place in a set of policy subsystems, which will remain stable in the absence of galvanizing external events.

A different set of understandings regarding how policy works for higher education would involve fundamentally restructuring the role of government in higher education to stop funding enrollment and start funding completion. None of the existing groups, such as the American Council on Education or for-profit institutions, even considers this as a policy option. Such a change would need to come from outside the current subsystem. In Tennessee, the new performance funding plan proposed by the Tennessee Higher Education Commission and enacted by the legislature promises to come much closer to funding on the basis of completion than any previously implemented policy.

Existing institutions will play a key role in making changes in the existing policy regime. We highlight the role of several institutions in the policy realm of higher education: institutions of higher education, think tanks, foundations, and nongovernmental organizations (NGOs).

Institutions of higher education. One of the paradoxes of reforming higher education is that institutions of higher education themselves are often the originators of reforms in other areas. Those working within higher education have instigated major changes in many areas of society. Yet institutions of higher education have rarely been at the forefront of pushing for major changes in higher education policy, for entirely understandable reasons.

Think tanks, foundations, and other NGOs. Earlier in this chapter we describe the process of regime change in K–12 education, particularly the use of an "elite" strategy by conservative foundations to change the dominant discourse around education reform. The same strategy could be used to push for higher education reform. Foundations and external organizations—including the Lumina Foundation for Education, the Bill & Melinda Gates Foundation, the Broad Foundation, and the Walton Family Foundation—are already outsize players in higher education and education reform movements. Their ability to leverage change depends on connections with both governmental agencies and possible constituencies such as the business community.

What Would It Take to Achieve Major Change in Higher Education Politics and Policy Making?

What would it take to bring major change to postsecondary education? For example, could a new policy regime feature student progress, learning, and completion?

Greater transparency regarding how higher education works, and particularly the level of performance of higher education, could generate more public demand for fundamental reforms in higher education. Efforts such as the National Center for Public Policy and Higher Education's Measuring Up report cards have helped to shape the public agenda for higher education in many states. However, they have not generated (and were not designed to generate) a groundswell of public concern about higher education.

One lesson that we derive from the experience of policy reform in K–12 is the importance of building a media campaign designed to change public opinion, starting with "elite" audiences. Lenkowsky and Piereson (2007), who led conservative organizations, provide a detailed analysis of the fifty-year role and impact of conservative foundations. These foundations used an elite strategy. The principal targets were professionals, scholars, policy makers, journalists, and similar elites. The goal was to have elites think differently about the problems and solutions for K–12 education. Traditional postsecondary policy and opinions focus on access for students and are only beginning to change to student success through the supply side of state systems and institutions (Kirst & Wirt, 2009, McGuinn, 2006). There is some evidence that the elite opinion strategy helped cause the policy sea change that McGuinn chronicles in his 1965–2005 analysis for K–12.

The higher education community needs to come to greater clarity on the nature of the problem or problems that face us in terms of educational progress, completion, and learning. What evidence is there that these problems can be solved with greater funding? With changes in curriculum? With changes in organizational structures? With changes in personnel? Although evidence is building, we know very little right now about the nature of these problems and the kinds of interventions that would be most effective in increasing performance.

The Past as Guide to Policy Making

In the beginning of this chapter we detail the major drivers of reform in K–12 education, including the role of federal and state governments—driven by real electoral pressures—in pushing for changes in the internal operations of schools, including what students are taught, who teaches students, and how teaching occurs. We show how various theories of political change can account for this reform movement in primary and secondary education. However, as we survey the higher education landscape, we do not find that the same kinds of pressures exist. While the public is increasingly skeptical of the value of higher education, we do not see the kind of widespread public dissatisfaction that our various theories suggest might drive major policy change. We also have not observed the kind of focusing events in higher education that might serve as the opening for a policy window. These factors, combined with the generally low salience of higher education as a policy issue, point us toward emphasizing the role of laying the groundwork for changes in public opinion as opposed to acting on public opinion at this point.

The Past May Not Be a Guide to the Future

We write at a time of great uncertainty for higher education. As the introduction and Chapter 2 document, the past may be no guide to the future when it comes to policy making for open-access institutions. Many close observers (e.g., Kamenetz) have suggested that higher education is on the brink of massive disruption (Christensen & Eyring, 2011). This disruption will be generated first by the advent of high-quality free content. The second great disruption, related to the first, is the advent of new forms of assessment and certification of learning, which do not rely on seat time and the credit hour but instead on assessing what students know and are able to do. Such a disruption could diminish or even eliminate higher education's current role in certifying learning.

Public dissatisfaction with the costs of college coupled with increasing skepticism about the current model of providing postsecondary education could lead policy makers to fundamentally rethink how they interact with institutions. If current cost increases in higher education continue, state policy makers will have virtually no choice but to seek out lower-cost alternatives to fulfill the need for developing human capital.

At the state level, broad-access institutions would need to fundamentally change how they view their roles. Currently, these institutions serve as "one stop" operations for a variety of activities: providing content, delivering learning, supporting learning, providing peer groups, assessing learning, and certifying outcomes. With the advent of widely available and free high-quality course material, many of the activities of these institutions that were once viewed as "core" (i.e., creating courses, offering courses at certain times with a certain student-faculty ratio) could move to the periphery.

At the same time, many students will not be able to progress through the new forms of instruction without considerable outside help. This implies that many of the operations of broad-access institutions—such as supporting learning and providing peer groups—may need to move from the periphery to the core. In addition, the measurement of both faculty productivity and student learning through the use of credit hours may need to fall by the wayside, with student progress measured by attainment as opposed to seat time (Wellman & Ehrlich, 2003).

As more cost-effective forms of instruction become available, the current business model of broad-access institutions, wherein every campus creates and delivers its own courses, may no longer be viable. State systems of higher education may need to become state networks of higher education, with campuses sharing responsibility for the creation of coursework and each campus providing learning supports, peer groups, and other interventions designed to improve student success. As noted previously, in the 1960s and 1970s state policy responded to the demands of the moment by creating larger state systems of higher education. A similar change—from systems to networks—may be necessary to cope with the challenges ahead.

For federal policy makers, the largest decisions will have to do with how to award financial aid and how to decide which institutions are and should be eligible to receive financial aid. Currently, federal aid policy dictates that only institutions that are regionally accredited will be eligible for federal financial aid dollars. Accreditation, while changing, is still based primarily on input-based measures. One possible option that has been suggested is that aid be awarded not to institutions on the basis of student seat time but to individuals on the basis of completed competencies.

Regardless of the form it takes, policy will continue to play a key role in funding and organizing higher education. The technological changes currently under way in the delivery of higher education will not result in a wholesale reshaping of the organization and financing of higher education without the intervention and active participation of policy makers. The choice is not whether policy makers will play a role but how they will cope with the changing landscape.

Note

1. For many years of polls, see http://pdkintl.org/programs-resources/poll/pdkgallup-poll-question-archive.

PART IV

A NEW RESEARCH AGENDA

9

UNDERSTANDING HUMAN RESOURCES IN BROAD-ACCESS HIGHER EDUCATION

Susanna Loeb, Agustina Paglayan, and Eric Taylor

Broad-access higher education institutions play a large and increasing role in American human capital development, yet our knowledge of how these institutions function and of the factors that contribute to their effectiveness is sparse. If instructors and managers play a central role in promoting human capital development at the higher education level—as they do in elementary and secondary schools—then research efforts to understand what it takes to recruit, develop, and retain effective educators are likely to be useful. In this chapter we identify lines of research related to instructors and managers of broad-access higher education that are likely to be productive both for understanding the effectiveness of these institutions and for identifying possible avenues for improvement.

Higher education institutions pursue multiple goals. Human capital development, most notably through classroom instruction for students, is clearly one of those goals. Providing additional services to aid students in their development of human capital—through such mechanisms as tutoring, mentoring, child care, and thoughtful scheduling—also can support this goal. Many institutions also provide services to the local community and many have knowledge production goals through faculty research programs. In this chapter we focus exclusively on the first goal, human capital production, and the role of instructors and managers in achieving this goal. Yet even within this narrower definition of the goal of broad-access institutions, the meaning of success or effectiveness is difficult to define or measure.

In this chapter we use extant research and some descriptive data to identify promising areas of research for understanding human resources in broad-access institutions. We focus primarily on the recruitment, assignment, development, and retention of instructors and the role of managers in these processes. Differentiating and assessing personnel and personnel practices is easier when we share an understanding of instructor effectiveness. Therefore, we begin in the next section with a discussion about the variation and distribution of instructor effectiveness, highlighting issues both in definition of effectiveness and in measurement. Next, we address personnel practices and policies—in particular the recruitment and selection, assignment, development, and retention of instructors. Third, we attend to the role of leaders or managers in these personnel practices, how these roles are different in higher education than they are in K–12 schools, and the systems and workforce dynamics that likely influence the quality of management in these organizations. We conclude with an overview of our main suggestions for further research, recognizing that while we choose to focus on one set of factors that are likely to contribute to human capital development in this chapter, there are many more influences and inputs into successful student outcomes.

Measuring Instructional Effectiveness

A central feature of many human resource decisions is information on employee and organizational performance. Effectiveness measures are inputs to the processes we discuss shortly but can also serve as outcome measures in research. Thus a first-order area of research is the following: *What measures of instructional effectiveness are feasible, reliable, and valid, and what is the distribution of effectiveness within and across broad access higher education institutions?*

A logical definition of instructor effectiveness is the extent to which the instructor helps students reach the goals for which the institution exists—for our purposes, human capital development. Notably, however, each institution's human capital goals are multidimensional, changing, different across students, and often difficult to measure. Thus, we often must turn to proxy or partial measures. We briefly discuss four approaches to approximating instructional effectiveness: direct measurement of student outcomes, judgments based on observed performance, observable characteristics of instructors, and inference from labor supply.

Direct Measurement of Student Outcomes

Substantial research effort, much of it in the past decade, has demonstrated large and consistent variation in elementary and middle school teachers' ability to promote student test score growth (Hanushek & Rivkin, 2010).[1] It is not unreasonable to expect similar between-instructor variation in broad-access college instruction. College and primary schooling are different on most dimensions, but the key instructional practices are far more similar: planning lessons, lecturing, asking questions, responding to confusion, managing time, and so on. Work by Carrell and West (2010) studying early college math classes, albeit at a highly selective institution, does find instructor variation similar to elementary teachers.

Moreover, while K–12 research generally focuses on teachers' contribution to learning as measured by test scores,[2] the college setting permits analysis of a wider set of student outcomes, though student learning outcomes are still central to higher education goals. Persistence, graduation, and choice of major field are important, quantifiable outcomes that are at least partly a function of the quality of instruction students receive (Bettinger & Long, 2010). Labor market outcomes are far more proximate and empirically tractable in this setting.

Observed Instructor Performance

Measuring employee performance by direct observation of how they carry out their work—a long-standing practice in the education sector—has recently been the focus of new empirical research. Research finds that observation-based assessments of performance in the classroom can predict more objective measures of student learning (on formal evaluation, see Grossman, Loeb, Cohen, & Wyckoff, 2013; Kane, Taylor, Tyler, & Wooten, 2011; on subjective evaluation, see Jacob & Lefgren, 2008; Rockoff, Staiger, Kane, & Taylor, 2012). Students' assessments of teachers also predict student learning in some cases (Bill & Melinda Gates Foundation, 2010; Hoffman & Oreopoulos, 2009).

Observation-based measures can be applied across a wide range of classes and can provide practical information on what good instructors do differently. Both are useful characteristics for broad-access settings, but institutions and researchers should remain cautious. Observer bias is a particular concern. Observers may favor some instructors over others (Jacob & Lefgren, 2008). Student evaluations may favor instructors who give good grades over instructors who are tough graders but contribute more to students' long-run success (Carrell & West, 2010).

Observable Characteristics of Instructors

When more direct measures of instructor effectiveness are unavailable or when their imprecision and potential biases cannot be mitigated, managers and researchers often turn to observable proxies: instructor characteristics correlated with direct measures. The history of research in K–12 settings is that the intuitive proxies are not necessarily useful proxies (Hanushek, 1986, 1997; Jacob, 2007; Rockoff, Jacob, Kane, & Staiger, 2011). Teachers with more years of teaching experience, and in particular, non-novice teachers, tend to be more effective (Chetty et al., 2011; Kruger, 1999; Rockoff, 2004).[3] There is also some evidence that knowledge of content and pedagogy predicts teachers' effectiveness (Boyd, Grossman, Lankford, Loeb, & Wyckoff, 2009a; Rockoff et al., 2011; Ronfeldt, 2012). By contrast, higher levels of educational attainment—in particular, holding a master's versus a bachelor's degree—do not predict student learning (Hanushek, 1986). The K–12 findings suggest an important question: are college instructors' educational degrees—in particular, holding a doctoral versus a master's degree—predictive of effectiveness? Similarly, it would be worthwhile to know whether instructors' appointment type is a good proxy for effectiveness. Bettinger and Long (2010) found that students assigned adjunct instructors were more likely to continue studying the subject, especially in professional fields. Hoffman and Oreopoulos (2009) found minimal differences in student achievement between tenure-track and non-tenure-track instructors. Evaluating potential proxy measures is a high-return investment of research effort because these measures can inform decision making.

Inference from Labor Supply

At any point in time, the faculty of an institution is, at least in part, a reflection of the labor supply available to that institution. In the absence of direct measures of performance, researchers can use labor supply measures as proxies for the quality of instructors to answer some, though clearly not all, questions of interest. These measures of labor supply may be useful for measuring quality when comparing across large groups of instructors: within an institution over time, across institutions, across fields, or among large geographic areas.

Better applicants reflect better employees, unless institutions specifically choose less-effective workers. A large, high-quality applicant pool likely signals an appealing job. Similarly, high turnover rates of employees often signal a lower-quality workforce, not just because turnover is disruptive but because turnover indicates a less appealing job. As a result, even if some measure, such as instructors' undergraduate institution competitiveness, is not a good direct measure of instructional effectiveness, it may nevertheless measure the opportunities workers have in alternative jobs. Thus comparing that measure across jobs and institutions can provide insight into the level of skill needed by an instructor at a given college.

We have described four approaches that vary in precision, in cost and feasibility, and, likely, in biases. A research agenda for broad-access higher education institutions that seeks to *(a) develop alternative measures, (b) understand the advantages and disadvantages of these measures, and (c) describe observed characteristics of individuals, institutions, and areas associated with these measures* would provide substantially more direction for reform than is currently available. Measurement is also a first step for understanding institutional processes and, in particular, the role of leaders and managers in these institutions.

Managing the Instructor Workforce

Being able to identify highly effective instructors or instruction is not enough to create an institution composed of such instructors and instruction. Research in K–12 education has highlighted the important role of both school leadership in general, and personnel practices in particular (Grissom & Loeb, 2011; Horng, Klasik, & Loeb, 2010; Loeb, Béteille, & Kalogrides, 2012).

In this section we discuss four elements of human resource management that are likely to be important for higher education institutions: (1) recruitment and selection of instructors, (2) assignment or use of instructors across courses, (3) development of instructional skills, and (4) retention, particularly of highly effective workers. Like the previous discussion, this one draws on relevant research from across education. While management structure at colleges can be quite different from K–12 schools, as when the faculty self-manage or select one of their own to serve for a time as department chair, these human resource tasks remain salient.

Recruitment and Selection

The effectiveness of broad-access institutions is partly a function of their ability to attract instructors who can motivate and support student learning. K–12 schools and higher education institutions vary in their ability to attract workers. Part of this variation is a result of factors outside the control of the institution, such as its geographic location and the needs and characteristics of the students that it serves. However, managers can improve the pool of instructors available to the institution both through direct recruitment efforts and by affecting the appeal of jobs.

A number of lessons emerge from research on K–12 schools regarding the role of recruitment and selection policies in promoting student learning. First, recruitment processes matter. Aggressive recruitment strategies attract a larger pool of candidates, and districts that make job offers early hire the most effective teachers (Boyd, Lankford, Loeb, Rockoff, & Wyckoff, 2008; Levin & Quinn, 2003). K–12 recruitment strategies may target the obvious candidates (i.e., individuals enrolled in a teacher preparation program), but increasingly, they also target candidates who had not previously considered the teaching profession. Although the effectiveness of candidates recruited through these alternative routes varies, their recruitment substantially increases the pool of applicants, enabling districts to be more selective (Boyd, Grossman, Lankford, Loeb, & Wyckoff, 2006; Darling-Hammond, Holtzman, Gatlin, & Heilig, 2005; Decker, Mayer, & Glazerman, 2004; Laczko-Kerr & Berliner, 2002; Raymond, Fletcher, & Luque, 2001). We know of no research that has addressed the recruitment and selection process in broad-access higher education institutions, let alone how the process differs when hiring for adjunct and part-time positions versus tenure-track faculty.

Second, salaries affect who is attracted into teaching (Figlio, 2002; Loeb & Page, 2000; Manski, 1987). What matters is not the absolute level of salaries but how they compare to the salaries in plausibly alternative professions. While elementary and secondary schools are largely constrained in their ability to offer different salaries to different applicants, broad-access institutions likely have more flexibility. Offering competitive salaries may be particularly important in fields like math, physics, chemistry, and engineering, where qualified individuals often have attractive job alternatives outside higher education.

To get a sense of the extent to which higher education institutions offer competitive salaries and benefits, we use data from the Current Population Survey (CPS) to identify a nationally representative sample of higher education instructors and workers in other sectors.[4] Figure 9.1 compares the average compensation of higher education instructors, all workers with a doctoral degree, and all secondary education teachers, over the period 1989–2009. The

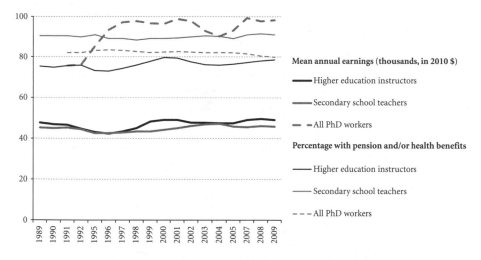

FIGURE 9.1. Evolution of salary and nonsalary benefits over time, 1989–2009. Annual earnings correspond to the total earnings from an individual's main job in the calendar year before the survey among individuals who reported that their main job in that year was as higher education teachers (or the other professions included). Pension and health benefits are also reported for the calendar year before the survey. Source: Authors' calculations based on U.S. Census Bureau Current Population Surveys of 1990–2010.

average annual earnings from teaching at the postsecondary level were $47,500 in 2010 dollars, considerably below the earnings of workers with doctoral degrees ($95,600).[5] This suggests that postsecondary teachers who hold doctoral degrees may have attractive alternatives besides working in the higher education industry. Our analysis also suggests differences in the attractiveness of jobs *within* the higher education industry. Specifically, we find that public and private sector institutions tend to offer similar levels of compensation, but instructors in technical and vocational schools tend to earn substantially less than other higher education instructors, and are also far less likely to have pension or health benefits.

Third, working conditions also affect recruitment. Teachers in K–12 education demonstrate preferences for schools with higher-achieving students; white teachers tend to prefer schools with a larger proportion of white students; and teachers in general prefer to work in schools that are located close to where they live or where they were raised (Boyd, Lankford, Loeb, & Wyckoff, 2005a, 2005b; Hanushek, Kain, & Rivkin, 2004; Loeb, Darling-Hammond, &

Luczak, 2005; Scafidi, Sjoquist, & Stinebrickner 2007). School characteristics, particularly the quality of school leadership, also affect teachers' career decisions in K–12 settings (Boyd et al., 2011; Grissom, 2011; Ladd, 2011). These and other factors might play a role in individual decisions on whether (and where) to teach at the higher education level. For example, applicants might be less worried about working "close to home" but more worried about the job prospects of spouses if they move to a new area or the prestige of the institution. Or they might be more worried than K–12 teachers about the availability of specific resources such as libraries, academic and professional workshops, or opportunities for regular interaction with local businesses and policy makers. These location and facilities dimensions also may play out very differently when instruction occurs online.

The stability and the flexibility of a job also can affect the extent to which an individual is attracted to it. On one hand, tenure-track positions might be more attractive than non-tenure-track ones, because of the stability that they confer. On the other hand, some highly qualified individuals might prefer to complement teaching with other nonacademic activities, and might value contracts that give them the flexibility to engage in those activities. Attracting individuals who are interested in nonacademic activities might be relevant to some higher education programs (e.g., technical/vocational programs, professional degree programs) more than to others.

Using data from the Integrated Postsecondary Education Data System (IPEDS) for the period 2002–2009, we compare broad-access higher education institution instructors to those at more competitive higher education institutions. As shown in Figure 9.2, in both the public and for-profit private sectors the proportions of tenured and full-time adjunct professors at less competitive four-year colleges are greater than the corresponding proportions among more competitive colleges, while the proportion of part-time adjunct faculty is lower. This pattern is consistent throughout the period of analysis (see Figure 9.3), and may be relevant in light of research that suggests that tenured and full-time instructors can be more effective than non-tenured and part-time faculty (Bettinger & Long, 2006, 2010; Ehrenberg & Zhang, 2005). Still, tenured faculty at less competitive institutions are likely to differ meaningfully from tenured faculty at competitive or more competitive institutions. In particular, research productivity is likely to be more of a factor in tenure at more competitive institutions. To date, research comparing tenure-track to non-tenure-track faculty has made comparisons only within institutions.

Distribution of instructor types: public institutions

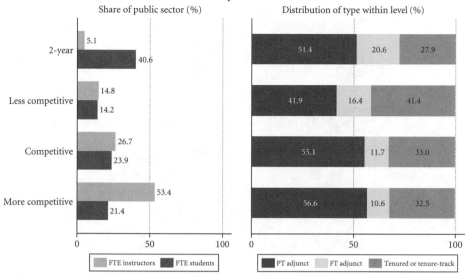

Share of public sector (%)

Distribution of type within level (%)

Distribution of instructor types: private nonprofit institutions

Share of private nonprofit sector (%)

Distribution of type within level (%)

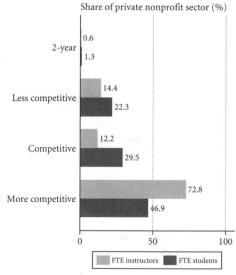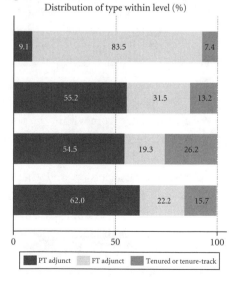

(*continued*)

FIGURE 9.2. (*continued*)

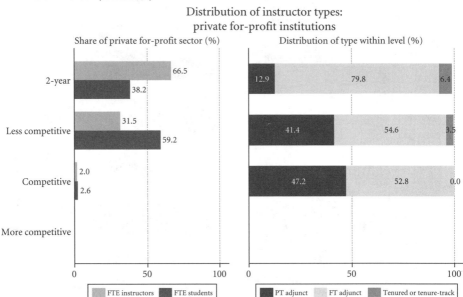

FIGURE 9.2. Relative importance of types of instructor across different types of higher education institutions, 2002–2009. All calculations based on full-time equivalents: part-time students counted as one half, part-time instructor positions counted as one half, and joint research-teaching positions counted as one half. Categories are based on Barron's 2009 competitiveness rankings. Source: Authors' calculations based on Integrated Postsecondary Education Data System data, 2002–2009.

The discussion so far presumes that institutions will be able to identify the best candidates from within the pool of applicants, but this is not at all obvious. The process through which managers or hiring committees choose from among competing candidates, the type of information and criteria they rely on to make this decision, and whether they revise their hiring strategies based on lessons from past hiring experiences can all affect selection. As discussed in the previous section, the hiring authority can rely on observable characteristics such as the educational attainment of candidates and their academic (including teaching) and nonacademic work experience. They can also obtain information about their expertise in a specific subject or a specific area within a subject, and their connections to the local business community. Moreover, they can rely on references to assess a candidate's interpersonal skills, ability, willingness to engage with students, and motivation to teach, and they can try

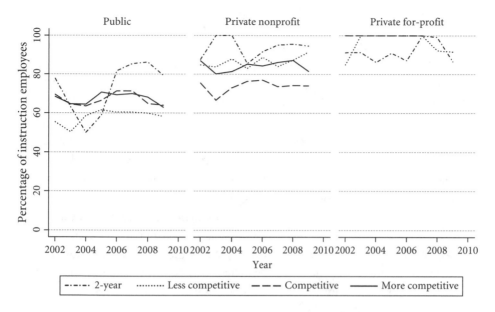

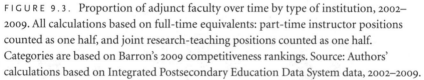

FIGURE 9.3. Proportion of adjunct faculty over time by type of institution, 2002–2009. All calculations based on full-time equivalents: part-time instructor positions counted as one half, and joint research-teaching positions counted as one half. Categories are based on Barron's 2009 competitiveness rankings. Source: Authors' calculations based on Integrated Postsecondary Education Data System data, 2002–2009.

to "guess" the extent to which a particular candidate will be good fit for the institution and its culture. We know very little about what characteristics of candidates are valued in the hiring process in higher education institutions, in general, and in broad-access institutions, in particular.

The preceding discussion suggests at least four promising areas for further research to help us understand the role of human resource policies in broad-access higher education institutions: *What are the recruitment strategies used by these institutions to attract a large pool of candidates into teaching? What processes, information, and criteria are used to choose among these candidates? To what extent are the different kinds of benefits offered by these institutions (salaries, nonsalary benefits, working conditions, job stability and flexibility, other incentives) effective in terms of matching the preferences of candidates and attracting effective teachers? Are particular recruitment strategies pursued, and particular benefits offered, to attract individuals into subjects that face a critical shortage of qualified staff?*

Job Assignment

Broad-access institutions must also decide how to allocate their faculty—with varying qualifications, experience, and skill—to different courses, sections, and other responsibilities. In K–12 settings teacher effectiveness is often not equally distributed across schools (Boyd et al., 2009a; Hanushek, 1986) or equally distributed within schools between different classes (Clotfelter, Ladd, & Vigdor, 2006; Kalogrides, Loeb, & Béteille, 2013). The least effective teachers, as measured directly or by proxies like experience, are generally assigned to schools and classes where students are furthest ahead of their grade level, suggesting these assignments are not optimal for equitable student outcomes.

Job assignment decisions are likely also a salient human resource decision for leaders at broad-access institutions. Using data from Ohio's public four-year colleges and universities, Figure 9.4 shows the proportion of courses, weighted by enrollment, taught by instructors of four different appointment types: tenured or tenure-track, graduate students, part-time adjunct, and

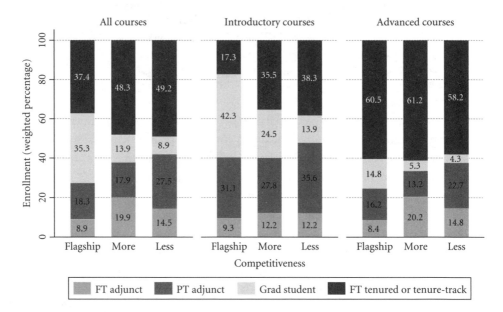

FIGURE 9.4. Distribution of instructor types by type of institution and type of course taught. Competitiveness categories are based on Barron's 2009 competitiveness rankings: "Less" is Barron's "less competitive"; "More" is all higher rankings. Source: Authors' calculations based on Ohio Board of Regents administrative data on first-time freshman cohorts at public four-year institutions in Ohio, fall 1998 and fall 1999.

full-time adjunct. We compare the relative proportions at more and less competitive institutions[6] and for introductory and advanced courses.[7] Across all courses (the leftmost panel), both competitive and less competitive institutions staff courses with more tenured or tenure-track faculty and fewer graduate students than does the flagship institution. Less competitive institutions use more part-time adjuncts and fewer full-time adjuncts, though the proportions of tenure-track faculty are similar.

The patterns are somewhat different when we compare introductory versus advanced courses. Introductory courses (the middle panel) are more likely to be taught by adjunct faculty, and less likely to be taught by tenured or tenure-track faculty than are advanced courses. At broad-access institutions, more introductory courses are taught by adjuncts than at more competitive institutions. Also noticeable, graduate students crowd out tenured and tenure-track faculty at more competitive institutions, partly because of their availability. In advanced courses (the rightmost panel) the patterns are reversed. Advanced courses are mostly taught by tenured and tenure-track faculty, and graduate students crowd out the adjunct positions at the flagship.

The evidence in Figure 9.4 points to substantial sorting of instructors across courses, even within institutions. The differences highlight different appointments as a key dimension in higher education human resources that is rare in K–12 settings. Yet this is not direct evidence of inequities in access to high-quality instruction. If graduate students and adjuncts are relatively better at introductory courses, then the patterns could reflect an efficient use of instructional resources. Alternatively, the patterns may be driven by senior faculty's preferences to teach advanced courses. A parallel analysis could investigate differences *across students*; any such patterns would have more implications for equity in access to quality.

These data from Ohio are, of course, just one brief example of status quo assignment patterns. But whatever the assignment patterns the decisions are likely to be consequential for student outcomes. Bettinger and Long (2010) find evidence that exposure to part-time adjunct instructors can influence students' decisions about what future courses to take and which major to choose. Borjas (2000) found that the undergraduate students of foreign-born graduate students had poorer outcomes in introductory economics classes, though results from other settings are mixed (Fleisher, Hashimoto, & Weinberg, 2002). Ehrenberg and Zhang (2006) report some evidence of lower graduation rates at institutions that use more nontenured faculty.

The research to date and the data presented suggest several research questions: *How do leaders in broad-access institutions decide which and what kind of faculty will teach different courses and sections? What are the objectives or goals in these decisions? On what information are these decisions based? What is the effect of these decisions on student success?*

One hypothesis for the sorting of teachers at the K–12 level is that a fixed salary schedule gives teachers an incentive to find easier teaching assignments as a way to increase their effective compensation. If colleges have and exercise greater flexibility in compensation, other patterns may emerge in broad-access institutions. Other dimensions that make assignments more or less preferable are also likely worth investigation: location, hours, class size, and student level.

Finally, traditional notions of job assignment, courses, and sections in higher education are being reconsidered where colleges are moving instruction online. The increasing use of technology to aid instruction may reprioritize which underlying skills constitute an effective instructor; generating discussion among students in a chat room may be very different from generating discussion in a classroom. Technology may also allow colleges to divide up tasks in new ways that leverage comparative advantage. The standardization implicit in some online course approaches could also reduce the variation in student outcomes attributable specifically to instructors. These are new questions, but the underlying management task of job assignment remains critical with similar goals for students.

Development and Supports

As described earlier, teachers, at least K–12 teachers, tend to improve with experience at the beginning of their careers (Rockoff, 2004) and perhaps later in their careers as well (Papay & Kraft, 2013). Recent research also provides evidence that teachers' improvement varies depending on the quality of their peers and the quality of the school in which they teach (Bruegmann & Jackson, 2009; Loeb, Béteille, & Kalogrides, 2012). There is some recent evidence that evaluation systems that include individualized feedback based on observed practice lead to improved teacher effectiveness among mid-career teachers (Taylor & Tyler, 2012). Moreover, a few intensive and sustained professional development programs have demonstrated substantial effects both on teaching and on student learning (Yoon, Duncan, Lee, Scarloss, & Shapley, 2007). All this evidence points to the potential for institutions to improve the effectiveness of current instructors. Yet much professional development, even well-touted programs, has shown little effect (see, for example, Garet et al., 2010, or Glazerman et al., 2009). The ability of an institution to improve its instructional workforce is likely to vary and is also likely to be consequential for overall institutional effectiveness.

To our knowledge, there is no research that systematically describes professional development in higher education—either instructional improvement or the programs and policies aimed at this improvement. A first-order question in understanding instructor development is this: *To what extent do instructors improve over time and how does this improvement vary across institutions, programs within institutions, and individuals?* If instructors in some contexts improve while those in other contexts do not, then the existing variation may shed light on useful approaches.

Professional development can take many forms, including formal coursework or degrees, in-service programs for individuals or groups, paid planning time for instructors to develop or refine courses, mentoring or coaching programs, individualized performance feedback, and others. While it is tempting to jump to measuring which professional development programs are effective, there is such a range of approaches to professional development—both formal and informal—that the effectiveness of a single program would likely tell us little about best practices or even the relative effects of that program.

Leaders of broad-access higher education institutions, like school leaders in the K–12 sector, can influence professional development opportunities for their instructors along at least four dimensions. First, they can influence the extent to which the professional development addresses the needs of the instructors it targets. A productive research line could assess the alignment between instructors' needs and the development resources they have access to. Second, institutional leaders can influence the extent to which professional development opportunities make use of high-quality approaches. A mentoring approach to professional development, for example, may be beneficial if the mentors are skilled, but it may not be if the mentors themselves do not have the knowledge to help mentees improve. Third, leaders can affect instructional improvement by incentivizing instructors to improve. If instructors are required to sit in classes, for example, they may have no incentive to learn the material covered. However, if they are evaluated on the extent to which they learn, they may be more inclined to learn. Performance improvements resulting from evaluation systems (Taylor & Tyler, 2012) may stem from the incentives imbedded in the evaluation system, even if those incentives are relatively weak or nonmonetary. Finally, institutional leaders can influence professional development by varying resources devoted to instructional improvement and by thoughtfully allocating those resources across different faculty. The optimal investment for a part-time adjunct on a short contract may differ from that for a new tenure-track assistant professor.

In keeping with these broad dimensions for the influence of institutional leaders on instructional improvement, research on professional development could productively shed light on at least four sets of questions. *First, what are common areas of weakness for instructors at broad-access higher education institutions, how do these needs vary, and how well are these needs targeted by current resources for improvement? Second, to what extent are broad-access higher education institutions making use of high-quality options for instructional improvement? Research can also shed light on which options are high quality. Third, to what extent are instructors incentivized to improve—for example, are they assessed on their effectiveness and are they rewarded for improvement? Fourth, how much do institutions spend on employee development and do they measure the returns to that investment?*

Retention and Turnover

While recruiting effective teachers and providing opportunities and incentives for improvement are two mechanisms for creating high-quality instruction for students, efforts to retain effective teachers are also an important aspect of ensuring high-quality instruction. Investments in recruitment and development will pay off only to the extent that, once identified and supported, these teachers stay in the institution.

Using CPS data for the period 1990–2010, we estimated turnover as the proportion of individuals who were postsecondary teachers in the previous calendar year who were no longer postsecondary teachers at the time of the survey. The estimates, which are reported in Figure 9.5, provide a sense of the incidence of year-to-year turnover from the postsecondary teaching profession. We find that on average for the whole period, 13 percent of postsecondary teachers left teaching each year. This rate is similar to the annual industry turnover rate among all workers who hold a doctoral degree (13.2 percent) and to the proportion of secondary education teachers who leave teaching each year (11.1 percent). Within higher education, the turnover rates of the public and private sectors are also similar.

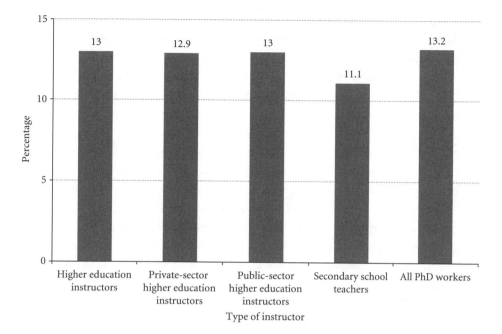

FIGURE 9.5. Average annual turnover from higher education teaching, 1990–2010.
Source: Authors' calculations based on U.S. Census Bureau Current Population Surveys
of 1990–2010.

It is unclear how much of the turnover observed in higher education is
detrimental to student learning and how much of it is beneficial. To assess
the effects, we would need to know who is more likely to leave the industry:
the most effective teachers, the least effective ones, or a group in between.
More broadly, research could seek to understand the determinants of the
decision to leave higher education. Much research on the determinants of
turnover among K–12 teachers provides evidence that teachers are more likely
to remain in the profession when they work in schools with high-performing
students and students whose race is the same as theirs (Boyd et al., 2005b;
Hanushek et al., 2004; Scafidi et al., 2007); when they perceive they are supported by their school leaders (Boyd et al., 2011; Grissom, 2011; Ingersoll, 2001;
Ladd, 2011); and when they earn higher salaries and receive pension benefits
from their employer (Hanushek et al., 2004; Harris & Adams, 2007; Murnane &
Olsen, 1989). Ehrenberg and colleagues (1991) found that higher levels of compensation are also associated with lower turnover among assistant and associate professors in higher education, although not for full professors. These

researchers find that the importance of salaries for retaining teachers is lower for institutions with graduate programs than for four-year undergraduate institutions, and it is lower for these institutions than for two-year colleges.

Observable teacher characteristics also predict retention in K–12 schools. In particular, the least experienced teachers are most likely to leave, and the most experienced teachers also leave at high rates because of retirement. In addition, and of importance for managing instructional quality, while both more effective and less effective teachers choose to leave, less effective teachers are somewhat more likely to leave, particularly during their first few years of teaching (Boyd, Grossman, Lankford, Loeb, & Wyckoff, 2009b; Goldhaber, Gross, & Player, 2007; Hanushek, Kain, O'Brien, & Rivkin, 2005).

The evidence on K–12 schooling, perhaps not surprisingly, suggests that many of the factors that are likely to attract individuals into teaching (e.g., salaries, nonsalary benefits, working conditions) are also likely to affect retention. However, the features that make teaching more appealing can make it more appealing for both effective and ineffective teachers. Much current debate in elementary and secondary education concerns school leaders' ability to dismiss ineffective teachers. Both legal and cultural factors hinder dismissal in K–12 schools and similar issues may (or may not) hold in higher education institutions. As shown in Table 9.1, the proportion of tenured teachers in less selective higher education institutions is high. We know of no research that assesses the effects of tenure laws per se on instructional quality in either K–12 or higher education. Still, institutional features such as tenure do play a role in staffing decisions, if only by constraining those decisions, and may be a lever for productive reform.

Overall, this discussion suggests at least four promising areas for research in broad-access higher education: *What is the level of teacher turnover among broad-access higher education institutions? What characteristics of teachers, their jobs, and the institutions in which they work are associated with a higher (lower) probability of retaining teachers? How does turnover affect student learning? To what extent are managers able to dismiss ineffective teachers and retain the most effective teachers?*

Managers' Work and Workforce

Throughout this chapter we have discussed the importance of personnel practices for managers and leaders in broad-access institutions. The set of

TABLE 9.1 Average earnings, nonsalary benefits, annual turnover, and proportion of workers with professional or doctoral degrees

	Annual earnings (in thousands, 2010 dollars), 1989–2009	Percentage of workers who receive pension and/or health benefits, 1989–2009	Annual turnover, 1990–2010	Percentage of workers with professional or doctoral degrees, 1992–2010
Teachers				
Higher education instructors	47.5	76.5	13.0	40.7
Private sector HE instructors	49.4	74.1	12.9	43.0
Public sector HE instructors	46.5	78.2	13.0	39.3
College and university HE instructors	47.7	77.0	—	41.1
Technical-vocational HE instructors	38.6	45.9	—	4.3
Secondary school teachers	44.8	90.0	11.1	3.2
Managers				
Higher education managers	59.6	88.7	17.7	17.2
Elementary and secondary school managers	65.3	91.8	12.4	11.0
All PhD workers	95.6	82.1	13.2	100.0

SOURCE: Authors' calculations based on the U.S. Census Bureau Current Population Surveys of 1989–2010.

individuals with responsibility for human resource decisions at colleges and universities, whom we have been calling managers and leaders, is noticeably different from K–12 schools. In higher education institutions these tasks are often partly managed by the faculty as a whole, or by one faculty member serving part-time as a department chair. Nevertheless, the list of human resource tasks remains. To conclude we recognize four additional factors concerning higher education managers, even if that role is distributed, and their effects on students: nonclassroom resources and direct interactions, management skills and dispositions, the role of unions and collective bargaining, and the workforce dynamics of managing the managers themselves.

Educational institution leaders can affect students in ways unrelated to the quality of classroom instruction. In K–12 settings, leaders interact with students in hallways, provide access to support services such as tutoring, enhance parent engagement, and so on. In higher education institutions the importance of such nonclassroom resources are likely to have at least as much effect on student success. Availability of child care, clarity of financial aid options, scheduling of classes, library resources, writing centers, and counseling each may affect students' human capital accumulation. For example, Bettinger and Baker (2011) find that students who were randomly assigned to receive coaching services were more likely to persist during the treatment period and were more likely to be attending the university one year after the coaching had ended. Similarly, Webber and Ehrenberg (2009) find that student service expenditures affect graduation and first-year persistence rates.

Managers and leaders of higher education institutions are drawn from and fill a diverse set of roles. It is far beyond the scope of this paper (and the expertise of the authors) to differentiate these roles and the skills and behaviors needed to perform them well. While quite a few studies address organizational *structures* in higher education (e.g., Altbach, 2005; Birnbaum, 1988), the research on the effectiveness of higher education leaders and, particularly, on the middle management of higher education appears to be even sparser than the research on higher education instructors.[8] As a starting point for research in this area, we suggest a mapping of typical management and leadership roles linked with their potential effects on students. With such a mapping could come a better understanding of the skills, dispositions, and behaviors needed to effectively manage a diverse group of teaching and nonteaching staff, including graduate student instructors, adjunct faculty, tenure-track faculty, and tenured faculty, as well as administrative and support staff.

The discussion of instructors' career paths in the previous section high-lights the importance of both workforce dynamics (e.g., workers' preference for higher compensation) and institutional structures and behaviors (e.g., ad-ministrator support and direct recruitment efforts) for developing an effec-tive instructor workforce. The same factors hold true for managers. Research in K–12 schools shows that school leaders (principals) are as influenced by school characteristics, such as the achievement and poverty level of students, as are teachers. It also shows that incentives and policies can overcome these preferences and draw high-quality managers to seemingly less appealing posi-tions (Loeb, Kalogrides, & Horng, 2010).

We were unable to find research that describes the career paths to lead-ership roles in open-access institutions. Three features of career paths documented in K–12 education provide an initial focus for understanding the leadership workforce in these institutions: recruitment, advancement opportunities, and differential quality. First, until recently, there has been lit-tle effort at direct recruitment of school leaders for elementary and secondary schools. Instead, leaders came from the set of teachers who volunteer to take administration training courses because they are interested or because they were "tapped" informally by current leaders (Myung, Loeb, & Horng, 2011). Informal processes emerged that may be inefficient for the organizations. For example, homophily in the form of principals tapping or encouraging teach-ers of their own race to become principals is evident, at least in some areas (Myung et al., 2011). Second, and in keeping with this lack of recruitment, the organizational structures of elementary and secondary schools provide few opportunities for potential leaders to practice or demonstrate the skills they need to be successful leaders. Almost all school principals were teachers (often a requirement). Yet teaching is quite different from school leadership, and good teachers may not make good principals. Third, the school leaders in low-income elementary and secondary schools are measurably different, on average, from those in schools serving higher-income students, with less leadership experience, a higher probability of interim or temporary status, and college degrees from less competitive institutions (Loeb et al., 2010).

While managers at all levels of education may play an important role in shaping the quality of instruction, their actions are often constrained by the need to bargain with teacher unions. Higher education is no exception: ap-proximately 40 percent of faculty are represented by a union (Julius, 2011). Whether union participation has positive or negative consequences for the quality of instruction remains an open and challenging question. While some studies find that unionism and collective bargaining reduce student learning in K–12 settings (Hoxby, 1996), others find no discernible impact on learning (Lovenheim, 2009), and yet others suggest that collective bargaining may have standardization effects that benefit most children but that are detrimental to kids at the very bottom or top of the achievement distribution (Goldhaber, 2006). As scholars move forward to study how unions influence higher education, a lesson from K–12 research that may prove useful is that cross-sectional studies that, for example, compare institutions with higher and lower union participation rates may be deceiving because these institutions likely differ for other reasons as well (Paglayan, 2013).

This section argues for at least four productive research paths. *(1) What are the nonclassroom features of higher education institutions that impact student human capital accumulation and how do institutions and managers differ in their choice and implementation of these features? (2) What are typical leadership roles within broad-access higher education institutions that influence student learning; what tasks do these leaders perform; and what skills and behaviors are necessary to perform these tasks effectively? (3) What are the typical paths to leadership roles; is there direct recruitment for these roles; and do potential leaders have opportunities to develop and demonstrate the skills they need to fill these roles? (4) What is the distribution of effective school leaders across and within institutions and what institutional factors (e.g., salaries, prestige, location, management) support or mitigate these differences?*

Conclusion

The goal of this chapter is to identify research topics related to instructors and managers in broad-access higher education institutions that are likely to be productive both for understanding the effectiveness of these institutions and for identifying useful levers for reform. Research in K–12 schools points to the importance of teachers and school leaders for student success. While teachers directly affect students in classrooms, school leaders form the teacher workforce through recruitment, assignment, development, and retention of teachers. In this chapter we focus primarily, though not exclusively, on the role of managers in these human resource dynamics. These are clearly not the only important roles for leaders of these institutions, but it is the focus here.

The most evident result from our undertaking is that surprisingly little research has examined the instructor workforce in higher education institutions. Work on measurement or definition of instructional effectiveness is sparse. Similarly, little research has described the characteristics of instructors, how these vary across institutions, or how institutional or manager characteristics predict this distribution. In contrast, there is a large literature in both these areas for K–12 schooling.

The research challenge is in some ways compounded and in some ways reduced by recent rapid growth in online education, particularly at the college level and at broad-access institutions. To the extent that technology changes how schools carry out instruction, those changes will have ripple effects on how schools recruit, develop, measure, and retain faculty. Some new questions in personnel management will emerge, the optimal strategies may change, and the number of faculty jobs may shrink. However, the fundamental human resource tasks, and accompanying research questions outlined in this chapter, will remain. Moreover, the data that online education provides can shed light on many of the questions identified here by providing greater detail on instructional practices and student behaviors and learning.

The studies that we reviewed suggest several potentially productive research areas, highlighting seven in particular. The first would generate a better understanding of instructional effectiveness, asking questions such as these: What measures of instructional effectiveness are feasible, reliable and valid, and how is effectiveness distributed within and across broad-access higher education institutions? A second productive area would address the recruitment of instructors, identifying processes as well as malleable (e.g., salary or recruitment) and nonmalleable (e.g., location or students) characteristics of the institution that affect the supply of high-quality instructors. A third, perhaps smaller, research agenda would seek to understand how leaders decide which faculty teach which courses and the effects of these choices on student success. Fourth, our understanding of instructional quality at higher education institutions and the role of managers in this quality would benefit from a better understanding of instructor development: identifying typical areas of weakness as well as high-quality options for improvement, resources spent, and incentives for instructors aligned with improvement. A fifth research area would explore instructor turnover and the role of the institution in this turnover, specifically differentiating the turnover of more and less effective instructors. A sixth, somewhat vast, research line would map the diverse leadership roles in these institutions and potential mechanisms by which these leaders might influence student learning and progression. Eventually, this line would also include an analysis of the leadership or management skills needed for these mechanisms to run smoothly. This agenda would provide insights into the influence of leadership in student learning that does not flow through classroom instruction. A seventh and final research goal would be to better understand the career paths of leaders themselves, identifying their preferences as well as the institutional features that promote or hinder the recruitment, development, and retention of good leaders.

Notes

1. These measures, often called value-added measures, are not without open methodological concerns (Chetty, Friedman, & Rockoff, 2013; Rothstein, 2010). Indeed, concerns about the nonrandom selection of students into particular schools and classrooms may be more salient in a college setting. Thus, the methods of such measurement are themselves an important area of research in broad-access higher education.

2. Exceptions include Chetty et al., 2011, and Dynarski, Hyman, & Schanzenbach, 2011, which study the college and career effects of students' earliest schoolteachers.

3. Newer research suggests that gains may continue well into a teacher's career (Papay & Kraft, 2013). Carrell and West (2010) suggest that instructor experience may have more complex effects on student outcomes.

4. Higher education instructors correspond to employed individuals who report that they work as "post-secondary teachers" in one of the following industries: "colleges and universities, including junior colleges," "vocational schools," or "business, technical, and trade schools and training."

5. All reported differences are statistically significant at the $p < .05$ level or below.

6. Competitiveness measured by Barron's selectivity rankings. More competitive includes Barron's "Competitive" or higher, and less competitive is Barron's "Less Competitive" or lower. We also show the flagship institution, Ohio State, separately.

7. Introductory courses are courses in which 75 percent of students are in their first year of college. Advanced courses are courses in which 75 percent of students are in their third or fourth years.

8. In a rare exception, Goodall (2008) finds that the research quality of higher education institutions improves, on average, when better scholars are appointed as leaders, but this result sheds no light on broad-access institutions and the goal of student learning.

10

IMPROVING COLLEGIATE OUTCOMES AT BROAD-ACCESS INSTITUTIONS

Lessons for Research and Practice

Michal Kurlaender, Jessica S. Howell, and Jacob Jackson

Today's broad-access colleges and universities are grappling with considerable pressures to improve collegiate outcomes—in particular, students' rates of completion and time-to-degree. Although more people are entering college than ever before, degree completion has stagnated. College completion is particularly low in open-access or less selective postsecondary institutions, where time-to-degree has also been on the rise (Bound, Lovenheim, & Turner, 2012). Many of these institutions are struggling with what policies, practices, or programs to implement in order to improve completion rates among their students.

The purpose of this chapter is to outline how campuses can use data to identify and evaluate promising practices to improve college completion. As indicated in the introduction, we believe there exists a tremendous opportunity to better connect *academic* research and *institutional* research in order to drive real improvements in student outcomes. The principles and strategies we present are focused on using institutional data to inform cost-benefit analyses and are applicable to any number of goals postsecondary institutions may have, not just raising degree completion rates. Therefore, we hope the lessons are transferable and will serve to improve data-based decision making and leadership in broad-access higher education institutions. Moreover, we present the strategies using specific data examples from the nation's largest public higher education system—the California State University (CSU) system. The CSU system, with twenty-three campuses, is the largest BA-granting public higher education system in the country, educating about one in ten California high school graduates and roughly 5 percent of the undergraduates enrolled in public four-year colleges in the entire nation.[1] Improving college completion has long been on the radar of CSU campuses.[2] CSU students come from urban, suburban, and rural areas and attended public high schools that are both among the best and among the worst in the nation. While California may not be a typical state, it reflects well the student populations of other states in the United States and the mainstream public colleges that educate them.

The chapter is organized as follows. In the first section, we provide some background and context to the college completion objective, emphasizing the important role of institutions in achieving these goals. In the second section, we focus on quality data—how to get appropriate data, combine data from various sources, and track students longitudinally to answer important questions about the institutional policies and practices that drive student success. In the third section, we discuss how to analyze existing programs and policies, providing specific examples using institutional data from one CSU campus. In the fourth section, we discuss how institutions might better evaluate newly implemented programs and efforts. The final section concludes by summarizing several key principles that are transferable to a host of other possible institutional goals.

Background and Context

Students who enter college fail to complete a degree for many reasons: loss of interest in college, lack of preparation or academic ability to persist, financial constraints, and/or institutional practices. First, not all students who enroll in college want to spend enough years there to acquire a credential or degree. Students choose to enroll and subsequently complete a college degree based on an interaction of their preferences, academic ability, resources, and a variety of other factors. Thus, students regularly (i.e., each term when they register) have the opportunity to weigh the additional benefits of staying enrolled—such as increases in knowledge, potential earnings, and collegiate experiences—against additional costs such as tuition, forgone earnings, and time spent in classes they dislike. If, at any point, this new information causes the perceived incremental costs associated with college to outweigh the incremental benefits of continuing, a student may choose to drop out or enroll part time (at least temporarily).

Second, academic skills and preparation in high school are key predictors of college completion and success (Adelman, 1999, 2006; Dougherty, Mellor,

& Jian, 2006; Fletcher & Tienda, 2009; Long, Conger, & Iatarola, 2012; Mattern, Marini, & Shaw, in press). It is no surprise that CSU freshmen with higher high school GPA and higher SAT scores are more likely to complete their college degree than their lower-performing counterparts (Kurlaender, Jackson, & Howell, 2012). Many students arrive at college unprepared for college-level work (Kurlaender & Howell, 2012; Snyder, Tan, & Hoffman, 2004), and students who arrive at college in need of remediation are less likely to persist in college when compared to their peers who arrive better prepared academically (Bettinger & Long, 2009; Boatman & Long, 2011; Calcagno & Long, 2008; Martorell & McFarlin, 2011). At California State University, over half of all students are identified as in need of remediation in English and/ or math as entering freshmen.[3] CSU students identified in need of remediation in English and/or mathematics at entry are less likely to complete college than those who arrive at college prepared for college level work (Howell, Kurlaender, & Grodsky, 2010).

Third, financial constraints remain a barrier to college completion. Researchers have found direct evidence of the causal impacts of college costs and financial aid on college outcomes. Several studies have demonstrated that reducing college costs increases college enrollment (Bound & Turner, 2002; Dynarski, 2003; Kane, 1994) and influences students' choice of institution (Hurwitz, 2012), especially among students with lower family incomes (Avery et al., 2006; Hurwitz, 2012). Income has become a more powerful determinant of college attendance over time, as well as of the quality of the colleges students attend (Belley & Lochner, 2007). Less is known about the causal impact of college cost on college completion, but what we do know suggests that costs matter (Bettinger, 2004; Dynarski, 2005). Overall, this body of work suggests that financial constraints matter; however, financial considerations beyond the direct costs of college require closer examination (Carneiro & Heckman, 2002; Stinebrickner & Stinebrickner, 2009).

Finally, institutional policies and practices may also play an important role in predicting degree receipt. Colleges vary widely with respect to the share of entering freshmen that they graduate within four, five, or six years. What practices might account for institutional variation in rates of freshman completion and time-to-degree? Prior research suggests that student interaction with faculty, student peers and sense of community, active engagement with the institution, and mentoring all contribute to higher rates of persistence (Astin, 1993; Habley, Bloom, & Robbins, 2012; Lotkowski, Robbins,

& Noeth, 2004; Tinto, 1993). Although they provide promising directions for future research, many of these studies fail to adequately control for observable and unobservable differences between students who select different kinds of colleges or collegiate experiences (Astin, 1993; Braxton, 2000; Tinto, 1993) and thus likely conflate the contributions of student characteristics to institutional rates of postsecondary persistence with those of institutional practices. College selectivity accounts for an appreciable share of the institutional variation in college graduation overall (Melguizo, 2008; Small & Winship, 2007; J. I. Smith, 2013), though work focusing specifically on community colleges has found less consistent evidence on the role of institutional quality measures on students' outcome (Calcagno, Bailey, Jenkins, Kienzl, & Leinbach, 2008; Sandy, Gonzalez, & Hilmer, 2006; Smith & Stange, 2013; Stange, 2012). More recently, several papers have suggested that cohort crowding and declining resources (particularly at less selective public institutions) may also lead to reductions in rates of college completion and increases in time to degree (Bound, Lovenheim, & Turner, 2010, 2012).

Although comparisons between colleges have shed light on the relative contributions of policies and student characteristics to graduation rates, most college campuses only have access to data on their own student body. It is nevertheless likely that all colleges wish to improve degree completion rates and that individual campuses attract and admit similar students from year to year. Thus, colleges are uniquely suited to investigate the impacts of their campus-specific policies and programs, especially with more and more data being collected at the local level.

In the example we use throughout this chapter, we analyze policies that may affect degree completion at a California State University campus. Specifically, we use student-level application, program participation, and degree data from one CSU campus to demonstrate methods of analyzing the impacts of three different campus programs or polices on completion: a freshman orientation program, declaring a major at college entry, and Summer Bridge.[4] We describe the analyses in detail within each section of this chapter.

Quality Data

Data-driven decision making is now a ubiquitous component of K–12 school improvement. Unfortunately, this approach has not been fully transferred to higher education. College campuses often have better data on their alumni and potential donors than on the educational backgrounds of their existing students. There may be many reasons for data limitations in postsecondary schooling. In particular, higher education has not been the focus of intense accountability efforts as in K–12 and, therefore, has had little incentive to invest in detailed data systems or the professional capacity necessary to maintain and analyze them. This may be changing with increased focus on college readiness as part of the Common Core State Standards movement and increased national policy attention on college attainment outcomes as a means of maintaining the competitiveness of the U.S. economy (Obama, 2009).[5] Moreover, higher education data systems are often highly decentralized, such that admissions offices collect information from student applications; financial aid offices collect only financial aid data; registrar offices collect only current registration information, and so on.

Collecting quality data is critical to addressing many of the most pressing issues facing higher education, including college completion. We present several important principles in assembling quality data to answer institutional questions. First, consider the source. This is essential for thinking about both data generalizability and data validity. Specifically, is the source providing the data (e.g., a survey given at summer orientation) representative of the general campus? And is the data source a valid measure of what analysts are trying to capture? For example, students' self-reported data on family income is not as reliable a source of information on students' potential financial constraints as is data available from the financial aid office that originates from the Free Application for Federal Student Aid (FAFSA).

Second, there are important advantages to combining data to provide a rich description of the student. Campus data sources are often dispersed, as each serves a function for one respective department or another; application data may serve admissions, while degree data may be used by the registrar. Gathering all available data about a student means either streamlining collection and storage of data or merging data after the fact. In our example, we use data from four different sources within the same university. First, we use application data for information on detailed student characteristics. Second, we use term-by-term data to determine declared major. Third, we use program participation data to determine orientation and Summer Bridge status. Last, we use degree data for a student's graduation status. Only through combining these distinct data sources are we able to investigate more fully the impacts of programs and policies on our student outcome of interest.

Third, build longitudinal data files to be able to more fully describe students' experiences prior to entering the institution. This is particularly important when those experiences may influence their postsecondary success. Many states (including California) do not yet have integrated data systems that allow researchers and education leaders to easily investigate students across the education pipeline. However, working separately with California's different education segments (i.e., K–12, community colleges, baccalaureate-granting institutions), we have been able to assemble longitudinal data files to track California's high school students entering one of the 23 CSU campuses of the CSU or one of the 112 California Community Colleges. In doing so, we have been able to investigate one of CSU's goals of improving college readiness among high school students (Kurlaender et al., 2012; Howell et al., 2010). For these studies we had to build a longitudinal data file connecting California high school juniors' school records with their later postsecondary outcomes at CSU and at the community college. It is also important that longitudinal data track students for as long as possible to determine if they ever obtain a degree at a different postsecondary institution and, importantly, how their postsecondary schooling experiences may have influenced later occupational outcomes. Many states that already have an integrated data system have been able to do this more easily. Moreover, the importance of such an endeavor is underscored by the recent establishment of the Center for Analysis of Postsecondary Education and Employment, funded the U.S. Department of Education.[6]

Analyzing Existing Programs and Practices

Postsecondary institutions across the country are committed to improving student outcomes, in particular, degree receipt. Many have established new committees, programs, and task forces addressing college attrition and delayed time-to-degree (e.g., see efforts such as Complete College America). CSU is no exception, with a heavy systemwide focus on raising six-year college completion rates, particularly for underrepresented minority groups. In this section, we offer some important guidance on how institutions might effectively identify and analyze existing programs and practices that may improve college completion. Again, we note that the lessons here are transferable to a host of other institutional goals and objectives.

Principles for Identification

Campuses often begin their efforts by simply identifying promising programs, policies, and practices. We suggest that identification be based on a purposeful approach that may include one, if not several, of four simple principles. First, particular programs and/or policies should be based on evidence from the existing literature that is suggestive (if not convincing) that such programs, policies, and/or practices work, at least at other similar campuses.[7] Second, different programs, policies, and practices come at varying costs to the institution; therefore, institutional leaders should be aware of such costs in conjunction with their consideration of the benefits of existing programs. Third, institutions often survey their students for helpful insights about programs and policies that may aid, or possibly hinder, their academic progress. For example, student surveys might be helpful in streamlining registration processes, understanding obstacles to particular majors, or providing a broad picture of student (dis)satisfaction with campus policies, procedures, and even programs. Finally, institutions can rely on their own administrative data and utilize an empirically based approach to investigate existing programs' success and the impact of policies and practices. Ideally these approaches work together; that is, programs and policies often exist because they are based on what we know from the literature about student success and what we hear from student feedback via surveys, are transparent regarding differential cost, and rely on more regular quantitative evaluation of effects on measurable student outcomes.

Using the preceding criteria and rich data from one typical CSU campus, we now provide a concrete example of three such programs/practices that are often employed or considered at many postsecondary institutions. Specifically, we investigate this campus's freshman orientation program, the practice of driving students toward an early declaration of a major, and participation in Summer Bridge. These three practices exist on most broad-access college campuses, and there is reason to believe that any or all of these programs could have an impact on college degree completion. They range from relatively low cost (mandating that all students declare a major at entry) to relatively high cost (expanding a Summer Bridge program).

Evaluating Existing Programs and Practices

Many campuses likely collect the necessary data to evaluate the effectiveness of existing programs, policies, and practices. However, when such data do not exist, it is critical to have a data collection strategy that would yield reliable information about who participates in what programs and who might be implicated by particular policies.

We use data on two first-time freshman cohorts attending this CSU campus in the 2002 and 2003 academic years and begin by examining who participates in these three programs. As Table 10.1 details, 60 percent of students at this CSU campus participated in freshman orientation, 75 percent of first-time freshmen had declared a major by the end of their first year, and 4 percent participated in the targeted Summer Bridge program.

It may be helpful to begin by examining the outcomes of interest for program participants and nonparticipants. Such data can show immediately promising candidates for expansion or contraction; however, such simple comparisons of outcomes can also be misleading and should not be relied on without closer inspection, as we demonstrate next. Table 10.2 compares the six-year degree completion rates of these 2002 and 2003 first-time freshman cohorts. Those who participate in freshman orientation have a 56 percent completion rate compared to a 39 percent completion rate among nonpartici-

TABLE 10.1 Programs/policies at one CSU campus, pooled 2002 and 2003 first-time freshmen

	Freshman orientation	Declare major	Summer Bridge
Number participating	3,909	4,855	241
Percentage participating	60	75	4

SOURCE: Authors' calculations from data provided by the California State University Chancellor's Office, Analytic Studies.
NOTE: The total sample size is 6,466 students.

TABLE 10.2 Six-year completion rates at one CSU campus, by program/policy, pooled 2002 and 2003 first-time freshmen

	Freshman orientation	Declare major	Summer Bridge
Number of students participating	3,909	4,855	241
Percentage of participants completing degree	56	50	43
Percentage of nonparticipants completing degree	39	46	50
Difference (in percentage points)	**17**	**4**	**−7**

SOURCE: Authors' calculations from data provided by the California State University Chancellor's Office, Analytic Studies.

pants (a difference of 17 percentage points). Among all freshmen who declare a major in their first year, 50 percent of students graduate within six years compared to 46 percent among those who declare their major later (a difference of 4 percentage points). Finally, among all first-time freshman students who participate in Summer Bridge, 43 percent ultimately graduate compared to the 50 percent graduation rate among nonparticipants (a difference of −7 percentage points). Although the difference in graduation rates between Summer Bridge participants and nonparticipants is negative, suggesting that the program may have the opposite effect of its intended goals, these raw differences may be misleading because of the important differences that distinguish program participants from nonparticipants across all of these programs (a critical point we turn to next). Similarly, the 17-percentage-point advantage between those who participate in freshman orientation and those who do not may lead one to believe that the program is doing a great job at helping students to graduate, but orientation participants may be markedly different from nonparticipants in ways that skew this simplistic interpretation of the data.

Considering Selection into Program Participation

In general, students do not randomly decide to participate in programs or engage in particular practices. Some programs attract certain types of students and some are only targeted at specific student populations. Considering who is likely to participate in a program nearly always explains some of the observed relationship between program participation and student outcomes. This is crucial to consider when analyzing differences in student outcomes like those displayed in Table 10.2. In our example, recall that degree completion rates among freshman orientation participants were 17 percentage points higher than for nonparticipants. In the top panel of Table 10.3, we present information about the characteristics of those who participate in freshman orientation and those who do not, noting where those differences are statistically significant. Students who participate in freshman orientation are different from those who do not; specifically, they are more likely to be white or Asian, to be female, to be exempt from needing remediation in math and English, and to have a higher high school grade point average and SAT score, and they are less likely to be from a lower-income household or to have parents with a high school diploma or less.

Although only 25 percent of first-time freshmen do not declare a major by the end of their first year, the second panel of Table 10.3 indicates that

TABLE 10.3 Mean differences in student characteristics at one CSU campus, by program/policy, pooled 2002 and 2003 first-time freshmen

Panel 1: Freshman Orientation	Participant	Nonparticipant	Difference
Underrepresented Minority	0.31	0.42	−0.11***
Male	0.38	0.41	−0.03**
Math Exempt	0.78	0.63	0.15***
English Exempt	0.57	0.44	0.13***
HS GPA	3.28	3.14	0.15***
SAT	994	948	46.68***
Low Income	0.19	0.31	−0.12***
Missing Income	0.10	0.10	0.00
First Generation	0.17	0.28	−0.11**
Missing Parent Ed	0.07	0.08	−0.01**
Disability	0.02	0.02	0.00
Panel 2: Declare Major	Yes	No	Difference
Underrepresented Minority	0.36	0.35	0.01
Male	0.39	0.40	0.00
Math Exempt	0.73	0.68	0.05***
English Exempt	0.53	0.47	0.06***
HS GPA	3.24	3.18	0.06***
SAT	981	962	18.71***
Low Income	0.24	0.23	0.01
Missing Income	0.10	0.10	0.00
First Generation	0.21	0.23	−0.02**
Missing Parent Ed	0.07	0.08	−0.01
Disability	0.02	0.01	0.01
Panel 3: Summer Bridge	Participant	Nonparticipant	Difference
Underrepresented Minority	0.74	0.34	0.40***
Male	0.32	0.40	−0.07**
Math Exempt	0.62	0.72	−0.10***
English Exempt	0.71	0.51	0.20***
HS GPA	2.89	3.24	−0.35***
SAT	839	981	−142.24***
Low Income	0.63	0.22	0.41***
Missing Income	0.10	0.10	0.00
First Generation	0.58	0.20	0.37***
Missing Parent Ed	0.07	0.08	0.00
Disability	0.02	0.02	0.00

SOURCE: Authors' calculations from data provided by the California State University Chancellor's Office, Analytic Studies.

NOTE: Asterisks indicate statistical significance at the following levels: * = 0.10, ** = 0.05, *** = 0.01.

students who wait to declare a major appear to have significantly weaker academic credentials relative to those who do declare a major within their first year (e.g., more likely to need remediation in English and/or math, lower high school GPA and lower SAT scores) and are significantly more likely to be first-generation college students. Finally, we note that Summer Bridge is (as intended) a highly targeted program, and therefore students who participate in Summer Bridge are significantly different from those who do not along a host of dimensions.

In particular, the third panel of Table 10.3 indicates that Summer Bridge students are more likely to be from underrepresented minority groups (Latino or African American), to be female, and to have lower academic credentials (except for English remediation), and are significantly more likely to be from a lower socioeconomic background (based on family income and parental education levels).

It is critical to account for these observable student and family differences when evaluating the impact of these programs and practices on student outcomes for two primary reasons. First, the student characteristics associated with participating in freshman orientation or Summer Bridge and for declaring a major early are the same characteristics associated with college completion. In other words, first-generation college students may not only be less likely to attend freshman orientation than students whose parents have higher educational attainment, but first-generation students are also less likely to finish college more generally. Similarly, students who need remediation in college may be less likely to declare a major in their freshman year than those who do not need remediation, and so it is hard to disentangle whether it is the fact that they didn't declare a major in their first year or their lack of academic readiness that keeps them from graduating at the same rate as those who do declare a major early in their college career. Of course, a host of other unobserved characteristics that may be associated with college completion, such as student motivation, may also be associated with selection into these programs. It is much more difficult to account for factors that we do not observe, but it is nonetheless important to consider what these factors might be and how they probably interact with both program participation and our outcome—college completion.[8]

If participation in a program is conflated with the effectiveness of the program, we need to attempt to separate those effects in our analysis. This is accomplished, to a large extent, by accounting for the characteristics of participants in a regression analysis framework.[9] These "regression adjusted" differences in completion rates for participants compared to nonparticipants are presented in Table 10.4.

In our example, the raw differences in completion rates between students who participated in freshman orientation and those who did not

TABLE 10.4 Regression-adjusted program/policy effects

	Freshman orientation	Declare major	Summer Bridge
Number of students	3,909	4,855	241
Percentage of participants	56	50	43
Percentage of nonparticipants	39	46	50
Raw difference (in percentage points)	17	4	−7
Regression-adjusted difference (in percentage points)	**11.5*****	**2.4**	**8.7***

SOURCE: Authors' calculations from data provided by the California State University Chancellor's Office, Analytic Studies.
NOTE: Asterisks indicate statistical significance at the following levels: * = 0.10, ** = 0.05, *** = 0.01.

(17 percentage points in Table 10.2) is substantially reduced to an 11.5 percentage point difference when we account for student characteristics associated with orientation participation in Table 10.4. Similarly, when we control for differences in student characteristics in our comparison of freshman students who declare a major by the end of their first year with those who do not, the graduation rate among those who declare a major early is only 2.4 percentage points higher than those who do not (a difference that not only is smaller than the 4-percentage-point raw difference from Table 10.2 but is also no longer statistically different from zero [Table 10.4]). Finally, when we adjust for the characteristics of students who are selected into the Summer Bridge program, we now find a positive relationship with college completion. Specifically, among similar students who meet the Summer Bridge criteria, participating students have a significantly higher college graduation rate than those who do not participate in Summer Bridge (a difference of 8.7 percentage points in Table 10.4 compared to the misleading negative estimated effect in Table 10.2).

The second reason it is so critical to think about who participates in particular programs is because it provides campuses with vital information about how their specific student population may respond to changes in programs, policies, and practices. In other words, campuses need better information about the characteristics of their students who engage in particular activities in order to assess whether altering those programs is likely to yield desired changes or have unintended consequences. Having such detailed information about students also allows for useful forecasts into the future. Campuses can project what might happen to completion rates given changing demographics of their student population.

Simulating Changes in Policy

Adjusting program effects to account for student characteristics and selection into program participation can help identify which programs may have favorable impacts and for what types of students. In addition, campuses can use similar methods of analysis (based on student characteristics and program participation) to project student outcomes in the future and to simulate what might happen to student outcomes if a particular campus program were expanded or cut. The 2025 California Goal Dashboard is a good example of a prediction tool that is a more advanced version of the reporting tools that are increasingly known as "data dashboards."[10] Such prediction tools harness regression modeling techniques and student-level data to forecast what might happen to various outcomes of interest when we change some of the inputs.

In our example in this chapter thus far, we have used completion data from the 2002 and 2003 freshmen at one CSU campus to build a model that suggested that students who participated in a freshman orientation program on a specific CSU campus were 11.5 percentage points more likely to graduate than students who did not, even after adjusting for important demographic and academic characteristics of students who participate. Because this regression-adjusted figure is quite large, this campus may be interested in making the freshman orientation program mandatory to boost students' rates of degree completion. Before implementing such a policy change, however, the campus could go one step further and predict what might happen if they go forward with a mandatory orientation program. We now use the same models from the previous section to simulate what would have happened if freshman orientation had been made mandatory on that campus, causing all students to participate in the program.[11] First, we apply the model generated by our regression analysis in Table 10.4 to the pooled 2002 and 2003 data with true information on program participation to generate a baseline projection. As expected, the model accurately predicts the completion rate of the pooled 2002 and 2003 cohorts at 49.4 percent in Table 10.5 (with the actual graduation rate at 49.2).

Next, we simulate what would have happened to graduation rates if everyone in the 2002 and 2003 freshman cohorts participated in freshman orientation. To do so, we generate a modified data set in which each student appears to have participated in freshman orientation. We apply the same model parameters from our regression analysis to the modified data and calculate

TABLE 10.5 Baseline and simulated graduation rates at one CSU campus, pooled 2002 and 2003 first-time freshmen

Baseline graduation rate (predicted based on existing cohort characteristics)	49.4%
Simulated graduation rate (based on 100% freshman orientation participation)	53.9%
Projected gain in degree completion from policy change (in percentage points)	**4.5**

SOURCE: Authors' calculations from data provided by the California State University Chancellor's Office, Analytic Studies.

the expected increase in completion rates on this campus (also presented in Table 10.5). The results from our simulation suggest that we would expect a graduation rate near 54 percent for these cohorts, which is a predicted increase in the college completion rate of roughly four to five percentage points.

Why does the simulation project only a 4.5-percentage-point gain in the completion rate rather than the 11.5-percentage-point gain the campus may have hoped for given the regression-adjusted program effects presented in Table 10.4? The simulated completion rate is substantially lower simply because most students already attend freshman orientation, and those who do not have a variety of characteristics associated with lower odds of graduation, including lower SAT and high school GPA (see Table 10.3). It is also likely, though nearly impossible to demonstrate with data, that the nonparticipants induced into orientation by such a policy have unobservable characteristics that are also associated with lower odds of graduation (e.g., lower motivation). Mandating the participation of those additional students cannot offset the negative influence of their other characteristics on completion. Thus, the simulation offers a more realistic picture of the expected change in graduation rates given the characteristics of students likely implicated by a mandate to participate in freshman orientation—namely, those who do not currently participate.

We could apply a similar simulation technique to early major declaration and/or Summer Bridge participation. Most students come into the institution with a declared major, but campuses could use the methodology described previously to predict what would happen if the campus made this a mandatory part of enrollment; as suggested earlier we would need to consider what might be different between those who do and do not choose to declare a major at entry. And, although it may not be sensible to simulate universal participation in Summer Bridge (since it is such a small and targeted program), we can nevertheless simulate what would happen if more students with the specific characteristics targeted by Summer Bridge (first-generation college students, often from underrepresented minority groups) participated in the program.

By narrowing the simulation to the population likely implicated in expanding a narrow program, campuses can get a more realistic picture of the potential effects of such action.

Expanding Programs: A Cautionary Tale?

In 2004, the CSU campus we have been using for our example decided to make freshman orientation a mandatory program. This policy change provides us with a unique opportunity to also examine the impact on college completion rates of an actual (rather than simulated) policy change and to compare our simulation model to actual data. As noted previously, about 60 percent of freshmen attended orientation in the 2002 and 2003 freshman cohorts. In 2004, when the campus made orientation mandatory, nearly all students (96 percent) participated. Other than orientation participation, there are few changes in student characteristics across the 2002, 2003, and 2004 cohorts. If our within-sample simulations in Table 10.5 showed a 4.5-percentage-point increase in graduation rates by making orientation a mandatory program, we would expect to see a similar increase in graduation rates for the 2004 cohort, when the program was actually formally expanded. What happened to the graduation rates of the 2004 freshmen for whom orientation was mandatory? The results are shown in Table 10.6. For the 2004 cohort, our simulation method predicts a graduation rate of 54.2 percent, which is a nearly 5-percentage-point projected increase above either simulated or actual 2002/2003 completion rates. Because this policy change was actually implemented, however, we know that the six-year graduation rate for the 2004 cohort was essentially unchanged at 49.5 percent despite the mandatory orientation policy.

Why didn't universal participation in freshman orientation lead to the expected improvement in graduation rates? Our simulation model tells us it is not because of demographic or academic changes in the students, since

TABLE 10.6 Projected versus actual six-year graduation rates following mandatory freshman orientation policy in 2004

	2002/2003	2004
Orientation participation (%)	60.7	96.3
Simulated graduation rate (%)	49.4	54.2
Actual graduation rate (%)	49.2	49.5

SOURCE: Authors' calculations from data provided by the California State University Chancellor's Office, Analytic Studies.

we account for these differences. So, what went wrong? First, it is nearly impossible to isolate this program change from other changes experienced by the university (changes in administration, economic conditions or other resources, etc.). Moreover, although our model accounts for the many observable characteristics associated with program participation and graduation, a host of other unobserved characteristics that may be associated with college completion, such as motivation, may also affect graduation rates. Finally, it is possible that, in the expansion of the orientation program to all students, the program was less effective because expansion changed the program in some way (e.g., led to weaker instructors for freshman orientation or a watered-down freshman orientation experience). A combination of several of these factors is likely at play, resulting in impacts that are smaller than expected and drawing attention to the importance of appropriately implementing the scale-up of programs and practices.

Although the simulation model did not match the actual data on completion rates following this policy change, it is important to reiterate the value of this methodology for making more accurate predictions than would have otherwise been available to campus decision makers. Figure 10.1 summarizes this important takeaway. If campus decision makers simply compared raw

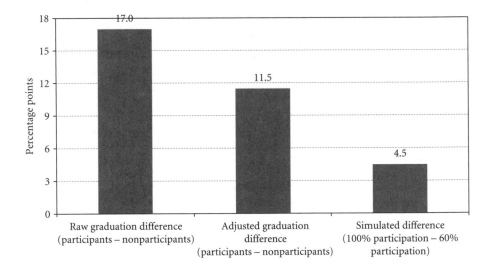

FIGURE 10.1. Differences in anticipated benefits of mandatory orientation policy, by methodology. Source: Authors' calculations from data provided by the California State University Chancellor's Office, Analytic Studies.

completion rate differences between participants and nonparticipants, they would have naïvely expected a mandatory orientation policy to boost completion rates by 17 percentage points.

If these same decision makers were more data savvy and thought to adjust the raw differences using regression analysis and the student characteristics associated with participation, they would have expected a mandatory orientation policy to boost completion rates by 11.5 percentage points. Finally, if decision makers used their regression results to simulate the effect of a mandatory orientation policy, they would have expected a 4.5-percentage-point increase in degree completion. Although all three methods overstate the true impact, observed to be zero in this case, the simulation method demonstrates the greatest potential to remove factors that are known to upwardly bias the anticipated benefits of the policy change. We argue that improved accuracy is a worthy goal when perfect accuracy is not possible.

New Directions for Institutional Program Evaluation

In this final section, we discuss how postsecondary institutions can employ some basic and critically important principles in implementing and evaluating programs and policies. Specifically, we focus on ensuring that programs implemented across college campuses can be grounded in existing literature about what works, a thoughtful cost-benefit analysis, and a more rigorous evaluation plan to identify program effects with improved accuracy.

Campuses do not necessarily have to reinvent the wheel when deciding what new programs and policy changes to initiate. As suggested previously, programs should be grounded in existing literature about what works and chosen with the current realities of the institution in mind. We suggest that a close investigation of institutional data is also important for identifying promising practices and programs. First, how similar are the student characteristics of your campus to those discussed in other settings where programs and policies were deemed successful? Second, institutions can use existing data to explore how many students would be implicated by a new program, which may be targeted (such as Summer Bridge), or a policy change, such as establishing a new minimum credit load. All of this information is essential for both the design of a successful program and for subsequently understanding why programs may or may not have met their intended goals.

Another critical step in the process of identifying promising programs for expansion or removal is a cost-benefit analysis.[12] This chapter identifies a method of projecting the benefits of policy and programmatic changes, but those benefits must be put on a "per dollar" basis using project costs to appropriately compare alternatives. Although an analysis of the direct costs of expanding a program is beyond the scope of this chapter (largely because of data availability), individual campuses can probably obtain the necessary information on the direct costs of programs more readily (and perhaps from campuses that have already implemented such changes). The real strength of the cost-benefit analysis is that campus decision makers are then able to weigh the impact on their degree completion rates of an additional dollar spent various different ways. Imagine the power of knowing how an additional dollar invested in freshman orientation, an initiative to declare majors in the first year, or Summer Bridge is differentially predicted to influence completion rates. On larger campuses, larger sample sizes would even enable decision makers to examine how to move the completion needle for particular subgroups of interest: first-generation students, English language learners, racial/ethnic minorities, and so on.

Institutions, often with good intentions to solve existing problems, frequently undertake major changes or implement new programs based on limited information. We offer a strong suggestion to pilot new programs and/or policy changes when at all possible. This provides valuable information about how new programs (or changing policies) may function on the ground, who is affected, and the intended and unintended consequences of such changes. Although the focus of this chapter has been on quantitative evidence, campuses should also collect qualitative information during the pilot phase on the specifics of implementation, which will be crucial if the results of the pilot lead the campus to scale up to a larger portion of the student body.

Once campuses decide to implement or expand a new program, or to alter an existing policy or practice, it is vital to establish an appropriate comparison group to effectively evaluate the change.[13] The examples we provide in the previous section yield some initial insights about why this is important. Mainly, program participants are significantly different from nonparticipants in both observable and unobservable ways, either because some programs are targeted toward certain students (such as Summer Bridge for first-generation, underrepresented minority students) or because programs are optional (freshman orientation in 2002 and 2003). As a result, participation in such programs is not random, and this lack of randomness implies that there may not be a simple control group available for comparison without some proactive design prior to implementing changes.[14]

Randomized control trials are the only way to establish a true causal relationship between programs and outcomes. Only by randomly assigning some students to be program participants and others to not be can we confidently conclude whether observed changes in student outcomes are the result of participation in the program. Randomized experiments are difficult to accomplish in higher education and are often not feasible for a variety of reasons. Campus leaders are often adamantly against depriving students of a particular experience if there is enough room to accommodate all those interested and sufficient anecdotal evidence that the program will improve student outcomes. Even when there are program constraints, a first-come, first-served basis often feels like the most reasonable way to distribute resources; yet students who volunteer to participate first are potentially substantially different from those who do not, and we have demonstrated in this chapter that self-selection by students biases the interpretation of the data in ways that challenge the goal of rigorous data-driven decision making. Finally, changes in procedures or policies are nearly impossible to assign to some students and not to others in a campus environment, making the separation of treatment and control groups a very difficult hurdle.

In the absence of randomized experiments, it is useful to engage in some basic counterfactual thinking to design a solid evaluation plan (i.e., what would college completion look like in the absence of this program or change in policy?). Among social science researchers, these sorts of evaluations are described as quasi-experimental. Over the past two decades there have been important developments in education research and related fields in the use of quasi-experimental methods for program evaluation; these techniques aim to approximate the underlying logic of the experiment without random assignment (Murnane & Willett, 2011). These methods rely on finding comparisons that may exist naturally rather than being assigned to them randomly (Shavelson & Towne, 2002). For example, a natural comparison group to evaluate the impact of a universal change in the minimum credit load on time-to-degree may be the cohorts of students enrolled right before the change in policy was implemented (assuming that no other changes occurred simultaneously that may have also influenced time-to-degree). Similarly, in evaluating the effects of collegiate remediation, many scholars compare students just above and just below the score cutoff for remediation placement, hypothesizing that at some level the cutoff is arbitrary (random) for students in the narrow band right around it. These approaches are fundamentally about eliminating the potential influence of observable and unobservable factors that may be confounded with the program effect (or the policy/program change) primarily because it enables decision makers to have a more accurate view of the benefits against which to compare costs.

While we do not have actual data on the per-student cost of expanding the orientation program to be mandatory for all new freshmen at our sample CSU campus, we can assume a figure to easily demonstrate the substantial differences in cost-benefit analysis based on the results summarized in Figure 10.1. For example, assume that this CSU campus determined that orientation cost $50 per student and that the mandatory policy would add roughly 2,500 additional students to orientation, for a total estimated (and hypothetical) cost of the policy of $125,000. The return on this investment under the simplistic analysis that identified a 17-percentage-point boost in degree completion is 0.136 percentage points per $1,000 invested. Under the more rigorous simulation, which predicted a much more modest 4.5-percentage-point boost in completion, the return on investment is 0.036 percentage points per $1,000. The simulation-based estimate of return on investment is 36 percent smaller than the simplistic analysis would indicate. When compared to what other investments could be made with $1,000 on a college campus, these differences matter.

Conclusion and Implications for Practices

Today more than ever, colleges and universities are focused on improving persistence and degree completion for their students. Thus, it is imperative that such efforts be guided by some basic principles of design and evaluation if postsecondary institutions are to reap the benefits of the investment. First, postsecondary institutions need to have better knowledge of their student body. Campuses collect a large amount of information from students in admission about students' prior academic performance, financial aid forms about student socioeconomic status, and enrollment practices (e.g., declaration of major, on-time degree accumulation, major, and academic performance). This information is useful for providing richer and more detailed data about the student body, and of particular subgroups of interest (first-generation students, part-time students, etc.) by the desired outcomes—in this case, persistence, degree completion, and time-to-degree. In obtaining greater knowledge about the student body, campuses can more adequately identify differences among subpopulations to target the practices that may be more effective.

Second, campuses seek to identify promising practices and interventions. In so doing, they can initiate new programs or policies (e.g., offer a freshman experience course), expand an existing one (e.g., make a voluntary program such as freshman orientation mandatory), or reduce or eliminate a practice or policy that may present obstacles for students (e.g., reducing the number of required general education credits). In each of these cases it is critical for campuses to consider which students are affected by such a policy or practice change, and by what mechanism should the proposed change lead to improved outcomes.

Finally, campuses must be diligent in monitoring and evaluating the effects of new practices to determine whether they have had the desired effects on student outcomes. In so doing there are some basic questions that are useful to consider:

Who is affected?

- Who currently participates in such programs or activities and are they the "typical" student?

- If creating a new program, will it be voluntary, and if so, who might likely participate?

- What are the differences between participants and nonparticipants in background characteristics and enrollment practices?

- Is there any enforcement regarding who participates? Are there any consequences for not participating?

Change by what mechanism?

- Why might the change in policies or programs lead to desired effects?

- What are the specific inputs of resources (smaller classes, mentoring program, priority registration, etc.) that are to alter outcomes?

- Is there any evidence of compliance for the program and/or policy change?

How to track change?

- What did these student outcomes look like before the new policy or program came into place?

- Did any other policies or programs get initiated or change at the same time, and which of these may be conflating the changes observed in the data?

- What else changed about the institution and the student body that may either magnify or reduce the desired changes brought about by a new program or policy?

In closing, we encourage campus leaders and decision makers to recognize that they have potentially untapped resources on their campuses that may be of great help in implementing the types of analyses described in this chapter. It is well known that institutional research offices, particularly at broad-access institutions, are understaffed and existing resources may be exhausted by federal and state reporting requirements. All campuses, however, employ a wide variety of quantitatively inclined instructional faculty in their departments of economics, education, public policy, sociology, and statistics (among other disciplines). Social science researchers, particularly those looking to engage their particular skills in ways that serve the campus community, are ripe for engagement in data-driven decision making of the type that we outline here. We encourage campuses to think outside the box and remove the silos that exist between the academic and student services sides of their campuses to embrace the methods outlined in this chapter with the resources they already have at their disposal.

Notes

The work presented here is based on a collaboration between the authors and the CSU Chancellor's Office. It is part of a larger project funded by the Bill & Melinda Gates Foundation. We thank Desdemona Cardoza, Philip Garcia, Jeff Gold, and Marsha Hirano-Nakanishi at the CSU Chancellor's Office for help with access to the data and for helpful comments on different iterations of this work. Opinions reflect those of the authors and do not necessarily reflect those of the funder, the state agency providing the data, or of the College Board.

1. This calculation is based on a published CSU enrollment of 411,000 students in 2010 (California State University, 2010) and an enrollment of 7.92 million students in public four-year colleges nationwide in 2010 (U.S. Department of Education, National Center for Education Statistics, 2012b).

2. The CSU system was awarded a competitive Complete College America state innovation challenge grant program. For more information on the program, see http://www.completecollege.org/path_forward/innovation_challenge/.

3. This is in some part because of CSU's more rigorous cutoffs on college entrance exams (such as the SAT) in order to exempt from remedial coursework.

4. Freshman orientation programs seek to familiarize students with registration procedures, course offerings, and academic requirements and generally assist students with their adjustment to college. Analyses of important milestones and momentum points have identified the timely declaration of a major as an indicator of progress toward a degree (see, for example, Moore & Shulock, 2011). Summer Bridge programs are intensive, residential orientation programs for entering students who are not fully prepared to meet the demands of college coursework. Summer Bridge is one among many enrichment programs targeted toward first-generation college students or other students deemed "at risk" for college attrition or failure.

5. When President Obama declared that "by 2020, America will once again have the highest proportion of college graduates in the world" (Obama, 2009), a substantial number of college completion initiatives and efforts were already under way, and more sprang up accordingly. For an overview of major U.S. college completion initiatives, see Russell, 2011.

6. See the center's website at http://capseecenter.org.

7. The quality of evidence in the research literature lies along a spectrum from correlational (suggestive) to causal (prescriptive). Because causal evidence is preferred but more challenging to generate, campus decision makers will likely have to rely on suggestive evidence in many instances. The What Works Clearinghouse (http://ies.ed.gov/ncee/wwc) is an initiative of the U.S. Department of Education's Institute of Education Sciences (IES) that is designed to be a central and trusted source of scientific evidence for what works in education. Although the What Works Clearinghouse is a much richer resource for interventions in K–12 settings than postsecondary settings, it nonetheless has some studies on postsecondary programs and can be a useful resource to examine for causal evidence on similar policies, programs, and practices under consideration on college campuses.

8. For example, relatively more motivated students are likely the ones who participate in freshman orientation when it is optional, and their motivation also arguably propels them to greater success in their coursework and in completing a degree. Although it is challenging to quantify the impact of motivation, we note that the direction of its effect is clear, allowing an understanding of bias associated with mandating freshman orientation. If students who are induced to participate in freshman orientation when it becomes mandatory are relatively less motivated students, then the impact of the mandate on student academic outcomes will be mitigated by this unobservable factor that we believe exists but cannot directly incorporate into the analyses.

9. Regression analysis is a statistical technique for quantifying the relationships between variables that are observable in data. In multiple regression, the effect of changing one variable (e.g., high school GPA) on the outcome of interest (e.g., college completion) is isolated by holding constant other variables that also influence the outcome (parental education, income, etc.). Regression analysis, although usually conducted by researchers using specialized statistical software, is also available in Excel using the Data

Analysis Toolpack add-in. Excel would almost always be sufficient for the data analysis needs of a typical campus.

10. Other states (e.g., Virginia; see http://research.schev.edu/default.asp?select1= Reports) and the U.S. Department of Education (see http://dashboard.ed.gov/dash board.aspx) also have data dashboards that report the sort of data that could be harnessed for the type of simulation and prediction available on the 2025 California Goal Dashboard (which is available at http://californiacompetes.org/home/calculator).

11. Simulation methods vary; information about the specifications used in this analysis can be obtained from the authors.

12. A good source on cost-benefit analysis in education is Levin & McEwan, 2001.

13. For an excellent discussion of this, see Light, Singer, & Willett, 1990.

14. We recommend *Identifying and Implementing Educational Practices Supported by Rigorous Evidence* (Coalition for Evidence-Based Policy, 2003), a user-friendly publication that describes many of these issues in a nontechnical way.

11

A RESEARCH FRAMEWORK
FOR U.S. HIGHER EDUCATION

Daniel Klasik, Kristopher Proctor, and Rachel Baker

U.S. higher education is a complex ecology. Within it, a great variety of actors—students, faculty, administrators, governing entities, funders, and even researchers—cooperate and compete for survival and prestige. Each type of actor has its own goals and motivations, yet the fate of each is connected with many others. Paradoxically, this very complexity makes the limiting assumptions of higher education research necessary. It would be difficult to say anything useful about the ecology without somehow narrowing the scope and context of any given research agenda. In this chapter we provide a framework for higher education research that organizes the field in a way that allows researchers to focus on particular dimensions of the ecology while also making simplifying assumptions more explicit. We hope that greater precision and variety in research will help move public discourse on higher education productively. While we focus primarily on questions of consequence for broad-access schools, our orienting ideas can fruitfully inform inquiry of the entire ecology.

As illustrated in Table 11.1, the framework is a matrix of topical domains and analytic levels. We proceed by first broadly introducing the domains: fields, markets, governance, learning, and careers. Next we move through three analytic levels and describe how the domains manifest in each one.

Fields. Following Scott in Chapter 1, we inherit this idea from sociologists DiMaggio and Powell, who define organizational fields to be "those organizations that, in the aggregate, constitute a recognized area of institutional life: key suppliers, resource and product consumers, regulatory agencies, and other

TABLE 11.1 A research framework for U.S. higher education

	Field	Markets	Governance	Learning	Careers
Organizations	What are the varieties of organizations, and how do they relate to and interact with each other? (Scott, Chapter 1; Ruef & Nag, Chapter 4)	How do organizations compete for students, employees, prestige, and legitimacy? (Fain & Lederman, Chapter 3)	What are the regulatory systems that shape organizations? How does this governance occur? (Doyle & Kirst, Chapter 8)	How do organizations learn from past success or failure, from their peers or competitors, or from the larger environment? (Kurlaender, Howell, & Jackson, Chapter 10)	How do the ecological positions of organizations change over time? (Scott, Chapter 1; Ruef & Nag, Chapter 4)
Leaders/faculty/staff	What do labor politics look like? How are the roles of academic workers evolving? (Scott, Chapter 1; Kamenetz, Chapter 2)	How do leaders/faculty/staff find and compete for jobs? (Loeb, Paglayan, & Taylor, Chapter 9)	To whom are leaders/faculty/staff accountable? What are the limits of governance of leaders/faculty/staff?	How do leaders/faculty/staff learn from their own experience, peers, or specific training? (Loeb, Paglayan, & Taylor, Chapter 9)	What do the careers of leaders/faculty/ staff look like? How do these careers vary across sectors? (Loeb, Paglayan, & Taylor, Chapter 9)
Students	How do students become connected with different types of schools? How does this vary with different definitions of diversity? (Deil-Amen, Chapter 6)	How do students make choices among different types of schools? How do colleges from different sectors locate and recruit students? (Ruef & Nag, Chapter 4)	Who holds students accountable for their success or failure? (Arum & Roksa, Chapter 7)	How do students learn best? What constitutes a classroom or campus? How should learning be measured? (Kamenetz, Chapter 2; Arum & Roksa, Chapter 7)	How do students move into and through college across the course of their lives? (Settersten, Chapter 5; Deil-Amen, Chapter 6)

organizations that produce similar services or products" (1983, p. 148). The field concept enables us to remember that many different kinds of actors contribute to higher education. These actors are responsible for resource flows, have the power to legitimate higher education activity, and regulate and govern educational practice. As Scott explains in detail in Chapter 1, the whole of the field is something different from the sum of its parts, and the field concept enables us to keep the complexity of this whole in mind.

Markets. In a strict economic sense, *markets* refers to supply- and demand-clearing interactions of buyers and sellers of particular goods and services. While this concept often implies monetary exchange, markets in higher education do not necessarily involve money. For example, the competitive market for faculty will set monetary prices for faculty hires, but only if we consider financial aid a price does the market for students imply financial transaction. Colleges maintain a demand for students and try to acquire students in many ways, for example by offering a variety of academic, social, and athletic activities, or by offering convenient amenities such as parking and child care. Simultaneously students sate their demand for education by paying tuition, but they may also contribute other assets to the exchange, such as impressive test scores or grade point averages (Winston, 1999). In many broad-access schools, access to government subsidy is another crucial resource students bring to these transactions.

Governance. Governance concerns the ways in which oversight and accountability influence the behavior of school leaders, faculty, staff, and students. Higher education is composed of many governing agents, including state and federal regulators, independent accreditation agencies, and professional associations. We emphasize that governance includes regulative, normative, and cultural-cognitive dimensions (Scott, 2008). The regulative dimension includes the rules, laws, or sanctions that coerce desired behaviors. Colleges are subject to many regulations. The U.S. Department of Education (ED), for example, requires all colleges to be accredited by ED-recognized accreditation agencies to be eligible for federal student financial aid programs. The normative dimension includes the degree to which expectations, obligations, values, and morality influence behavior. Normative concerns can often be as influential as regulatory ones. For example, the mission statements of religious schools often reflect doctrinal values that direct such fundamental organizational practices such as student admissions, faculty hiring and firing, and employee benefit allocations. The cultural-cognitive dimension of governance emphasizes how shared understandings influence both how people make sense of organizational reality and how they make decision according to that reality. The annual *U.S. News and World Report* rankings, for example, deeply influence perceptions of the relative quality of schools and shape a wide array of student and administrator choices (Sauder & Espeland, 2009).

These different aspects of governance often work simultaneously. For example, for-profit schools have long been shaped by a widespread (cultural-cognitive) belief that they are categorically inferior to nonprofit colleges and that their profit motive works against normative ideals of education as a public good. At the same time, for-profit schools may be subject to different government regulations than nonprofit ones. The aim of research in this domain should be to understand how the different types of governance interact with one another to shape organizational and individual behavior.

Learning. Questions of learning involve how, from whom, and how well organizations and individuals learn and how such learning is assessed and evaluated. Learning takes place at multiple empirical levels. Faculty and students may learn from explicit training, while institutions may learn from their own successes and failures or from the experiences of peers and competitors. Questions of learning vary for different domains in the ecology. There is a lot of research on learning in some domains: standardized student assessments are becoming more widely used for accountability and measurement, for example. Faculty training also has received considerable scholarly attention. Many other questions, such as how college leaders read signals from the larger environment, or what a "classroom" is in the age of digital education, remain largely unexamined.

Careers. Careers are sequenced trajectories of people and organizations over time. For faculty and other college employees we might think of careers in the most familiar sense: working lives unfolding over years, from first job through promotions and transfers and ultimate retirement. Students and colleges also have careers, and these vary across demographic and organizational space. Students in broad-access schools, for example, are more prone to periodically enter and leave college and attend multiple institutions (McCormick, 2003). Schools themselves also evolve over time, expanding or shrinking in size, gaining or losing prestige and visibility, and always at some risk of closure. All of these dynamics are amenable to systematic analysis.

We now turn to the different analytic levels of the framework to more fully specify the research domains.

Organizations

At the organization level, colleges themselves are actors: shaped by their environments, seeking to survive and prosper, and evolving over time.

Fields. Colleges are beholden to multiple governmental agencies, publics, and resource providers. Good examples of research assessing how field-level factors influence organizational behavior include Kraatz, Ventresca, and Deng's (2010) demonstration that the consolidation of admissions and financial aid offices in liberal arts colleges led to the adoption of similar practices by competing schools. Likewise, research by Brint and colleagues (2011) showed that the adoption of new academic programs is influenced by factors such as the number of schools within a region adopting the same program, or the number of people residing in the geographic region of the school. In Chapter 4, Ruef and Nag go about the work of classifying the varied organizations in the field and demonstrate both the difficulty of such a task and the power of sophisticated analytic techniques for confronting the challenge.

Markets. Colleges compete with one another for material resources and prestige. There is a great deal of excellent educational economics in this domain but much to be done specifically regarding the market dynamics of broad-access schools. Breneman, Pusser, and Turner (2006) have capably described how market forces led to the proliferation of for-profit colleges in recent decades. Brint and colleagues (2012) explored how curricular changes and the growth of academic fields in four-year colleges are influenced by student demand, donor preferences, and labor market signals.

Governance. Colleges typically enjoy a great deal of official autonomy, even while they are beholden to a wide variety of external constituencies. There is much less systematic understanding of college governance than there should be. Part of why so little attention has been paid to organizational governance may come from the relative lack of public scrutiny U.S. higher education has historically received. As described by Doyle and Kirst in Chapter 8, public approval of higher education has largely kept colleges free of many of the accountability pressures that have been applied to the K–12 sector. In the work that has been done on organizational governance, Richardson and Martinez (2009) describe the various ways in which several states organize their higher education systems, with the relative control of particular state agencies and actors differing significantly across states. Weisbrod, Ballou, and Asch (2008) examined how the missions and finances of universities inform their operations.

Preliminary research by Scott, Proctor, and Baker (2011) revealed how many actors external to colleges—including various governmental agencies, alumni, private foundations, professional associations, unions, religious organizations, and accrediting agencies—influence intramural operations. More research is needed to answer questions such as these: To which actors are colleges most responsive? How do the various dimensions of governance affect day-to-day academic operations? How do these governance systems influence outcomes such as student retention and completion?

Learning. Students are not the only learning agents in higher education. Colleges and universities also must absorb information and knowledge from their environments to survive and flourish in changing times (see Stinchcombe, 1990). One way in which organizations learn is by compiling information about themselves in response to expectations from outside agencies. Schools compile data in offices of institutional research and report large amounts of information to accreditors and the government to maintain accreditation and eligibility for federal financial aid. Helping colleges learn has itself become a thriving market. A wide array of consulting services caters to schools eager to enhance their reputations and maintain productivity. Yet as Kurlaender, Howell, and Jackson explain in Chapter 10, many schools lack the resources to conduct or commission any but the most basic research required by regulators. How does learning capacity vary across schools? What information is most useful for institutional decision making? Is there evidence of organizations learning from past successes or mistakes or those of their peers and competitors?

Careers. Questions of organizational career concern how schools' ecological positions change over time. Historians in particular have given this area of research good attention. Labaree (2010), for example, discusses how new colleges and universities tend to be founded at the bottom of the postsecondary hierarchy but slowly build prestige as new schools develop below them. Some researchers have also considered the trajectories of community colleges and other broad-access schools.

Many community colleges originally prepared students to attend baccalaureate-granting institutions, so their curriculum largely served to educate students in the liberal arts (Dougherty, 1994). However, the desire of community college leaders to transform their schools into vocational institutions, combined with increased demand by students for employment credentials rather than transfer credit in the 1970s, led to the vocationalization of the community college curriculum (Brint & Karabel, 1989, 1991). In another example of evolving organizational careers, many U.S. institutions originally founded as normal schools evolved into teachers colleges, and then into comprehensive universities, as states sought to expand public higher education during the Cold War years (Dunham, 1969). More research on organizational careers should enable school leaders and policy makers to help colleges evolve in adaptation to changing national priorities.

Leaders, Faculty, and Staff

The middle tier of the matrix focuses specifically on school personnel: leaders, faculty, and staff. We use these terms broadly. College leaders include presidents, deans, provosts, department chairs and top administrative staff. Faculty refers to teaching staff in general and may include nontenured or adjunct teachers. Staff includes anyone else on payroll. We recognize that the boundaries between these categories can be fuzzy. Devoting serious research attention to the human capital that constitutes U.S. colleges and universities is essential if we want to know what draws capable people to careers in broad-access higher education and what encourages them to stay and succeed over time.

Fields. The field level is where we see what Scott calls "arenas of contestation for power among players with diverse interests and agendas"—in other words, labor politics (Chapter 1). Scott notes how the actions of colleges are often shaped by broader social movements. In Chapter 2, Kamenetz points out how the spread of digital media is disrupting well-worn patterns of labor relations throughout the entire ecology. This level is where research can fruitfully investigate how the biographies of particular leaders, faculty, and staff, and of whole categories of academic workers, are shaped by the ongoing evolution of the entire ecology.

Markets. Colleges compete, often fiercely, for the leaders and faculty and staff they need. As has proven true for systemic improvement in K–12 education, raising organizational performance in postsecondary schools will require clear understanding of how the best employees find jobs they like, how their performance is assessed, and how they are rewarded for work well done. In Chapter 9, Loeb, Paglayan, and Taylor provide a broad synthesis of current knowledge in this domain. They note how little research investigates the recruitment and selection of leaders and faculty at broad-access schools, or of what characteristics are most valued by institutional decision makers. More scholarship on academic labor markets is sorely needed if policy makers hope to better motivate high-capacity workers to enter and remain in broad-access schools.

Governance. Questions of governance consider for what and to whom college leaders, faculty, and staff are accountable. For leaders and faculty, recent history raises large questions about the extent to which the privilege of self-governance can be sustained in light of growing calls for new forms of academic accountability. For staff—who constitute the numerical majority of the academic labor force but receive the least research attention—a central question will be how performance is encouraged and rewarded in different sectors of the ecology. There already are many new opportunities in the rapidly growing for-profit sector. For example, the wide frontier of proprietary education technology is drawing ambitious new talent. Yet these new jobs will almost certainly not come with the employment protections that were hard-won in the public sector through years of union activity. Who makes the rules for the future that these tech-savvy higher education workers will inherit?

Learning. While it seems natural that questions of learning would apply mostly to college students, there are important reasons also to study the learning of college leaders, faculty, and staff. K–12 researchers have long been concerned with the factors associated with effective instruction in order to improve teacher training. In the broad-access sector it is similarly important to understand effective learning and training for leaders, faculty, and staff. The bulk of existing research about learning among college workers concerns the training of administrators. Hull and Keim (2007) compare the different leadership training programs undergone by leaders at community colleges. Hankin (1996) explores the training needs of community college leaders after they leave graduate school. Loeb, Paglayan, and Taylor (Chapter 9) find no analogous literature about the training of faculty.

The large open questions about learning include how academic personnel learn from their own experiences and through collegial exchange. Are certain types of professional development more or less effective? When and how do college personnel use data to inform and improve what they do? How is effective leadership or teaching best measured?

Careers. Career approaches can only enrich studies of faculty, staff, and administrative labor markets, enabling the development of policy that will honor the professional cultures of workers in broad-access schools and reward improved worker performance over entire career arcs. Variation is important here.

Careers at broad-access schools can be quite different from those at four-year universities. In Chapter 7, Arum and Roksa point out how research productivity often trumps teaching performance in determining career advancement at research universities. But at Western Governors University, as Kamenetz notes in Chapter 2, professors are rewarded on the basis of student performance. Studies of academic careers should track such variation and assess how different kinds of workers respond to different kinds of career cues.

Students

Students' paths through college are probably the most thoroughly studied features of U.S. higher education. There is a great deal of scholarship on students' college search, application, and attendance decisions, and on factors influencing student persistence and completion. Yet for all its strengths, research on students in higher education suffers from three major weaknesses. First, it tends to be bimodal; much is known about students at highly selective schools and those at community colleges. Students at schools in the broad middle are dramatically underrepresented in the scholarly literature, as Deil-Amen points out in Chapter 6. Second, many studies of student careers presume that for any given student, college is ideally a single destination. How any given student moves through multiple organizations over time is much less well understood. Third, the current very fluid relationship between college and the adult life course described by Settersten in Chapter 5 is poorly represented in the scholarship on students' academic careers.

Fields. An important field-level question is how different kinds of students get connected with different kinds of schools. A great deal of descriptive research has addressed this matter in some way. Scholars have compared the characteristics of students in community colleges versus for-profits, and selective versus broad-access schools (e.g., Bailey, Badway, & Gumport, 2001; Breneman, Pusser, & Turner, 2006; Carnevale & Rose, 2004). Unfortunately, similarly nuanced descriptions of students at schools throughout the postsecondary status distribution are hard to find. As Deil-Amen points out, research has typically focused on a select few measures of diversity, such as race and socioeconomic status. More research needs to attend to other types of diversity such as age, household composition, and marital status, and the distribution of these identities across the postsecondary ecology.

Markets. The demand side of the academic marketplace is another of the most thoroughly studied aspects of U.S. higher education. Researchers have long considered how students think about their college options and decide where to apply or attend (e.g., An, 2009; Grodsky & Reigle-Crumb, 2010; Hossler & Gallagher, 1987), how students navigate the steps to selective four-year college enrollment (Klasik, 2012), how much and in what way cost is a factor in decision making (An, 2009; Avery & Hoxby, 2004; Beattie, 2002), and how all of this has changed over time (Hoxby, 2009).

Important gaps remain nevertheless. Most research has focused on the application decisions of students attending selective colleges (Avery, Glickman, Hoxby, & Metrick, 2004) and those on the margin between community colleges and four-year schools (Bers & Galowich, 2002; De La Rosa, 2006; Kurlaender, 2006). Much less is known about how students make choices among different kinds of broad-access options. As the postsecondary ecology continues to nurture a wider variety of educational choices, particularly in the booming proprietary sector Fain and Lederman describe in Chapter 3, research examining how students make finer distinctions among academic options is certainly warranted.

Governance. Questions of governance for students often relate to accountability. Specifically: Who is responsible for learning, persistence, and completion in college? The parallel question in K–12 education has been answered definitively: teachers and schools, not students and parents, are primarily responsible for student failure. The answer is much less clear in higher education. Few scholars have directly addressed the essentially normative question of who gets credit for student success or failure in college. This is an important problem for educational ethics and policy making.

Learning. Measures of college teaching and learning are startlingly underdeveloped. This is all the more notable in comparison with K–12 education. What research there is has typically focused on selective schools (Arum & Roksa, 2011; Chambliss & Takacs, 2014). Studies in more selective colleges have examined topics such as the impact of full-time versus part-time instructors and how school leaders can affect student learning (see Chapter 9 for a review). The rise of for-profit and online education has brought more attention to student learning at a wider range of schools (e.g., Bailey et al., 2001), but there is still much work to do. Newly pressing questions about the spatial and temporal organization of instruction remain largely unanswered: What is a "classroom"? What is a "campus," and is a physical one required to produce college learning?

How do online and brick-and-mortar ones compare? Should we define "basic skills" for college students, regardless of where and how they attend?

Careers. As material returns to higher education continue to rise (Baum & Ma, 2007; Card, 2001) and holding a stable job increasingly requires college training, college enrollment has grown to include an ever wider plurality of Americans. While the expansion of college access is unquestionably a mark of progress, it raises large and important new questions: What is the range of ways in which college attendance fits into the life course? Is there one ideal way or multiple good ways? At what points in the life course is college most beneficial, and does this vary by occupation, household composition, or other dimensions of difference? How is technological change affecting what students expect from college and what colleges might properly expect of students? How does college debt shape other occupational and life decisions?

Conclusion

U.S. colleges and universities face formidable challenges. Shrinking state budgets are restricting the ability of many public institutions to maintain their broad-access mission. Growing numbers of students enter college needing remedial or developmental coursework. People continue to enter college at different points in their lives, with varied goals: some seek degrees, others plan to transfer, still others seek to hone skills or gain nondegree certifications as they navigate dynamic labor markets. There is clear and mounting pressure from state legislatures and from Washington to increase college "completion"— whatever that might mean. All the while, the growth of digital instructional media is challenging long-standing presumptions about how, where, and by whom higher education should properly be delivered.

While change and challenge are always unsettling, they also provide opportunities for high hopes and new dreams. We are optimistic about the future of higher education in America. Ours is perhaps the most varied and flexible academic ecology the world has ever known. Understanding its dynamics is essential to preserve its vitality.

REFERENCES

Abbott, A. (1988). *The system of professions: An essay on the division of expert labor.* Chicago, IL: University of Chicago Press.

Abbott, A. (2002). The disciplines and the future. In S. Brint (Ed.), *The future of the city of intellect: The changing American university* (pp. 206–230). Stanford, CA: Stanford University Press.

Adelman, C. (1996, October 4). The truth about remedial work: It's more complex than windy rhetoric and simple solutions suggest. *The Chronicle of Higher Education,* p. A56.

Adelman, C. (1999). *Answers in the tool box: Academic intensity, attendance patterns, and bachelor's degree attainment.* Washington, DC: U.S. Department of Education.

Adelman, C. (2006). *The toolbox revisited: Paths to degree completion from high school through college.* Washington, DC: U.S. Department of Education.

Albert, S., & Whetten, D. (1985). Organizational identity. In L. Cummings & B. Staw (Eds.), *Research in organizational behavior* (pp. 263–295). Greenwich, CT: JAI Press.

Aldrich, H. E. (1979). *Organizations and environments.* Englewood Cliffs, NJ: Prentice-Hall.

Aldrich, H. E., & Ruef, M. (2006). *Organizations evolving* (2nd ed.). London, UK: Sage.

Allen, I. E., & Seaman, J. (2011). *Going the distance: Online education in the United States, 2011.* Babson Park, MA: Babson Survey Research Group.

Allen, N. (2010). *A cover to cover solution: How open textbooks are the path to textbook affordability.* Boston: Student PIRGS.

Altbach, G. P. (2005). Patterns in higher education development. In P. G. Altbach, R. O. Berdahl, & P. J. Gumport (Eds.), *American higher education in the twenty-first century: Social, political, and economic challenges* (2nd ed., pp. 15–37). Baltimore, MD: Johns Hopkins University Press.

An, B. P. (2009). The relations between race, family characteristics, and where students apply to college. *Social Science Research, 39*(2), 310–323.

Apollo Group. (2013, October 22). Apollo Group, Inc. reports fourth quarter and fiscal year 2013 results [Press release]. Retrieved from http://investors.apollo.edu/phoenix.zhtml?c=79624&p=irol-newsArticle&ID=1866956&highlight=

Apollo Group Q4 2012 earnings call. (2012, October 16). *NASDAQ*. Retrieved from http://www.nasdaq.com/aspx/call-transcript.aspx?StoryId=928351&Title=apollo -group-management-discusses-q4-2012-results-earnings-call-transcript

Arbona, C., & Nora, A. (2007). The influence of academic and environmental factors on Hispanic college degree attainment. *The Review of Higher Education, 30*(3), 247–269.

Arkansas Association of Two-Year Colleges. (2012, April 1). Community colleges establish Southwest Arkansas Regional Consortium [Press release]. Retrieved from http://www.aatyc.org/about-us/archive-news/114-community-colleges-establish -southwest-arkansas-regional-consortium.html

Armstrong, E. A., & Hamilton, L. T. (2013). *Paying for the party: How college maintains inequality.* Cambridge, MA: Harvard University Press.

Arum, R., Gamoran, A., & Shavit, Y. (2007). Inclusion and diversion in higher education: A study of expansion and stratification in 15 countries. In Y. Shavit, R. Arum, & A. Gamoran (Eds.), *Stratification in higher education: A comparative study* (pp. 1–35). Stanford, CA: Stanford University Press.

Arum, R., & Roksa, J. (2011). *Academically adrift: Limited learning on college campuses.* Chicago, IL: University of Chicago Press.

Arum, R., & Roksa, J. (2014). *Aspiring adults adrift: Tentative transitions of college graduates.* Chicago, IL: University of Chicago Press.

Association of American Colleges and Universities. (n.d.). Liberal Education and America's Promise (LEAP). Retrieved March 28, 2014, from http://www.aacu.org/leap/ vision.cfm

Association of American Colleges and Universities. (2007). *College learning for the new global century.* Washington, DC: Author.

Astin, A. (1984). Student involvement: A developmental theory for higher education. *Journal of College Student Personnel, 25*(4), 297–308.

Astin, A. (1993). *What matters in college? Four critical years revisited.* San Francisco, CA: Jossey-Bass.

Attewell, P., & Lavin, D. (2007). *Passing the torch: Does higher education for the disadvantaged pay off across the generations?* New York, NY: Russell Sage Foundation.

Attewell, P., Lavin, D., Domina, T., & Levey, T. (2006). New evidence on college remediation. *The Journal of Higher Education, 77*(5), 886–924.

Aud, S., Hussar, W., Johnson, F., Kena, G., Roth, E., Manning, E., . . . Zhang, J. (2012). *The condition of education 2012* (NCES 2012-045). Washington, DC: U.S. Department of Education, National Center for Education Statistics.

Aud, S., Hussar, W., Planty, M., Snyder, T., Bianco, K., Fox, M., . . . Drake, L. (2010). *The condition of education 2010* (NCES 2010-028). Washington, DC: U.S. Department of Education, National Center for Education Statistics.

Avery, C., Glickman, M., Hoxby, C., & Metrick, A. (2004). *A revealed preference ranking of U.S. colleges and universities* (National Bureau of Economic Research Working Paper No. 10803).

Avery, C., & Hoxby, C. (2004). Do and should financial aid packages affect students' college choices? In C. Hoxby (Ed.), *College choices: The economics of where to go, when to go, and how to pay for it* (pp. 239–299). Chicago, IL: University of Chicago Press.

Avery, C., Hoxby, C., Jackson, C., Burek, K., Pope, G., & Raman, M. (2006). *Cost should be no barrier: An evaluation of the first year of Harvard's financial aid initiative* (National Bureau of Economic Research Working Paper No. 12029).

Avery, C., & Turner, S. (2012). Student loans: Do college students borrow too much—or not enough? *The Journal of Economic Perspectives, 26*(1), 165–192.

Baber, L. D. (2010). Beyond structural diversity: Centering "place" among African American students in predominantly White campuses. In T. E. Dancy, II (Ed.), *Managing diversity: (Re)visioning equity on college campuses* (pp. 221–242). New York, NY: Lang.

Bailey, T. (2009). Challenge and opportunity: Rethinking the role and function of developmental education in community college. *New Directions for Community Colleges, 145*, 11–30.

Bailey, T., Badway, N., & Gumport, P. (2001). *For-profit higher education and community colleges.* Stanford, CA: National Center for Postsecondary Improvement.

Barrow, L., & Rouse, C. (2005). Does college still pay? *Economist's Voice, 2*(4), 1–8.

Bastedo, M. N., & Bowman, N. A. (2009). *U.S. News & World Report* college rankings: Modeling institutional effects on organizational reputation. *American Journal of Education, 116*(2), 163–183.

Baum, J. A. C., & Shipilov, A. V. (2006). Ecological approaches to organizations. In S. R. Clegg, C. Hardy, T. B. Lawrence, and W. R. Nord (Eds.), *The Sage handbook of organization studies* (2nd ed., pp. 55–110). Thousand Oaks, CA: Sage.

Baum, S., & Ma, J. (2007). *Education pays: The benefits of higher education for individuals and society.* Washington, DC: College Board.

Baumgartner, F. R., & Jones, B. D. (2002). *Policy Dynamics.* Chicago, IL: University of Chicago Press.

Beach, J. M. (2009). A critique of human capital formation in the U.S. and the economic returns to sub-baccalaureate credentials. *Educational Studies, 45*, 24–38.

Beattie, I. (2002). Are all adolescent econometricians created equal? Racial, class, and gender differences in college enrollment. *Sociology of Education, 75*(1), 19–43.

Beck, U. (2000). Living your own life in a runaway world: Individualisation, globalisation, and politics. In W. Hutton and A. Giddens (Eds.), *Global capitalism* (pp. 164–174). New York, NY: New Press.

Belfield, C., & Bailey, T. (2011). The benefits of attending community college: A review of the evidence. *Community College Review, 39*(1), 46–68.

Bell, B. S., & Federman, J. E. (2013). E-learning in postsecondary education. *The Future of Children, 23*(1), 165–185.

Belley, P., & Lochner, L. (2007). The changing role of family income and ability in determining educational achievement. *Journal of Human Capital, 1*(1), 37–89.

Berman, E. P. (2012). *Creating the market university: How academic science became an economic engine.* Princeton, NJ: Princeton University Press.

Bers, T. H., & Galowich, P. M. (2002). Using survey and focus group research to learn about parents' roles in the community college search process. *Community College Review, 29*(4), 67–82.

Bettinger, E. P. (2004). How financial aid affects persistence. In C. Hoxby (Ed.), *College choices: The economics of where to go, when to go, and how to pay for it* (pp. 207–238). Chicago, IL: University of Chicago Press.

Bettinger, E. P., & Baker, R. B. (2011). *The effects of student coaching in college: An evaluation of a randomized experiment in student mentoring* (National Bureau of Economic Research Working Paper No. 16881).

Bettinger, E. P., & Long, B. T. (2006). The increasing use of adjunct instructors at public institutions: Are we hurting students? In R. G. Ehrenberg (Ed.), *What's happening to public higher education?* (pp. 51–70). Westport, CT: American Council on Higher Education.

Bettinger, E. P., & Long, B. T. (2009). Addressing the needs of underprepared students in higher education: Does college remediation work? *The Journal of Human Resources, 44*(3), 736–771.

Bettinger, E. P., & Long, B. T. (2010). Does cheaper mean better? The impact of using adjunct instructors on student outcomes. *Review of Economics and Statistics, 92*(3), 598–613.

Betton, J., & Dess, G. (1985). The application of population ecology models to the study of organizations. *Academy of Management Review, 10*(4), 750–757.

Bill & Melinda Gates Foundation. (2010). *Learning about teaching: Initial findings from the Measures of Effective Teaching Project.* Seattle, WA: Author.

Birnbaum, R. (1988). *How colleges work: The cybernetics of academic organization and leadership.* San Francisco, CA: Jossey-Bass.

Blaich, C., & Wise, K. (2011). *From gathering to using assessment results: Lessons from the Wabash national study.* Champaign, IL: National Institute for Learning Outcomes Assessment.

Bledstein, B. J. (1976). *The culture of professionalism: The middle class and the development of higher education in America.* New York, NY: Norton.

Blei, D. (2012). Probabilistic topic models. *Communications of the ACM, 55*(4), 77–84.

Blei, D., Ng, A., & Jordan, M. (2003). Latent Dirichlet allocation. *Journal of Machine Learning, 3,* 993–1022.

Bloom, D. (2010). Programs and policies to assist high school dropouts in the transition to adulthood. *The Future of Children, 20*(1), 89–108.

Boatman, A., & Long, B. T. (2011, August). Does remediation work for all students? How the effects of postsecondary remedial and developmental courses vary by level of academic preparation. *National Center for Postsecondary Research Brief.* Retrieved from http://www.postsecondaryresearch.org/i/a/document/17998_Aug2011 Brief.pdf

Bok, D. (2006). *Our underachieving colleges: A candid look at how much students learn and why they should be learning more.* Princeton, NJ: Princeton University Press.

Borjas, G. J. (2000). Foreign-born teaching assistants and the academic performance of undergraduates. *The American Economic Review, 90*(2), 355–359.

Bound, J., Lovenheim, M., & Turner, S. (2010). Why have college completion rates declined? An analysis of changing student preparation and collegiate resources. *American Economic Journal: Applied Economics, 2*(3), 129–157.

Bound, J., Lovenheim, M., & Turner, S. (2012). Increasing time to baccalaureate degree in the United States. *Education Finance and Policy, 7*(4), 375–424.

Bound, J., & Turner, S. (2002). Going to war and going to college: Did World War II and the GI Bill increase educational attainment for returning veterans? *Journal of Labor Economics, 20*(4), 784–815.

Bourdieu, P. (1986). The forms of capital. In J. G. Richardson (Ed.), *Handbook of theory and research for the sociology of education* (pp. 242–258). New York, NY: Greenwood Press.

Bourdieu, P., & Wacquant, L. J. D. (1992). *An invitation to reflexive sociology.* Chicago, IL: University of Chicago Press.

Bowen, W. G., Chingos, M. M., & McPherson, M. S. (2009). *Crossing the finish line: Completing college at America's public universities.* Princeton, NJ: Princeton University Press.

Boyd, D., Grossman, P., Ing, M., Lankford, H., Loeb, S., Rockoff, J., & Wyckoff, J. (2011). The influence of school administrators on teacher retention decisions. *American Educational Research Journal, 48*(2), 303–333.

Boyd, D., Grossman, P., Lankford, H., Loeb, S., & Wyckoff, J. (2006). How changes in entry requirements alter the teacher workforce and affect student achievement. *Journal of Education Finance and Policy, 1*(2), 176–216.

Boyd, D., Grossman, P., Lankford, H., Loeb, S., & Wyckoff, J. (2009a). Teacher preparation and student achievement. *Educational Evaluation and Policy Analysis, 31*(4), 416–440.

Boyd, D., Grossman, P., Lankford, H., Loeb, S., & Wyckoff, J. (2009b). *Who leaves: Teacher attrition and student achievement* (Center for Analysis of Longitudinal Data in Education Research Working Paper 23).

Boyd, D., Lankford, H., Loeb, S., Rockoff, J., & Wyckoff, J. (2008). The narrowing gap in New York City teacher qualifications and its implications for student achievement in high-poverty schools. *Journal of Policy Analysis and Management, 27*(4), 793–818.

Boyd, D., Lankford, H., Loeb, S., & Wyckoff, J. (2005a). The draw of home: How teachers' preferences for proximity disadvantage urban schools. *Journal of Policy Analysis and Management, 24*(1), 113–132.

Boyd, D., Lankford, H., Loeb, S., & Wyckoff, J. (2005b). Explaining the short careers of higher-achieving teachers in schools with low-performing students. *The American Economic Review, 95*(2), 166–171.

Boyer, E. L. (1990). *Scholarship reconsidered: Priorities of the professoriate.* Princeton, NJ: Carnegie Foundation for the Advancement of Teaching.

Bragg, D. (2012). *Career and technical education: Understanding community colleges.* London, UK: Routledge/Taylor Francis.

Braxton, J. M. (Ed.). (2000). *Reworking the student departure puzzle.* Nashville, TN: Vanderbilt University Press.

Braxton, J. M., Hirschy, A. S., & McClendon, S. A. (2004). *Understanding and reducing college student departure.* San Francisco, CA: Jossey-Bass.

Breneman, D. W., Pusser, B., & Turner, S. (2006). The contemporary provision of for-profit higher education: Mapping the competitive market. In D. W. Breneman, B. Pusser, and S. E. Turner (Eds.), *Earnings from learning: The rise of for-profit universities* (pp. 3–22). Albany: State University of New York Press.

Brint, S. (2002). The rise of the "practical arts." In S. Brint (Ed.), *The future of the city of intellect: The changing American university* (pp. 231–259). Stanford, CA: Stanford University Press.

Brint, S., & Karabel, J. (1989). *The diverted dream: Community colleges and the promise of educational opportunity in America, 1900–1985.* New York, NY: Oxford University Press.

Brint, S., & Karabel, J. (1991). Institutional origins and transformations: The case of American community colleges. In W. W. Powell & P. J. DiMaggio (Eds.), *The new institutionalism in organizational analysis* (pp. 337–360). Chicago, IL: University of Chicago Press.

Brint, S., Proctor, K., Hanneman, R. A., Mulligan, K., Rotondi, M. B., & Murphy, S. P. (2011). Who are the early adopters of new academic fields? Comparing four perspectives on the institutionalization of degree granting programs in U.S. four-year colleges and universities, 1970–2005. *Higher Education, 61*(5), 563–585.

Brint, S., Proctor, K., Murphy, S. P., & Hanneman, R. A. (2012). The market model and the growth and decline of academic fields in U.S. four-year colleges and universities, 1980–2000. *Sociological Forum, 27*(2), 275–299.

Brint, S., Riddle, M., & Hanneman, R. (2006). Reference sets, identities, and aspirations in a complex organizational field: The case of American four-year colleges and universities. *Sociology of Education, 79*(3), 229–252.

Brint, S., & Rotondi, M. B. (2008, August). *Student debt, the college experience, and transitions to adulthood.* Paper presented at the annual meeting of the American Sociological Association, Boston, MA.

Brock, T. (2010). Young adults and higher education: Barriers and breakthroughs to success. *The Future of Children, 20*(1), 109–132.

Bruegmann, E., & Jackson, L. (2009). Teaching students and teaching each other: The importance of peer learning for teachers. *American Economic Journal: Applied Economics, 1*(4), 85–108.

Burawoy, M. (2012). The great American university. *Contemporary Sociology, 41*(2), 139–149.

Burd, S. (2009, November–December). The subprime student loan racket. *Washington Monthly.* Retrieved from http://www.washingtonmonthly.com/features/2009/0911.burd.html

Bushaw, W. J., & Lopez, S. J. (2011). Betting on teachers: The 43rd annual Phi Delta Kappa/Gallup poll of the public's attitudes toward the public schools. *Phi Delta Kappan, 93*(1), 8–26.

Calcagno, J. C., Bailey, T., Jenkins, D., Kienzl, G., & Leinbach, T. (2008). Community college student success: What institutional characteristics make a difference? *Economics of Education Review, 27*(6), 632–645.

Calcagno, J. C., & Long, B. T. (2008). *The impact of postsecondary remediation using a regression discontinuity approach: Addressing endogenous sorting and noncompliance* (National Bureau of Economic Research Working Paper No. 14194).

California State University. (2010). Table 1: Total enrollment by sex and student level, fall 2010. Retrieved from http://www.calstate.edu/as/stat_reports/2010-2011/f10_01.htm

Card, D. (2001). Estimating the returns to schooling: Progress on some persistent econometric problems. *Econometrica, 69*(5), 1127–1160.

Carey, K. (2004). *A matter of degrees: Improving graduation rates in four-year colleges and universities.* Washington, DC: Education Trust.

Carini, R. M., Kuh, G. D., & Klein, S. P. (2006). Student engagement and student learning: Testing the linkages. *Research in Higher Education, 47*(1), 1–32.

Carnegie Commission on Higher Education. (1973). *A classification of institutions of higher education.* Berkeley, CA: Author.

Carnegie Foundation for the Advancement of Teaching. (2011, January). Updated Carnegie Classifications show increase in for-profits, change in traditional landscape. Retrieved from http://www.carnegiefoundation.org/newsroom/press-releases/updated-carnegie-classifications

Carneiro, P., & Heckman, J. J. (2002). The evidence on credit constraints in postsecondary schooling. *The Economic Journal, 112*(482), 705–734.

Carnevale, A. P. (1987). *The learning enterprise.* Washington, DC: U.S. Department of Labor.

Carnevale, A. P., & Rose, S. J. (2004). Socioeconomic status, race/ethnicity, and selective college admissions. In R. D. Kahlenberg (Ed.), *America's untapped resource: Low-income students in higher education* (pp. 101–156). New York, NY: Century Foundation Press.

Carnevale, A. P., Smith, N., & Strohl, H. (2010). *Help wanted: Projections of jobs and education requirements through 2018.* Washington, DC: Georgetown University, Center on Education and the Workforce.

Carrell, S. E., & West, J. E. (2010). Does professor quality matter? Evidence from random assignment of students to professors. *Journal of Political Economy, 118*(3), 409–432.

Carroll, G. R., & Hannan, M. T. (1995). *Organizations in industry: Strategy, structure, and selection.* New York, NY: Oxford University Press.

Cater, D. (1964). *Power in Washington.* New York, NY: Vintage Books.

Chambliss, D. F., & Takacs, C. G. (2014). *How college works.* Cambridge, MA: Harvard University Press.

Cherlin, A. (2005). American marriage in the early 21st century. *The Future of Children, 15*(2), 33–55.

Chetty, R., Friedman, J., Hilger, N., Saez, E., Schanzenbach, D. W., & Yagan, D. (2011). How does your kindergarten classroom affect your earnings? Evidence from Project STAR. *The Quarterly Journal of Economics, 126*(4), 1593–1660.

Chetty, R., Friedman, J. N., & Rockoff, J. E. (2013). *Measuring the Impacts of Teachers I: Evaluating Bias in Teacher Value-Added Estimates.* (National Bureau of Economic Research Working Paper No. 19423).

Christensen, C. M., & Eyring, H. J. (2011). *The innovative university: Changing the DNA of higher education from the inside out.* San Francisco: Jossey-Bass.

Clark, B. R. (1972). The organizational saga in higher education. *Administrative Science Quarterly, 17*(2), 178–184.

Clark, B. R. (1983). *The higher education system: Academic organization in cross-national perspective.* Berkeley: University of California Press.

Clawson, D. (2009). Tenure and the future of the university. *Science, 324,* 1147–1148.

Clotfelter, C. T., Ladd, H. F., & Vigdor, J. (2006). Teacher-student matching and the assessment of teacher effectiveness. *The Journal of Human Resources, 41*(4), 778–820.

Coalition for Evidence-Based Policy. (2003). *Identifying and implementing educational practices supported by rigorous evidence: A user friendly guide.* Washington, DC: U.S. Department of Education, Institute of Education Sciences.

Cole, J. C. (2009). *The great American university: Its rise to preeminence, its indispensable national role, and why it must be protected.* New York, NY: Public Affairs.

Coleman, J. S., Campbell, E. Q., Hobson, C. J., McPartland, J., Mood, A. M., Weinfeld, F. D., & York, R. L. (1966). *Equality of educational opportunity.* Washington, DC: U.S. Department of Health, Education, and Welfare.

Collatos, A., Morell, E., Nuno, A., & Lara, R. (2004). Critical sociology in K–16 early intervention: Remaking Latino pathways to higher education. *Journal of Hispanic Higher Education, 3*(2), 164–179.

College Board. (2013). *Trends in college pricing, 2013.* Princeton, NJ: Author. Retreived from http://trends.collegeboard.org/sites/default/files/college-pricing-2013-full-report.pdf

Confessore, N. (2003, November). What makes a college good? *The Atlantic Monthly, 292*(4), 118–126.

Cook, C. E. (1998). *Lobbying for higher education: How colleges and universities influence federal policy.* Nashville, TN: Vanderbilt University Press.

Council for Adult and Experiential Learning. (n.d.). Who is CAEL. Retrieved March 28, 2014, from www.in.gov/che/files/LearningCountsorg.pdf

Council for Adult and Experiential Learning. (2010). *Fueling the race to postsecondary success: A 48-institution study of prior learning assessment and adult student outcomes.* Chicago: Author.

Council for Aid to Education. (n.d.). CLA+ overview. Retrieved March 28, 2014, from http://www.collegiatelearningassessment.org

Coursera. (n.d.). What is ACE CREDIT? Retrieved June 17, 2014, from http://help.coursera.org/customer/portal/articles/840056-what-is-ace-credit-

Coursera. (2013, October 23). A triple milestone: 107 partners, 532 courses, 5.2 million students and counting! *Coursera Blog.* Retrieved from http://blog.coursera.org/post/64907189712/a-triple-milestone-107-partners-532-courses-5-2

Cox, R. D. (2009). *The college fear factor: How students and professors misunderstand one another.* Cambridge, MA: Harvard University Press.

Cuyjet, M. J. (2006). *African American men in college.* San Francisco, CA: Jossey-Bass.

Damaske, S. (2009). Brown suits need not apply: The intersection of race, gender, and class in institutional network building. *Sociological Forum, 24*(2), 402–424.

Danziger, S. (2004). *Earnings by education for young workers, 1975 and 2002* (Data Brief No. 17). Philadelphia, PA: MacArthur Network on Transitions to Adulthood.

Danziger, S., & Ratner, D. (2010). Labor market outcomes and the transition to adulthood. *The Future of Children, 20*(1), 133–158.

Darling-Hammond, L., Holtzman, D. J., Gatlin, S. J., & Heilig, J. V. (2005). Does teacher preparation matter? Evidence about teacher certification, Teach for America, and teacher effectiveness. *Education Policy Analysis Archives, 13*(42). Retrieved from http://epaa.asu.edu/ojs/article/view/147/273

Davis, G. F., McAdam, D., Scott, W. R., & Zald, M. N. (Eds.). (2005). *Social movements and organization theory.* Cambridge, UK: Cambridge University Press.

Decker, P. T., Mayer, D. P., & Glazerman, S. (2004). *The effects of Teach for America on students: Findings from a national evaluation.* Princeton, NJ: Mathematica Policy Research.

Deil-Amen, R. J. (2011a). Beyond remedial dichotomies: Are "underprepared" college students a marginalized majority? In E. M. Cox & J. S. Watson (Eds.), *New Directions for Community Colleges: No. 155. Marginalized students* (pp. 59–71). San Francisco, CA: Jossey-Bass.

Deil-Amen, R. J. (2011b). Socio-academic integrative moments: Rethinking academic and social integration among two-year college students in career-related programs. *The Journal of Higher Education, 82*(1), 54–91.

Deil-Amen, R. J., & DeLuca, S. (2010). The underserved third: How our educational structures populate an educational underclass. *Journal of Education for Students Placed at Risk, 15*(1), 27–50.

Deil-Amen, R. J., & Goldrick-Rab, S. (2009, August). *Institutional transfer and the management of risk in higher education.* Paper presented at the annual meeting of the American Sociological Association, San Francisco, CA.

Deil-Amen, R. J., & Rios-Aguilar, C. (2012). Beyond getting in and fitting in: An examination of social networks and professionally-relevant social capital among Latina/o university students. *Journal of Hispanic Higher Education, 11*(2), 179–196.

Deil-Amen, R. J., Rios-Aguilar, C., Irwin, M., & Gonzalez Canche, M. (2010, November). *Living and working in college: Low-income students challenging prior models of college success and persistence.* Paper presented at the national conference of the Association for the Study of Higher Education, Indianapolis, IN.

De La Rosa, M. L. (2006). Is opportunity knocking? Low-income students' perceptions of college and financial aid. *American Behavioral Scientist, 49*(12), 1670–1686.

DeNavas-Walt, C., Proctor, B. D., & Smith, J. C. (2010). *Income, poverty, and health insurance coverage in the United States: 2009.* Washington, DC: U.S. Government Printing Office.

Desrochers, D. M., & Wellman, J. V. (2011). *Trends in college spending 1999–2009: Where does the money come from? Where does it go? What does it buy?* Washington, DC: Delta Cost Project.

Dillon, S. (2006, March 1). Online colleges receive a boost from Congress. *The New York Times.* Retrieved from http://www.nytimes.com/2006/03/01/national/01educ.html

DiMaggio, P. J. (1986). Structural analysis of organizational fields: A block model approach. In L. Cummings and B. Staw (Eds.), *Research in organizational behavior* (pp. 335–370). Greenwich, CT: JAI Press.

DiMaggio, P. J. (1991). Constructing an organizational field as a professional project: U.S. art museums, 1920–1940. In W. W. Powell & P. J. DiMaggio (Eds.), *The new institutionalism in organizational analysis* (pp. 267–292). Chicago, IL: University of Chicago Press.

DiMaggio, P. J., & Powell, W. W. (1983). The iron cage revisited: Institutional isomorphism and collective rationality in organizational fields. *American Sociological Review, 48*(2), 147–160.

Dougherty, C., Mellor, L., & Jian, S. (2006). *The relationship between Advanced Placement and college graduation.* Austin, TX: National Center for Educational Accountability.

Dougherty, K. J. (1994). *The contradictory college: The conflicting origins, impacts, and futures of the community college.* Albany: State University of New York Press.

Downs, A. (1957). *An economic theory of democracy.* New York, NY: Harper.

Doyle, W. R. (2007). The political economy of redistribution through higher education subsidies. In J. C. Smart (Ed.), *Higher education: Handbook of theory and research* (Vol. 22, pp. 335–409). Dordrecht, Germany: Springer.

Doyle, W. R. (2010a). The politics of public college tuition and state financial aid. *The Journal of Higher Education, 83*(5), 617–647.

Doyle, W. R. (2010b). U.S. senators' ideal points for higher education: Assessing the role of partisanship and change. *The Journal of Higher Education, 81*(5), 619–644.

Dunham, E. A. (1969). *Colleges of the forgotten America: A profile of state colleges and regional universities.* Hightstown, NJ: McGraw-Hill.

Dynarski, S. (2003). Does aid matter? Measuring the effect of student aid on college attendance and completion. *The American Economic Review, 93*(1), 279–288.

Dynarski, S. (2005). *Building the stock of college-educated labor* (National Bureau of Economic Research Working Paper No. 11604).

Dynarski, S., Hyman, J. M., & Schanzenbach, D. W. (2011). *Experimental evidence on the effect of childhood investments on postsecondary attainment and degree completion* (National Bureau of Economic Research Working Paper No. 17533).

Edin, K., & Kefalas, M. (2005). *Promises I can keep: Why poor women put motherhood before marriage.* Berkeley: University of California Press.

Edin, K., & Tach, L. (2012). Becoming a parent: The social context of fertility in young adulthood. In A. Booth, S. L. Brown, N. S. Landale, W. D. Manning, & S. M. McHale (Eds.), *Early adulthood in a family context* (pp. 185–208). New York, NY: Springer.

Ehrenberg, R. G., Kasper, H., & Rees, D. (1991). Faculty turnover at American colleges and universities: Analyses of AAUP data. *Economics of Education Review, 10*(2), 99–110.

Ehrenberg, R. G., & Zhang, L. (2005). Do tenured and tenure-track faculty matter? *The Journal of Human Resources, 40*(3), 647–659.

Ehrenberg, R. G., & Zhang, L. (2006). Do tenured and tenure-track faculty matter? In R. G. Ehrenberg (Ed.), *What's happening to public higher education?* (pp. 37–50). Westport, CT: American Council on Higher Education.

Eide, E., & Waehrer, G. (1998). The role of the option value of college attendance in college major choice. *Economics of Education Review, 17*(1), 73–82.

Emirbayer, M., & Mische, A. (1998). What is agency? *American Journal of Sociology, 103*(4), 962–1023.

Everett-Haynes, L. M., & Deil-Amen, R. J. (2011, April). *Redefining resiliency: Variations among African-American and Latino university students.* Paper presented at the annual meeting of the American Educational Research Association, New Orleans, LA.

Fain, P. (2012a, July 31). End of the beginning. *Inside Higher Ed.* Retrieved from http://www.insidehighered.com/news/2012/07/31/next-steps-harkin-and-profits

Fain, P. (2012b, May 7). New college, new model. *Inside Higher Ed.* Retrieved from http://www.insidehighered.com/news/2012/05/07/brandman-university-and-investment-fund-launch-hispanic-serving-college#sthash.a9CBCzWY.dpbs

Fain, P. (2012c, July 10). Rise of the accreditor? *Inside Higher Ed.* Retrieved from http://www.insidehighered.com/news/2012/07/10/profit-ashford-university-loses-accreditation-bid

Fain, P. (2013a, March 19). Beyond the credit hour. *Inside Higher Ed.* Retrieved from http://www.insidehighered.com/news/2013/03/19/feds-give-nudge-competency-based-education

Fain, P. (2013b, July 11). If at first you don't succeed. *Inside Higher Ed.* Retrieved from http://www.insidehighered.com/news/2013/07/11/ashford-earns-accreditation-western-association-second-try

Fain, P. (2013c, October 8). No aid, no problem. *Inside Higher Ed.* Retrieved from http://www.insidehighered.com/news/2013/10/08/universitynows-unique-approach-accreditation-and-federal-financial-aid

Fallows, J. (2003, November). The new college chaos. *The Atlantic Monthly, 292*(4), 106–114.

Fernandez, R., & Rogerson, R. (1995). On the political economy of education subsidies. *Review of Economic Studies, 62*(2), 249–262.

Figlio, D. N. (2002). Can public schools buy better-qualified teachers? *Industrial and Labor Relations Review, 55*(4), 686–699.

Fischer, C. S., & Hout, M. (2006). *Century of difference: How America changed in the last one hundred years.* New York, NY: Russell Sage Foundation.

Fitzpatrick, M., & Turner, S. E. (2007). Blurring the boundary: Changes in collegiate participation and the transition to adulthood. In S. Danziger and C. Rouse (Eds.), *The price of independence: The economics of early adulthood* (pp. 107–137). New York, NY: Russell Sage Foundation.

Fleisher, B., Hashimoto, M., & Weinberg, B. A. (2002). Foreign GTAs can be effective teachers of economics. *Journal of Economic Education, 33*(4), 299–325.

Fletcher, J. M., & Tienda, M. (2009). High school classmates and college success. *Sociology of Education, 82*(4), 287–314.

Fligstein, N. (2001). Social skill and the theory of fields. *Sociological Theory, 19*(2), 105–125.

Fligstein, N., & McAdam, D. (2012). *A theory of fields.* Oxford, UK: Oxford University Press.

Flowers, L. (2006). Effects of attending a 2-year institution on African-American males' academic and social integration in the first year of college. *Teachers College Record, 108*(2), 267–286.

Frank, D. J., & Gabler, J. (2006). *Reconstructing the university: Worldwide shifts in academia in the 20th century.* Stanford, CA: Stanford University Press.

Franzen, C. (2012, February 24). Kickstarter expects to provide more funding to the arts than NEA. *TPM.* Retrieved from http://talkingpointsmemo.com/idealab/kickstarter-expects-to-provide-more-funding-to-the-arts-than-nea

Freeman, J. L. (1965). *The political process: Executive bureau-legislative committee relations.* New York, NY: Random House.

Friedland, R., & Alford, R. A. (1991). Bringing society back in: Symbols, practices, and institutional contradictions. In W. W. Powell and P. J. DiMaggio (Eds.), *The new institutionalism in organizational analysis* (pp. 232–263). Chicago, IL: University of Chicago Press.

Fry, R. (2002). *Latinos in higher education: Many enroll, too few graduate.* Washington, DC: Pew Hispanic Center.

Fuller, A. (2012, September 14). In selecting peers for comparison's sake, colleges look upward. *The Chronicle of Higher Education,* pp. A19–A20.

Furstenberg, F. F., Jr. (2007). *Destinies of the disadvantaged: The politics of teenage childbearing.* New York, NY: Russell Sage Foundation.

Furstenberg, F. F., Jr. (2010). On a new schedule: Transitions to adulthood and family change. *The Future of Children, 20*(1), 67–87.

Fusarelli, B. C., & Cooper, B. S. (2009). *The rising state: How state power is transforming our nation's schools.* Albany: State University of New York Press.

Gándara, P., & Contreras, F. (2009). *The Latino education crisis: The consequences of failed social policies.* Cambridge, MA: Harvard University Press.

Garet, M. S., Wayne, A. J., Stancavage, F., Taylor, J., Walters, K., Song, M., . . . Warner, E. (2010). *Middle school mathematics professional development impact study: Findings after the first year of implementation.* Washington, DC: U.S. Department of Education.

Gerber, T. P., & Cheung, S. Y. (2008). Horizontal stratification in postsecondary education: Forms, explanations, and implications. *Annual Review of Sociology, 34,* 299–318.

Giddens, A. (1979). *Central problems in social theory: Action, structure and contradiction in social analysis.* Berkeley: University of California Press.

Giddens, A. (2002). *Runaway world: How globalization is reshaping our lives.* London, UK: Routledge.

Giordano, P. C., Manning, W. D., Longmore, M. A., & Flanigan, C. M. (2012). Developmental shifts in the character of romantic and sexual relationships from adolescence to young adulthood. In A. Booth, S. L. Brown, N. S. Landale, W. D. Manning, &

S. M. McHale (Eds.), *Early adulthood in a family context* (pp. 133–164). New York, NY: Springer.

GitHub. (n.d.). About. Retrieved March 28, 2014, from https://github.com/about

Gladieux, L. E., & Wolanin, T. R. (1978). *Congress and the colleges: The national politics of higher education.* Lexington, MA: Lexington Books.

Glazerman, S., Dolfin, S., Bleeker, M., Johnson, S., Isenberg, E., Lugo-Gil, J., . . . Ali, M. (2009). *Impacts of comprehensive teacher induction: Results from the first year of a randomized controlled study.* Washington, DC: U.S. Department of Education.

Glenny, L. A. (1959). *Autonomy of public colleges: The challenge of coordination.* New York, NY: McGraw-Hill.

Goldhaber, D. (2006). Are teacher unions good for students? In J. Hannaway & A. J. Rotherham (Eds.), *Collective bargaining in education: Negotiating change in today's schools* (pp. 141–157). Cambridge, MA: Harvard Education Press.

Goldhaber, D., Gross, B., & Player, D. (2007). *Are public schools really losing their best? Assessing the career transitions of teachers and their implications for the quality of the teacher workforce* (Center for Analysis of Longitudinal Data in Education Research Working Paper No. 12).

Goldin, C. D., & Katz, L. F. (1999). The shaping of higher education: The formative years in the United States, 1890 to 1940. *The Journal of Economic Perspectives, 13*(1), 37–62.

Goldin, C. D., & Katz, L. F. (2008). *The race between education and technology.* Cambridge, MA: Harvard University Press.

Goldrick-Rab, S. (2006). Following their every move: An investigation of social class differences in college pathways. *Sociology of Education, 79*(1), 61–79.

Goldrick-Rab, S., & Pfeffer, F. T. (2009). Beyond access: Explaining socioeconomic differences in college transfer. *Sociology of Education, 82*(2), 101–125.

Goldrick-Rab, S., & Roksa, J. (2008). *A federal agenda for promoting student success and degree completion.* Washington, DC: Center for American Progress.

Gonzalez, J. (2009, November 8). For-profit colleges, growing fast, say they are key to Obama's degree goals. *The Chronicle of Higher Education.* Retrieved from http://chronicle.com/article/For-Profit-Colleges-Say-They/49068

Goodall, A. H. (2008). *Highly cited leaders and the performance of research universities* (Cornell Higher Education Research Institute Working Paper No. 111).

Granovetter, M. (1973). The strength of weak ties. *American Journal of Sociology, 78*(6), 1360–1380.

Greenberg, D. (1998, June 1). Small men on campus: The shrinking college president. *The New Republic, 218*(22), 16–23.

Grissom, J. (2011). Can good principals keep teachers in disadvantaged schools? Linking principal effectiveness to teacher satisfaction and turnover in hard-to-staff environments. *Teachers College Record, 113*(11), 2552–2585.

Grissom, J., & Loeb, S. (2011). Triangulating principal effectiveness: How perspectives of parents, teachers, and assistant principals identify the central importance of managerial skills. *American Educational Research Journal, 48*(5), 1091–1123.

Grodsky, E., & Reigle-Crumb, C. (2010). Those who choose and those who don't: Social background and college orientation. *The ANNALS of the American Academy of Political and Social Science, 627,* 14–35.

Grossman, P., Loeb, S., Cohen, J. J., & Wyckoff, J. (2013). Measure for measure: The relationships between measures of instructional practice in middle school English language arts and teachers' value-added scores. *American Education Journal, 119*(3), 445–470.

Grubb, W. N. (1993). The varied economic returns to postsecondary education: New evidence from the class of 1972. *The Journal of Human Resources, 28*(2), 365–392.

Grubb, W. N. (1996). *Working in the middle: Strengthening education and training for the mid-skilled labor force.* San Francisco, CA: Jossey-Bass.

Grubb, W. N. (2002). Learning and earning in the middle, part I: National studies of pre-baccalaureate education. *Economics of Education Review, 21*(4), 299–321.

Guiffrida, D. A. (2006). Toward a cultural advancement of Tinto's theory. *The Review of Higher Education, 29*(4), 451–472.

Gumport, P. J. (2000). Academic restructuring: Organizational change and institutional imperatives. *Higher Education, 39*(1), 67–91.

Haas, J., Hall, R., & Johnson, N. (1966). Toward an empirically derived taxonomy of organizations. In R. V. Bowers (Ed.), *Studies on behavior in organizations* (pp. 157–180). Athens: University of Georgia Press.

Habley, W. R., Bloom, J. L., & Robbins, S. (2012). *Increasing persistence: Research-based strategies for college student success.* San Francisco, CA: Jossey-Bass.

Hacker, J. (2006). *The great risk shift.* New York, NY: Oxford University Press.

Hagedorn, L. S., Chi, W., Cepeda, R., & McLain, S. (2007). An investigation of critical mass: The role of Latino representation in the success of urban community college students. *Research in Higher Education, 48*(1), 73–91.

Hagedorn, L. S., Maxwell, W., & Hampton, P. (2002). Correlates of retention for African-American males in the community college. *Journal of College Student Retention: Research, Theory, and Practice, 3*(3), 243–263.

Hankin, J. N. (1996). The door that never closes: Continuing education needs of community college leaders. *New Directions for Community Colleges, 95,* 37–46.

Hannah, S. B. (1996). The higher education act of 1992: Skills, constraints, and the politics of higher education. *The Journal of Higher Education, 67*(5), 498–527.

Hannan, M. (2010). Partiality of memberships in categories and audiences. *Annual Review of Sociology, 36,* 159–181.

Hannan, M., & Freeman, J. (1977). The population ecology of organizations. *American Journal of Sociology, 82*(5), 929–964.

Hannan, M., & Freeman, J. (1986). Where do organizational forms come from? *Sociological Forum, 1*(1), 50–72.

Hannan, M., & Freeman, J. (1989). *Organizational ecology.* Cambridge, MA: Harvard University Press.

Hannan, M., Pólos, L., & Carroll, G. (2007). *Logics of organization theory: Audiences, codes, and ecologies.* Princeton, NJ: Princeton University Press.

Hanushek, E. A. (1986). The economics of schooling: Production and efficiency in public schools. *Journal of Economic Literature, 24*(3), 1141–1177.

Hanushek, E. A. (1997). Assessing the effects of school resources on student performance: An update. *Educational Evaluation and Policy Analysis, 19*(22), 141–164.

Hanushek, E. A., Kain, J. F., O'Brien, D. M., & Rivkin, S. G. (2005). *The market for teacher quality* (National Bureau of Economic Research Working Paper No. 11154).

Hanushek, E. A., Kain, J. F., & Rivkin, S. G. (2004). Why public schools lose teachers. *The Journal of Human Resources, 39*(2), 326–354.

Hanushek, E. A., & Rivkin, S. G. (2010). Using value-added measures of teacher quality. *The American Economic Review, 100*(2), 267–271.

Harper, S. R. (2008). Realizing the intended outcomes of *Brown*: High-achieving African American male undergraduates and social capital. *American Behavioral Scientist, 52*(7), 1030–1053.

Harper, S. R. (2009). Niggers no more: A critical race counternarrative on Black male student achievement at predominantly White colleges and universities. *International Journal of Qualitative Studies in Education, 22*(6), 697–712.

Harper, S. R., & Davis, H. F., III. (2012). They (don't) care about education: A counternarrative on Black male students' responses to inequitable schooling. *Educational Foundations, 26*(1), 103–120.

Harris, D. N., & Adams, S. J. (2007). Understanding the level and causes of teacher turnover: A comparison with other professions. *Economics of Education Review, 26*(3), 325–337.

Harris, F., III, & Harper, S. R. (2008). Masculinities go to community college: Understanding male identity socialization and gender role conflict. In J. Lester (Ed.), *New Directions for Community Colleges: No. 142. Gendered perspectives on community colleges* (pp. 25–35). San Francisco, CA: Jossey-Bass.

Hearn, J. C., & McLendon, M. K. (2012). Governance research: From adolescence toward maturity. In M. N. Bastedo (Ed.), *The organization of higher education: Managing colleges for a new era* (pp. 45–85). Baltimore, MD: Johns Hopkins University Press.

Higher Education Act of 1965, P.L. 89-329, 89th Cong., 2nd Sess. (1965).

Hodgkinson, H. (1971). *Institutions in transition: A profile of change in higher education.* New York, NY: McGraw-Hill.

Hoffmann, F., & Oreopoulos, P. (2009). A professor like me: The influence of instructor gender on college achievement. *The Journal of Human Resources, 44*(2), 479–494.

Horng, E., Klasik, D., & Loeb, S. (2010). Principal's time use and school effectiveness. *American Journal of Education, 116*(4), 491–523.

Hossler, D., & Gallagher, K. S. (1987). Studying college student choice: A three-phase model and implications for policymakers. *College and University, 62*(3), 207–221.

Hout, M. (2012). Social and economic returns to college education in the United States. *Annual Review of Sociology, 38*, 379–400.

Howell, J., Kurlaender, M., & Grodsky, E. (2010). Postsecondary preparation and remediation: Examining the effect of the Early Assessment Program at California State University. *Journal of Policy Analysis and Management, 29*(4), 726–748.

Hoxby, C. M. (1996). How teachers' unions affect education production. *Quarterly Journal of Economics, 111*(3), 671–718.

Hoxby, C. M. (2009). The changing selectivity of American colleges. *Journal of Economic Perspectives, 23*(4), 95–118.

Hubbard, L., Mehan, H., & Stein, M. K. (2006). *Reform as learning: School reform, organizational culture, and community politics in San Diego.* New York, NY: Routledge.

Hughes, K. L., Karp, M. M., & O'Gara, L. (2009). Student success courses in the community college: An exploratory study of student perspectives. *Community College Review, 36*(3), 195–222.

Hull, R. J., & Keim, M. C. (2007). Nature and status of community college leadership development programs. *Community College Journal of Research and Practice, 31*(9), 689–702.

Humanities, Arts, Science, and Technology Alliance and Collaboratory. (n.d.). Badges Work for Vets. Retrieved June 17, 2014, from https://www.hastac.org/competitions/winners/badges-work-vets

Hurtado, S., & Carter, D. F. (1997). Effects of college transition and perceptions of the campus racial climate on Latino college students' sense of belonging. *Sociology of Education, 70*(4), 324–345.

Hurwitz, M. (2012). The impact of institutional grant aid on college choice. *Educational Evaluation and Policy Analysis, 34*(3), 344–363.

Illich, I. (1971). *Deschooling Society.* London, UK: Boyars.

Immerwahr, J. (1999a). *Doing comparatively well: Why the public loves higher education and criticizes K–12.* Washington, DC: Institute for Educational Leadership.

Immerwahr, J. (1999b). *Taking responsibility: Leaders' expectations of higher education* (National Center Report #99-1). San Jose, CA: National Center for Public Policy and Higher Education.

Immerwahr, J. (2000). *Great expectations: How the public and parents—white, African-American, and Hispanic—view higher education.* San Jose, CA: National Center for Public Policy and Higher Education.

Immerwahr, J. (2004). *Public attitudes on higher education: A trend analysis, 1993 to 2003* (National Center Report #04-2). San Jose, CA: National Center for Public Policy and Higher Education.

Immerwahr, J., & Johnson, J. (2007). *Squeeze play: How parents and the public look at higher education today* (National Center Report #07-4). San Jose, CA: National Center for Public Policy and Higher Education.

Immerwahr, J., & Johnson, J. (2010). *Squeeze play 2010: Continued public anxiety on cost, harsher judgments on how colleges are run.* San Jose, CA: National Center for Public Policy and Higher Education.

Ingersoll, R. (2001). Teacher turnover and teacher shortages: An organizational analysis. *American Educational Research Journal, 38*(3), 499–534.

Institute of Higher Education. (2011). *Academic ranking of world universities—2011.* Shanghai, China: Jiao Tong University.

Institute for Higher Education Policy. (2012). *A new classification scheme for for-profit institutions.* Washington, DC: Author.

International Telecommunication Union. (2012). *Measuring the information society.* Geneva, Switzerland: Author.

Ishida, H., Spilerman, S., & Su, K. H. (1997). Educational credentials and promotion chances in Japanese and American organizations. *American Sociological Review, 62*(6), 866–882.

Jacob, B. A. (2007). The challenges of staffing urban schools with effective teachers. *The Future of Children, 17*(1), 129–54.

Jacob, B. A., & Lefgren, L. J. (2008). Principals as agents: Subjective performance measurement in education. *Journal of Labor Economics, 26*(1), 101–136.

Jacob, B., McCall, B., & Stange, K. (2013). *College as country club: Do colleges cater to students' preferences for consumption?* (National Bureau of Economic Research Working Paper No. 18745).

Jacobson, L., & Mokher, C. (2009). *Pathways to boosting the earnings of low-income students by increasing their educational attainment.* Arlington, VA: Hudson Institute and Center for Naval Analysis.

Jaggars, S., & Hodara, M. (2011). *The opposing forces that shape developmental education: Assessment, placement, and progression at CUNY community colleges* (Community College Resource Center Working Paper No. 36).

Jaschik, S. (2010, July 1). Standing up to "accreditation shopping." *Inside Higher Ed.* Retrieved from http://www.insidehighered.com/news/2010/07/01/hlc

Johnson, V. E. (2003). *Grade inflation: A crisis in college education.* New York, NY: Springer-Verlag.

Jones, S. (2011). Freedom to fail? The board's role in reducing college dropout rates. *Trusteeship, 19*(1), 2–5.

Jovic, E., & McMullin, J. (2011). Learning and aging. In R. A. Settersten, Jr., and J. L. Angel (Eds.), *Handbook of sociology of aging* (pp. 229–244). New York, NY: Springer Science.

Julius, D. J. (2011). Universities should continue to bargain. *Journal of Collective Bargaining in the Academy, 3*(1). Retrieved from http://thekeep.eiu.edu/jcba/vol3/iss1/1

Julius, D. J., & Gumport, P. J. (2003). Graduate student unionization: Catalysts and consequences. *The Review of Higher Education, 26*(2), 187–216.

June, A. W. (2011, September 23). Florida, with an eye on Texas, readies for next conflict over faculty productivity. *The Chronicle of Higher Education*, p. A17.

Kalogrides, D., Loeb, S., & Béteille, T. (2013). Systematic sorting: Teacher characteristics and class assignments. *Sociology of Education, 86*(2), 103–123.

Kamenetz, A. (2010). *DIYU: Edupunks, edupreneurs, and the coming transformation of higher education*. White River Junction, VT: Green.

Kamenetz, A. (2011a). Billy Sichone. *The Edupunks' Guide*. Retrieved from http://edu punksguide.org/stories/billy-sichone

Kamenetz, A. (2011b). C.4 open ed startups. *The Edupunks' Guide*. Retrieved from http:// edupunksguide.org/resources/open-ed-startups

Kamenetz, A. (2011c). C.5 reputation networks. *The Edupunks' Guide*. Retrieved from http://edupunksguide.org/resources/reputation-networks

Kamenetz, A. (2011d, June 16). Knewton's "adaptive learning" technology spreads to tens of thousands of students at ASU, Penn State, SUNY, more. *Fast Company*. Retrieved from http://www.fastcompany.com/1760309/knewtons-adaptive-learning-tech nology-spreads-tens-thousands-students-asu-penn-state-suny-mo

Kamenetz, A. (2011e). The transformation of higher education through prior learning assessment. *Change: The Magazine of Higher Learning, 43*(5), 7–13.

Kamenetz, A. (2012a, January 12). 5 resources for the 4-year career. *Fast Company*. Retreived from http://www.fastcompany.com/1799655/5-resources-4-year-career

Kamenetz, A. (2012b, August 8). How Coursera, a free online education service, will school us all. *Fast Company*. Retrieved from http://www.fastcompany.com/3000042/ how-coursera-free-online-education-service-will-school-us-all

Kamenetz, A. (2012c, February 7). Most innovative companies 2012: Southern New Hampshire University, for relentlessly reinventing higher ed, online and off. *Fast Company*. Retrieved from http://www.fastcompany.com/3017340/most-innovative -companies-2012/12southern-new-hampshire-university

Kamenetz, A. (2013, October 29). Are you competent? Prove it. Degrees based on what you can do, not how long you went. *The New York Times*. Retrieved from http:// www.nytimes.com/2013/11/03/education/edlife/degrees-based-on-what-you-can -do-not-how-long-you-went.html

Kane, T. J. (1994). College entry by blacks since 1970: The role of college costs, family background, and the returns to education. *Journal of Political Economy, 102*(5), 878–911.

Kane, T. J., & Rouse, C. (1995). Labor market returns to two- and four-year college. *The American Economic Review, 85*(3), 600–614.

Kane, T. J., & Rouse, C. (1999). The community college: Educating students at the margin between college and work. *The Journal of Economic Perspectives, 13*(1), 63–84.

Kane, T. J., Taylor, E. S., Tyler, J. H., & Wooten, A. L. (2011). Identifying effective classroom practice using student achievement data. *The Journal of Human Resources, 43*(3), 587–613.

Karabel, J. (2005). *The chosen: The hidden history of admission and exclusion at Harvard, Yale, and Princeton.* New York, NY: Houghton Mifflin.

Karp, M. M., & Hughes, K. L. (2009). Information networks and integration: Institutional influences on experiences and persistence of beginning students. *New Directions for Community Colleges, 144,* 73–82.

Karp, M. M., Hughes, K. L., & O'Gara, L. (2010). An exploration of Tinto's integration framework for community college students. *Journal of College Student Retention: Research, Theory, and Practice, 12*(1), 69–86.

Kerckhoff, A. C. (1995). Institutional arrangements and stratification processes in industrial societies. *Annual Review of Sociology, 21,* 323–347.

Kerr, C. (1991). *The great transformation in higher education, 1960–1980.* Albany: State University of New York Press.

Kerr, C. (2001). *The uses of the university* (5th ed.). Cambridge, MA: Harvard University Press.

King, B., Clemens, E. S., & Konty, M. F. (2011). Identity realization and organizational forms: Differentiation and consolidation of identities among Arizona's charter schools. *Organization Science, 22*(3), 554–572.

Kingdon, J. W. (1995). *Agendas, alternatives, and public policies* (2nd ed.). New York, NY: HarperCollins.

Kirst, M. W. (2013). *The Common Core meets state policy: This changes almost everything.* Stanford: Policy Analysis for California Education.

Kirst, M. W., Meister, G., & Rowley, S. R. (1984). Policy issue networks: Their influence on state policymaking. *Policy Studies Journal, 13*(2), 247–263.

Kirst, M. W., & Wirt, F. M. (2009). *The political dynamics of American education* (4th ed.). San Pablo, CA: McCutchan.

Klasik, D. (2012). The college application gauntlet: A systematic analysis of the steps to four-year college enrollment. *Research in Higher Education, 53*(5), 506–549.

Klein, S., Liu, O. L., & Sconing, J. (2009). *Test validity study (TVS) report.* Washington, DC: Fund for the Improvement of Postsecondary Education.

Knapp, L. G., Kelly-Reid, J. E., & Ginder, S. A. (2012). *Enrollment in postsecondary institutions, fall 2011; financial statistics, fiscal year 2011; and graduation rates, selected cohorts, 2003–2008: First look (preliminary data)* (NCES 2012-174). Washington, DC: U.S. Department of Education.

Knewton. (2011, June 15). Four universities select Knewton to power math college readiness courses [Press release]. Retrieved from http://www.knewton.com/press-releases/knewton-to-power-more-university-math-courses

Kraatz, M. S., Ventresca, M. S., & Deng, L. (2010). Precarious values and mundane innovations: Enrollment management in American liberal arts colleges. *Academy of Management Journal, 53*(6), 1521–1545.

Kruger, A. B. (1999). Experimental estimates of education production functions. *Quarterly Journal of Economics, 114*(2), 497–532.

Kurlaender, M. (2006). Choosing community college: Factors affecting Latino college choice. *New Directions for Community Colleges, 133,* 7–16.

Kurlaender, M., & Howell, J. (2012). College remediation: A review of the causes and consequences. *Advocacy and Policy Center Literature Brief.* New York, NY: College Board.

Kurlaender, M., Jackson, J., & Howell, J. (2012). K–12 postsecondary alignment and school accountability: High school responses to California's Early Assessment Program. *Advocacy and Policy Center Research Brief.* New York, NY: College Board.

Labaree, D. F. (1988). *The making of an American high school.* New Haven, CT: Yale University Press.

Labaree, D. F. (1997a). *How to succeed in school without really learning: The credentials race in American education.* New Haven, CT: Yale University Press.

Labaree, D. F. (1997b). Public goods, private goods: The American struggle over educational goals. *American Educational Research Journal, 34*(1), 39–81.

Labaree, D. F. (1997c). The rise of the community college: Markets and the limits of educational opportunity. In *How to succeed in school without really learning: The credentials race in American education* (pp. 190–222). New Haven, CT: Yale University Press.

Labaree, D. F. (2010). Understanding the rise of American higher education: How complexity breeds autonomy. *Peking University Education Review, 8*(3), 24–39.

Laczko-Kerr, I., & Berliner, D. C. (2002). The effectiveness of "Teach for America" and other under-certified teachers on student academic achievement: A case of harmful public policy. *Education Policy Analysis Archives, 10*(37). Retrieved from http://epaa.asu.edu/ojs/article/view/316/442

Ladd, H. F. (2011). Teachers' perceptions of their working conditions: How predictive of planned and actual teacher movement? *Educational Evaluation and Policy Analysis, 33*(2), 235–261.

Lagemann, E. (1992). *The politics of knowledge: The Carnegie Corporation, philanthropy, and public policy.* Chicago, IL: University of Chicago Press.

Lawrence, T. B., & Suddaby, R. (2006). Institutions and institutional work. In S. R. Clegg, C. Hardy, T. B. Lawrence, & W. R. Nord (Eds.), *The Sage handbook of organization studies* (2nd ed., pp. 215–254). Thousand Oaks, CA: Sage.

Lederman, D. (2005, July 15). "Good day" for for-profit colleges. *Inside Higher Ed.* Retrieved from http://www.insidehighered.com/news/2005/07/15/reauthorization

Lederman, D. (2011, March 11). More than Bridgepoint on trial. *Inside Higher Ed.* Retrieved from http://www.insidehighered.com/news/2011/03/11/senate_hearing_on _for_profit_colleges_singes_accreditors_as_well_as_bridgepoint

Lederman, D. (2012, October 10). Higher ed shrinks. *Inside Higher Ed.* Retrieved from www.insidehighered.com/news/2012/10/10/enrollments-fall-first-time-15-years

Lenkowsky, L., & Piereson, J. (2007). Education and the conservative foundations. In R. Bacchetti & T. Ehrlich (Eds.), *Reconnecting education and foundations: Turning good intentions into educational capital* (pp. 347–378). San Francisco, CA: Jossey-Bass.

Levendusky, M. (2009). *The partisan sort: How liberals became Democrats and conservatives became Republicans.* Chicago, IL: University of Chicago Press.

Levin, H., & McEwan, P. (2001). *Cost-effective analysis: Methods and applications* (2nd ed.). Thousand Oaks, CA: Sage.

Levin, J., & Quinn, M. (2003). *Missed opportunities: How we keep high-quality teachers out of urban classrooms.* New York, NY: New Teacher Project.

Lewin, T. (2011, September 27). College graduation rates are stagnant even as enrollment rises, a study finds. *The New York Times.* Retrieved from http://www.nytimes .com/2011/09/27/education/27remediation.html

Lewin, T. (2012, March 4). Instruction for masses knocks down campus walls. *The New York Times.* Retrieved from http://www.nytimes.com/2012/03/05/education/moocs -large-courses-open-to-all-topple-campus-walls.html

Light, R. J., Singer, J. D., & Willett, J. B. (1990). *By design: Planning research on higher education.* Cambridge, MA: Harvard University Press.

Loeb, S., Béteille, T., & Kalogrides, D. (2012). Effective schools: Teacher hiring, assignment, development, and retention. *Education Finance and Policy, 7*(3), 269–304.

Loeb, S., Darling-Hammond, L., & Luczak, J. (2005). How teaching conditions predict teacher turnover in California schools. *Peabody Journal of Education, 80*(3), 44–70.

Loeb, S., Kalogrides, D., & Horng, E. (2010). Principal preferences and the uneven distribution of principals across schools. *Educational Evaluation and Policy Analysis, 32*(2), 205–229.

Loeb, S., & Page, M. (2000). Examining the link between teacher wages and student outcomes: The importance of alternative labor market opportunities and nonpecuniary variation. *Review of Economics and Statistics, 82*(3), 393–408.

Long, M., Conger, D., & Iatarola, P. (2012). Effects of high school course-taking on secondary and postsecondary success. *American Educational Research Journal, 49*(2), 285–322.

Loss, C. P. (2012). *Between citizens and the state: The politics of American higher education in the twentieth century.* Princeton, NJ: Princeton University Press.

Lotkowski, V. A., Robbins, S. B., & Noeth, R. J. (2004). The role of academic and nonacademic factors in improving college retention. *ACT Policy Report,* 20–24.

Lovenheim, M. (2009). The effect of teachers' unions on education production: Evidence from union election certifications in three Midwestern states. *Journal of Labor Economics, 27*(4), 525–587.

Lowen, R. S. (1997). *Creating the Cold War university.* Berkeley: University of California Press.

Lumina Foundation for Education. (2011). *The degree qualifications profile.* Indianapolis, IN: Author.

MacArthur Foundation. (2012, March 3). Badges for Lifelong Learning Competition winners announced [Press release]. Retrieved from http://www.macfound.org/press/press-releases/badges-lifelong-learning-competition-winners-announced

Manning, W., Longmore, M., & Giordano, P. (2005). *The changing institution of marriage: Adolescents' expectations to cohabit and marry* (Center for Family and Demographic Research Working Paper No. 2005–11).

Manski, C. F. (1987). Academic ability, earnings, and the decision to become a teacher: Evidence from the National Longitudinal Study of the High School Class of 1972. In D. A. Wise (Ed.), *Public Sector Payrolls* (pp. 291–312). Chicago, IL: University of Chicago Press.

Martin, I. W. (2008). *The permanent tax revolt.* Stanford, CA: Stanford University Press.

Martin, J., Feldman, M., Hatch, M. J., & Sitkin, S. (1983). The uniqueness paradox in organizational stories. *Administrative Science Quarterly, 28*(3), 438–453.

Martinez, G., & Deil-Amen, R. J. (in press). College for all Latinos? The role of high school messages in facing college challenges. *Teachers College Record, 117*(6).

Martorell, P., & McFarlin, I. (2011). Help or hindrance? The effects of college remediation on academic and labor market outcomes. *Review of Economics and Statistics, 93*(2), 436–454.

Massy, W. F., & Zemsky, R. (1994). Faculty discretionary time: Departments and the academic ratchet. *The Journal of Higher Education, 65*(1), 1–22.

Mattern, K., Marini, J. P., & Shaw, E. J. (in press). *Are AP students more likely to graduate on time?* New York, NY: College Board.

McClenney, K. (2009, April 24). Helping community college students succeed: A moral imperative. *The Chronicle of Higher Education.* Retrieved from http://chronicle.com/article/Helping-Community-College/6536

McCormick, A. C. (2003). Swirling and double-dipping: New patterns of student attendance and their implications for higher education. *New Directions for Higher Education, 121*, 13–24.

McCormick, A. C., & Zhao, C. M. (2005). Rethinking and reframing the Carnegie Classification. *Change: The Magazine of Higher Learning, 37*(5), 50–57.

McDonnell, L. (2010). Creating the political conditions for education finance policy change. In J. E. Adams, Jr. (Ed.), *Smart Money* (pp. 237–266). Cambridge, MA: Harvard Education Press.

McGuinn, P. (2006). *No Child Left Behind and the transformation of federal education policy, 1965–2005.* Lawrence: University Press of Kansas.

McKelvey, B. (1975). Guidelines for the empirical classification of organizations. *Administrative Science Quarterly, 20*(4), 509–525.

McKelvey, B. (1982). *Organizational systematics: Taxonomy, evolution, classification.* Berkeley: University of California Press.

McLendon, M. K., & Cohen-Vogel, L. (2008). Understanding education policy change in the American states: Lessons from contemporary political science. In *Understanding the politics of education: AERA handbook of theory and research* (pp. 30–51). Washington, DC: American Educational Research Association and Lawrence Erlbaum.

McLendon, M. K., Hearn, J. C., & Deaton, R. (2006). Called to account: Analyzing the origins and spread of state performance-accountability policies for higher education. *Educational Evaluation and Policy Analysis, 28*(1), 1–24.

McLendon, M. K., Hearn, J. C., & Mokher, C. (2009). Partisans, professionals, and power: The role of political factors in state higher education funding. *The Journal of Higher Education, 80*(6), 686–713.

McPherson, M. (1983). The ecology of affiliation. *American Sociological Review, 48*(4), 519–532.

Melguizo, T. (2008). Quality matters: Assessing the impact of attending more selective institutions on college completion rates of minorities. *Research in Higher Education, 49*(3), 214–236.

Meyer, J. W. (1977). The effects of education as an institution. *American Journal of Sociology, 83*(1), 55–77.

Meyer, J. W., Ramirez, F. O., Frank, D. J., & Schofer, E. (2007). Higher education as an institution. In P. J. Gumport (Ed.), *The sociology of higher education: Contributions and their contexts* (pp. 187–221). Baltimore, MD: Johns Hopkins University Press.

Meyer, J. W., & Rowan, B. (1977). Institutionalized organizations: Formal structure as myth and ceremony. *American Journal of Sociology, 83*(2), 340–363.

Milkis, S. (1996). The New Deal, the modern presidency and divided government. In P. F. Galderisi, R. Q. Herzberg, & P. McNamara (Eds.), *Divided government: Change, uncertainty, and the constitutional order* (pp. 135–172). Lanham, MD: Rowman & Littlefield.

Milliron, M. (2012, October 1). Reflections on the first year of a new-model university. *The Chronicle of Higher Education.* Retrieved from http://chronicle.com/article/Reflections-on-the-First-Year/134670

Mills, C. W. (1959). *The sociological imagination.* New York, NY: Oxford University Press.

Mintrom, M. (1997). Policy entrepreneurs and the diffusion of innovation. *American Journal of Political Science, 41*(3), 738–770.

Mintrom, M. (2000). *Policy entrepreneurs and school choice.* Washington, DC: Georgetown University Press.

Mohr, J., & Guerra-Pearson, F. (2010). The duality of niche and form: The differentia-tion of institutional space in New York City, 1888–1917. *Research in the Sociology of Organizations, 31,* 321–368.

Moll, L., Amanti, C., Neff, D., & González, N. (1992). Funds of knowledge for teaching: Using a qualitative approach to connect homes and classrooms. *Theory into Practice, 31*(1), 132–141.

Moore, C., & Shulock, N. (2011). *Sense of direction: The importance of helping community college students select and enter a program of study.* Sacramento, CA: Institute for Higher Education Leadership and Policy.

Moore, G. E. (1965). Cramming more components onto integrated circuits. *Electronics, 38*(8), 4–7.

Morse, R. (2013). Best colleges ranking criteria and weights. *U.S. News & World Report.* Retrieved from http://www.usnews.com/education/best-colleges/articles/2013/09/09/best-colleges-ranking-criteria-and-weights

Mozilla. (2011, September 15). Mozilla launches open badges project. *The Mozilla Blog.* Retrieved from http://blog.mozilla.org/blog/2011/09/15/openbadges

Mullin, C. M. (2012). *Why access matters: The community college student body* (Policy Brief 2012–01PBL). Washington, DC: American Association of Community Colleges.

Murnane, R. J., & Olsen, R. J. (1989). The effects of salaries and opportunity costs on duration in teaching: Evidence from Michigan. *Review of Economics and Statistics, 71*(2), 347–352.

Murnane, R. J., & Willett, J. B. (2011). *Methods matter: Improving causal inference in edu-cational social science research.* New York, NY: Oxford University Press.

Myung, J., Loeb, S., & Horng, E. I. (2011). Tapping the principal pipeline: Identifying talent for future school leadership in the absence of formal succession management programs. *Education Administration Quarterly, 47*(5), 695–727.

Naffziger, M. E., & Rosenbaum, J. E. (2011, August). *Disappointment set-ups? Differ-ences in college expectations among middle, poor and working class high school seniors.* Paper presented at the annual meeting of the American Sociological Association, Las Vegas, NV.

National Center for the Study of Collective Bargaining in Higher Education and the Professions. (2006). *Directory of faculty contracts and bargaining agents in institu-tions of higher education.* New York, NY: Baruch College.

National Commission on Excellence in Education. (1983). A nation at risk: The impera-tive for educational reform. *The Elementary School Journal, 84*(2), 113–130.

National Governors Association. (2010). *Complete to compete: Common college com-pletion metrics.* Retrieved from http://www.nga.org/files/live/sites/NGA/files/pdf/1007COMMONCOLLEGEMETRICS.PDF

National Governors Association. (2011). *Degrees for what jobs? Raising expectations for universities and colleges in a global economy.* Washington, DC: Author.

National Student Clearinghouse Research Center. (2012). *Completing college: A national view of student attainment rates.* Retrieved from http://nscresearchcenter.org/signaturereport4

National Student Clearinghouse Research Center. (2013). *Current term enrollment report—fall 2013.* Retrieved from http://nscresearchcenter.org/currenttermenrollmentestimate-fall2013

National Survey of Student Engagement. (2007). *Experiences that matter: Enhancing student learning and success.* Bloomington: Center for Postsecondary Research, Indiana University–Bloomington.

National Survey of Student Engagement. (2008). *Promoting engagement for all students: The imperative to look within.* Bloomington: Center for Postsecondary Research, Indiana University–Bloomington.

Newman, K., & Aptekar, S. (2007). Sticking around: Delayed departure from the parental nest in Western Europe. In S. Danziger & C. Rouse (Eds.), *The price of independence: The economics of early adulthood* (pp. 207–230). New York, NY: Russell Sage Foundation.

Núñez, A.-M., Sparks, P. J., & Hernández, E. (2011). Latino access to community colleges and Hispanic-serving institutions: A national study. *Journal of Hispanic Higher Education, 10*(1), 18–40.

NYC Department of Education. (n.d.). NYC School Survey. Retrieved March 28, 2014, from http://schools.nyc.gov/Accountability/tools/survey/default.htm

Oakley, F. (1997). The elusive academic profession: Complexity and change. *Daedalus, 126*(4), 43–66.

Obama, B. (2009, February 24). Remarks of President Barack Obama—address to joint session of Congress. Washington, DC: White House Press Office.

Oblinger, D. (2012). *Game changers: Education and information technology.* Washington, DC: EDUCAUSE.

Oliver, C. (1991). Strategic responses to institutional processes. *Academy of Management Review, 16*(2), 145–179.

Onondaga Community College. (n.d.). Admission. Retrieved March 28, 2014, from http://admission.sunyocc.edu/?id=25211&collgrid=462

Onondaga Community College. (n.d.). Residence halls. Retrieved March 28, 2014, from http://admission.sunyocc.edu/explore.aspx?menu=782&id=1798

Padilla, R. (2007). *Camino de la universidad: The road to college.* Indianapolis, IN: Lumina Foundation for Education.

Paglayan, A. S. (2013, November). *Public sector collective bargaining in the United States: New evidence on an old debate.* Paper presented at the Association for Public Policy Analysis and Management Fall Research Conference, Washington, DC.

Papay, J. P., & Kraft, M. A. (2013). Productivity returns to experience in the teacher labor market: Methodological challenges and new evidence on long-term career growth.

Unpublished article. Retrieved from http://scholar.harvard.edu/files/mkraft/files/papay_kraft_-_rte_may_2013_-_v2.pdf

Pappano, L. (2012, November 2). The year of the MOOC. *The New York Times.* Retrieved from http://www.nytimes.com/2012/11/04/education/edlife/massive-open-online-courses-are-multiplying-at-a-rapid-pace.html

Parry, M. (2012, July 18). Big data on campus. *The New York Times.* Retrieved from http://www.nytimes.com/2012/07/22/education/edlife/colleges-awakening-to-the-opportunities-of-data-mining.html

Parsons, M. D. (1997). *Power and politics: Federal higher education policymaking in the 1990's.* Albany: State University of New York Press.

Parsons, T., & Platt, G. M. (1973). *The American university.* Cambridge, MA: Harvard University Press.

Pascarella, E. T., Blaich, C., Martin, G. L., & Hanson, J. M. (2011). How robust are the findings of "Academically Adrift"? *Change: The Magazine of Higher Learning, 43*(3), 20–24.

Pentland, B., & Rueter, H. (1994). Organizational routines as grammars of action. *Administrative Science Quarterly, 39*(3), 484–510.

Perrakis, A. I. (2008). Factors promoting academic success among African American and white male community college students. *New Directions for Community Colleges, 142,* 15–23.

Perrakis, A. I., & Hagedorn, L. S. (2010) Latino/a student success in community colleges and Hispanic-serving institutions. *Community College Journal of Research and Practice, 34*(10), 797–813.

Pettit, B., & Western, B. (2004). Mass imprisonment and the life course: Race and class inequality in U.S. incarceration. *American Sociological Review, 69,* 151–169.

Pew Research Center. (2011). *Is college worth It? College presidents, public assess value, quality and mission of higher education.* Washington, DC: Author.

Phillips, D. (2002). A genealogical approach to organizational life chances: The parent-progeny transfer among Silicon Valley law firms, 1946–1996. *Administrative Science Quarterly, 47*(3), 474–506.

Pierson, P. (2000). Increasing returns, path dependence, and the study of politics. *American Political Science Review, 94*(2), 251–267.

Pinder, C., & Moore, L. (1979). The resurrection of taxonomy to aid the development of middle range theories of organizational behavior. *Administrative Science Quarterly, 24,* 99–118.

Pope, M. L. (2006). Meeting the challenges to African-American men at community colleges. In M. J. Cuyjet (Ed.), *African-American men in college* (pp. 210–236). San Francisco, CA: Jossey-Bass.

Porter, S. (2000). The robustness of the "graduation rate performance" indicator used in the *U.S. News and World Report* college ranking. *International Journal of Educational Advancement, 1*(2), 10–30.

Porter, S. (2012). *Using student learning as a measure of quality in higher education.* Washington, DC: HCM Strategists.

Powell, W., & Owen-Smith, J. (2002). The new world of knowledge production in the life sciences. In S. Brint (Ed.), *The future of the city of intellect: The changing American university* (pp. 107–130). Stanford, CA: Stanford University Press.

Pugh, D., Hickson, D., & Hinings, C. R. (1969). An empirical taxonomy of structures of work organizations. *Administrative Science Quarterly, 14*(1), 115–126.

Raphael, S. (2007). Early incarceration spells and the transition to adulthood. In S. Danziger and C. Rouse (Eds.), *The price of independence: The economics of early adulthood* (pp. 278–306). New York, NY: Russell Sage Foundation.

Raymond, M., Fletcher, S., & Luque, J. (2001). *Teach for America: An evaluation of teacher differences and student outcomes in Houston, Texas.* Stanford, CA: Center for Research on Education Outcomes.

Redden, E., & Fain, P. (2013, October 10). Going global. *Inside Higher Ed.* Retrieved from http://www.insidehighered.com/news/2013/10/10/laureates-growing-global-network-institutions

Reed, D. S. (2001). *On equal terms: The constitutional politics of educational opportunity.* Princeton, NJ: Princeton University Press.

Rendón, L. I. (1994). Validating culturally diverse students: Toward a new model of learning and student development. *Innovative Higher Education, 19*(1), 33–51.

Rendón, L. I., Jalomo, R. E., & Nora, A. (2000). Theoretical considerations in the study of minority student retention in higher education. In J. M. Braxton (Ed.), *Reworking the student departure puzzle* (pp. 127–156). Nashville, TN: Vanderbilt University Press.

Renzulli, L. (2005). Organizational environments and the emergence of charter schools in the United States. *Sociology of Education, 78*(1), 1–26.

Reuben, J. A. (1996). *The making of the modern university: Intellectual transformation and the marginalization of morality.* Chicago, IL: University of Chicago Press.

Rhoades, G. (1998). *Managed professionals: Unionized faculty and restructuring academic labor.* Albany: State University of New York Press.

Rhoades, G. (2007). The study of the academic profession. In P. Gumport (Ed.), *The sociology of higher education: Contributions and their contexts* (pp. 113–146). Baltimore, MD: Johns Hopkins University Press.

Rhoades, G., & Slaughter, S. (1997). Academic capitalism, managed professionals, and supply-side higher education. *Social Text, 15*(2), 9–38.

Rhoades, G., & Sporn, B. (2002). Quality assurance in Europe and the U.S.: Professional and political economic framing of higher education policy. *Higher Education, 43*(3), 355–390.

Rice, A. (2012, September 11). Anatomy of a campus coup. *The New York Times.* Retrieved from http://www.nytimes.com/2012/09/16/magazine/teresa-sullivan-uva-ouster.html

Rich, M. (2010, September 16). A more nuanced look at poverty numbers. *The New York Times.* Retrieved from http://economix.blogs.nytimes.com/2010/09/16/a-more-nuanced-look-at-poverty-numbers

Richardson, R., & Martinez, M. (2009). *Policy and performance in American higher education.* Baltimore, MD: John Hopkins University Press.

Rio Salado College. (n.d.). Frequently asked questions. Retrieved March 28, 2014, from http://www.riosalado.edu/calendar/Pages/faqs.aspx

Rockoff, J. E. (2004). The impact of individual teachers on student achievement: Evidence from panel data. *The American Economic Review, 94*(22), 247–252.

Rockoff, J. E., Jacob, B. A., Kane, T. J., & Staiger, D. O. (2011). Can you recognize an effective teacher when you recruit one? *Education Finance and Policy, 6*(1), 43–74.

Rockoff, J. E., Staiger, D. O., Kane, T. J., & Taylor, E. S. (2012). Information and employee evaluation: Evidence from a randomized intervention in public schools. *The American Economic Review, 102*(7), 3184–3213.

Roksa, J. (2009, August). *Work, marriage, and parenthood: Life course transitions and inequality in higher education.* New Haven, CT: Research Committee on Social Stratification and Mobility (RC28), International Sociological Association.

Roksa, J., & Levey, T. (2010). What can you do with that degree? College major and occupational status of college graduates over time. *Social Forces, 89*(2), 389–416.

Ronfeldt, M. (2012). Where should student teachers learn to teach? Effects of field placement school characteristics on teacher retention and effectiveness. *Educational Evaluation and Policy Analysis, 34*(1), 3–26.

Rosenbaum, J. E., Deil-Amen, R. J., & Person, A. E. (2006). *After admission: From college access to college success.* New York, NY: Russell Sage Foundation.

Rosenthal, M. (2007). *The age of independence: Interracial unions, same sex unions, and the changing American family.* Cambridge, MA: Harvard University Press.

Rothstein, J. (2010). Teacher quality in educational production: Tracking, decay, and student achievement. *Quarterly Journal of Economics, 25*(1), 175–214.

Ruef, M. (2000). The emergence of organizational forms: A community ecology approach. *American Journal of Sociology, 106*(3), 658–714.

Ruef, M., & Patterson, K. (2009). Credit and classification: The impact of industry boundaries in 19th century America. *Administrative Science Quarterly, 54*(3), 486–520.

Rumbaut, R. G., & Komaie, G. (2010). Immigration and adult transitions. *The Future of Children, 20*(1), 43–66.

Russell, A. (2011, October). *A guide to major U.S. college completion initiatives.* Higher Education Policy Brief, American Association of State Colleges and Universities. Retrieved from http://www.aascu.org/policy/publications/policymatters/2011/collegecompletion.pdf

Ryu, M. (2010). *Twenty-fourth status report: Minorities in higher education 2009 supplement.* Washington, DC: American Council on Education.

Sabatier, P. A., & Jenkins-Smith, H. C. (1993). *Policy change and learning: An advocacy coalition approach.* Boulder, CO: Westview Press.

Saenz, V. B., Lee, K., Kim, S., Valdez, P., Bukoski, B., & Hatch, D. (2010, November). *Understanding Latino male community college student success: A hierarchical linear model approach.* Presented at the annual conference of the Association for the Study of Higher Education, Indianapolis, IN.

Saenz, V. B., & Ponjuan, L. (2009). The vanishing Latino male in higher education. *Journal of Hispanic Higher Education, 8*(1), 54–89.

Sandy, J., Gonzalez, A., & Hilmer, M. J. (2006). Alternative paths to college completion: Effect of attending a 2-year school on the probability of completing a 4-year degree. *Economics of Education Review, 25*(5), 463–471.

Sauder, M., & Espeland, W. N. (2009) The discipline of rankings: Tight coupling and organizational change. *American Sociological Review, 74*(1), 63–82.

Saunders, M., & Serna, I. (2004). Making college happen: The college experiences of first-generation Latino students. *Journal of Hispanic Higher Education, 3*(2), 146–163.

Scafidi, B., Sjoquist, D. L., & Stinebrickner, T. (2007). Race, poverty, and teacher mobility. *Economics of Education Review, 26*(2), 145–159.

Schneider, B., Judy, J., Mazuca, C. E., & Broda, M. (2014). Trust in elementary and secondary urban schools: A pathway for student success and college ambition. In D. Van Maele, P. B. Forsyth, & M. Van Houtte (Eds.), *Trust and school life: The role of trust for learning, teaching, leading, and bridging* (pp. 37–56). New York, NY: Springer.

Schoeni, R. F., & Ross, K. E. (2005). Material assistance from families during the transition to adulthood. In R. A. Settersten, Jr., F. F. Furstenberg, Jr., & R. G. Rumbaut (Eds.), *On the frontier of adulthood: Theory, research, and public policy* (pp. 396–416). Chicago, IL: University of Chicago Press.

Schwartz, C. R., & Mare, R. D. (2005). Trends in educational assortative marriage from 1940–2003. *Demography, 42*(4), 621–646.

Schwartz, J. L., Donovan, J., & Guido-DiBrito, F. G. (2009). Stories of social class: Self-identified Mexican male college students crack the silence. *Journal of College Student Development, 50*, 50–66.

Scott, W. R. (1994). Conceptualizing organizational fields: Linking organizations and societal systems. In H. Derlien, U. Gerhardt, & F. W. Scharpf (Eds.), *Systemrationalitat und Partialinteresse* (pp. 203–221). Baden-Baden, Germany: Nomos Verlagsgesellschaft.

Scott, W. R. (2008). *Institutions and organizations: Ideas and interests.* Thousand Oaks, CA: Sage.

Scott, W. R. (2013). *Institutions and organizations: Ideas, interests, and identities* (4th ed.). Los Angeles, CA: Sage.

Scott, W. R., & Davis, G. F. (2007). *Organizations and organizing: Rational, natural, and open systems perspectives.* Englewood Cliffs, NJ: Prentice Hall.

Scott, W. R., & Meyer, J. W. (1983). The organization of societal sectors. In *Organizational environments: Ritual and rationality* (pp. 129–153). Beverly Hills, CA: Sage.

Scott, W. R., & Meyer, J. W. (1991). The organization of societal sectors: Propositions and early evidence. In W. W. Powell & P. J. DiMaggio (Eds.), *The new institutionalism in organizational analysis* (pp. 108–140). Chicago, IL: University of Chicago Press.

Scott, W. R., Proctor, K., & Baker R. B. (2011, December 1–2). *Broad access schools in Silicon Valley.* Paper presented at Mapping Broad Access Higher Education conference, Stanford University, Stanford, CA.

Seaman, B. (2005). *Binge.* New York, NY: Wiley.

Sedlacek, W. E. (2004). *Beyond the big test: Noncognitive assessment in higher education.* San Francisco, CA: Jossey-Bass.

Selingo, J. J. (2013). *College unbound.* New York, NY: Houghton Mifflin/New Harvest.

Senate Committee on Health, Education, Labor, and Pensions. (2012). *For profit higher education: The failure to safeguard the federal investment and ensure student success* (Senate Report 112–37). Washington, DC: U.S. Government Printing Office. Retrieved from http://www.help.senate.gov/imo/media/for_profit_report/Contents.pdf

Settersten, R. A., Jr. (2012). The contemporary context of young adulthood in the United States. In A. Booth, S. L. Brown, N. S. Landale, W. D. Manning, & S. M. McHale (Eds.), *Early adulthood in a family context* (pp. 3–26). New York, NY: Springer.

Settersten, R. A., Jr. (2013, October 5). We need to invest in men (and get men to "woman up"). *The Oregonian.* Retrieved from http://www.oregonlive.com/opinion/index.ssf/2013/10/we_need_to_invest_in_men_and_g.html

Settersten, R. A., Jr., Furstenberg, F. F., Jr., & Rumbaut, R. G. (Eds.). (2005). *On the frontier of adulthood: Theory, research, and public policy.* Chicago, IL: University of Chicago Press.

Settersten, R. A., Jr., & Lovegreen, L. (1998). Educational opportunities throughout adult life: New hopes or no hope for life-course flexibility? *Research on Aging, 20*(4), 506–538.

Settersten, R. A., Jr., Ottusch, T. M., & Schneider, B. (forthcoming). Becoming adult: Meanings, markers, and contradictions. In R. A. Scott & S. M. Kosslyn (Eds.), *Emerging trends in the social and behavioral sciences.* Thousand Oaks, CA: Sage.

Settersten, R. A., Jr., & Ray, B. (2010). *Not quite adults: Why 20-somethings are choosing a slower path to adulthood, and why it's good for everyone.* New York, NY: Random House.

Shavelson, R. J., & Towne, L. (Eds.). (2002). *Scientific research in education: Committee on scientific principles for education research.* Washington, DC: National Academies Press.

Simon, H. A. (1997). *Administrative behavior: A study of decision-making processes in administrative organizations* (4th ed.). New York, NY: Free Press.

Small, M. L., & Winship, C. (2007). Black students' graduation from elite colleges: Institutional characteristics and between-institution differences. *Social Science Research, 36*(3), 1257–1275.

Smith, J. I. (2013). Ova and out: Using twins to estimate the educational returns to attending a selective college. *Economics of Education Review, 36*, 166–180.

Smith, J. I., & Stange, K. (2013, November). *The effects of college sector and peers on degree attainment.* Paper presented at the Association for Public Policy Analysis and Management Fall Research Conference, Washington, DC.

Smith, V. (2011, July 11). *Transparency drives online learning at Rio Salado College* [Blog post]. Retrieved from http://illinois.edu/blog/view/915/55126

Snyder, T. D., Tan, A. G., & Hoffman, C. M. (2004). *Digest of education statistics, 2003.* Washington, DC: U.S. Department of Education, National Center for Education Statistics.

Soares, J. (2007). *The power of privilege: Yale and America's elite colleges.* Stanford, CA: Stanford University Press.

Stack, C. B. (1997). *All our kin: Strategies for survival in a black community.* New York, NY: Basic Books.

Stange, K. (2012). Ability sorting and the importance of college quality to student achievement: Evidence from community colleges. *Education Finance and Policy, 7*(1), 74–105.

Steele, C. M., & Aronson, J. (1995). Stereotype threat and the intellectual test performance of African-Americans. *Journal of Personality and Social Psychology, 69*(5), 797–811.

Stevens, M. L. (2007). *Creating a class: College admissions and the education of elites.* Cambridge, MA: Harvard University Press.

Stevens, M. L., Armstrong, E. A., & Arum, R. (2008). Sieve, incubator, temple, hub: Empirical and theoretical advances in the sociology of higher education. *Annual Review of Sociology, 34*, 127–151.

Stinchcombe, A. L. (1965). Social structure and organizations. In J. G. Match (Ed.), *Handbook of organizations* (pp. 142–193). Chicago, IL: Rand McNally.

Stinchcombe, A. L. (1990). *Information and organizations.* Berkeley: University of California Press.

Stinebrickner, T., & Stinebrickner, R. (2009). *Learning about academic ability and the college drop-out decision* (National Bureau of Economic Research Working Paper No. 14810).

Stone, D. A. (2011). *Policy paradox: The art of political decision making.* New York, NY: Norton.

Strayhorn, T. L. (2010). When race and gender collide: Social and cultural capital's influence on the academic achievement of African-American and Latino males. *The Review of Higher Education, 33*(3), 307–332.

Taylor, E. S., & Tyler, J. H. (2012). The effect of evaluation on teacher performance. *American Economic Review, 102*(7), 3628–3651.

Thelin, J. R. (2004). *A history of American higher education.* Baltimore, MD: Johns Hopkins University Press.

Tierney, W. G. (1992). An anthropological analysis of student participation in college. *The Journal of Higher Education, 63*(6), 603–618.

Tierney, W. G. (1999). Models of minority college-going and retention: Cultural integrity versus cultural suicide. *Journal of Negro Education, 68*(1), 80–91.

Tinto, V. (1993). *Leaving college: Rethinking the causes and cures of student attrition* (2nd ed.). Chicago, IL: University of Chicago Press.

Toma, J. D. (2012). Institutional strategy: Positioning for prestige. In M. N. Bastedo (Ed.), *The organization of higher education: Managing colleges for a new era* (pp. 118–159). Baltimore, MD: Johns Hopkins University Press.

Torres, V. (2006). A mixed method study testing data-model fit of a retention model for Latino/a students at urban universities. *Journal of College Student Development, 47*(3), 299–318.

Tyack, D. B. (1991). Public school reform: Policy talk and institutional practice. *American Journal of Education, 100*(1), 1–19.

Tyack, D. B., & Cuban, L. (1995). *Tinkering toward utopia: A century of public school reform.* Cambridge, MA: Harvard University Press.

University of the People. (n.d.). Our students. Retrieved March 28, 2014, from http://www.uopeople.org/groups/our_students

U.S. Census Bureau. (2010). America's families and living arrangements: 2010. In *2010 Current Population Survey.* Washington, DC: Author.

U.S. Census Bureau. (2011). America's families and living arrangements: 2011. In *2011 Current Population Survey.* Washington, DC: Author.

U.S. Department of Education. (2006). *A test of leadership: Charting the future of U.S. higher education.* Washington, DC: Author.

U.S. Department of Education. (2011). *Program integrity: Gainful employment-debt measures.* Washington, DC: Author.

U.S. Department of Education, National Center for Education Statistics. (2009). *Digest of education statistics.* Washington, DC: U.S. Department of Education.

U.S. Department of Education, National Center for Education Statistics. (2010). *Digest of education statistics.* Washington, DC: U.S. Department of Education.

U.S. Department of Education, National Center for Education Statistics. (2012a). *Postsecondary institutions and price of attendance in 2011–12; degrees and other awards conferred, 2010–11; and 12-month enrollment, 2010–11.* Washington, DC: U.S. Department of Education.

U.S. Department of Education, National Center for Education Statistics. (2012b). Table 23: Actual and projected numbers for enrollment in public 4-year postsecondary degree-granting institutions, by sex and attendance status, fall 1996 through fall 2021. Retrieved from http://nces.ed.gov/programs/projections/projections2021/tables/table_23.asp

U.S. Department of Education, National Center for Education Statistics. (2013). Table 315.10: Number of instructional faculty in degree-granting postsecondary institutions, by employment status, sex, control, and level of institution: Selected years, fall 1970 through fall 2011. In *Digest of education statistics*. Retrieved from http://nces.ed.gov/programs/digest/d13/tables/dt13_315.10.asp

Villalpando, O., & Solorzano, D. G. (2005). The role of culture in college preparation programs: A review of the research literature. In W. G. Tierney, Z. B. Corwin, & J. E. Colyar (Eds.), *Preparing for college: Nine elements of effective outreach* (pp. 13–28). Albany: State University of New York Press.

Voluntary System of Accountability. (n.d.). About VSA. Retrieved March 28, 2014, from http://www.voluntarysystem.org/about

Wabash College. (n.d.). Wabash National Study, 2006–2009. Retrieved March 28, 2014, from http://www.liberalarts.wabash.edu/study-instruments

Wade, G. (2012, June). Interview by P. Fain.

Webber, D. A., & Ehrenberg, R. G. (2009). *Do expenditures other than instructional expenditures affect graduation and persistence rates in American higher education?* (Cornell Higher Education Research Institute Working Paper 121).

Weber, M. (1949). "Objectivity" in social science and social policy. In E. Shils & H. A. Finch (Eds.), *The methodology of the social sciences* (pp. 49–112). Glencoe, IL: Free Press.

Weick, K. (1976). Educational organizations as loosely coupled systems. *Administrative Science Quarterly, 21*(1), 1–19.

Weisbrod, B. A., Ballou, J. P., & Asch, E. D. (2008). *Mission and money: Understanding the university.* New York, NY: Cambridge University Press.

Wellman, J. V., & Ehrlich, T. (2003). The credit hour: The tie that binds. *New Directions for Higher Education, 2003*(122), 119–122.

West, H. C., & Sabol, W. J. (2009). *Prison inmates and mid-year 2008* (NCJ 22561). Washington, DC: Bureau of Justice Statistics.

Western, B., & Pettit, B. (2010). Incarceration and social inequality. *Daedalus, 139*(3), 8–19.

Western Governors University. (n.d.). About WGU. Retrieved March 28, 2014, from http://www.wgu.edu/about_WGU/overview

WGU Indiana. (2010, June 11). Governor Daniels announces new online university for Indiana. Retrieved from http://indiana.wgu.edu/about_WGU_indiana/governor_announces_university_6-11-10

Whetten, D. (2006). Albert and Whetten revisited: Strengthening the concept of organizational identity. *Journal of Management Inquiry, 15*(3), 219–234.

White House. (2013, August 22). *Fact sheet on the president's plan to make college more affordable: A better bargain for the middle class.* Retrieved from http://www.whitehouse.gov/the-press-office/2013/08/22/fact-sheet-president-s-plan-make-college-more-affordable-better-bargain-

Wight, V. R., Chau, M., Aratani, Y., Schwarz, S. W., & Thampi, K. (2010). *A profile of disconnected young adults in 2010.* New York, NY: National Center for Child in Poverty, Columbia University.

Wightman, P., Schoeni, R., & Robinson, K. (2010, January). *Familial assistance to young adults.* Ann Arbor: University of Michigan.

WikiEducator. (2012). SNHU creates innovation lab and partners with OERu. Retrieved from http://wikieducator.org/SNHU/SNHU_Creates_Innovation_Lab_and_Partners_with_OERu

Winston, G. C. (1999). Subsidies, hierarchy and peers: The awkward economics of higher education. *The Journal of Economic Perspectives, 13*(1), 13–36.

Wirt, F. M., & Kirst, M. W. (2009). *The political dynamics of American education* (4th ed.). Berkeley, CA: McCutchan.

Wirt, J., Choy, S., Gerald, D., Provasnik, S., Rooney, P., Watanabe, S., & Tobin, R. (2002). *The condition of education 2002.* Washington, DC: U.S. Government Printing Office.

Wlezien, C. (2004). Patterns of representation: Dynamics of public preferences and policy. *The Journal of Politics, 66*(1), 1–24.

Yelowitz, A. (2007). Young adults leaving the next: The role of cost-of-living. In S. Danziger & C. Rouse (Eds.), *The price of independence: The economics of early adulthood* (pp. 170–206). New York, NY: Russell Sage Foundation.

Yoon, K. S., Duncan, T., Lee, S. W., Scarloss, B., & Shapley, K. L. (2007). *Reviewing the evidence on how teacher professional development affects student achievement* (Issues and Answers Report, REL 2007-No. 033). Washington, DC: U.S. Department of Education.

Yosso, T. J. (2005). Whose culture has capital? A critical race theory discussion of community cultural wealth. *Race, Ethnicity and Education, 8*(1), 69–91.

Zell, M. C. (2009). Achieving a college education: The psychological experiences of Latina/o community college students. *Journal of Hispanic Higher Education, 9*(2), 167–186.

Zemsky, R. (2009). *Making reform work: The case for transforming American higher education.* New Brunswick, NJ: Rutgers University Press.

Zuckerman, E. (1999). The categorical imperative: Securities analysts and the illegitimacy discount. *American Journal of Sociology, 104*(5), 1398–1438.

Zumeta, W. (2001). Public policy and accountability in higher education: Lessons from the past and present for the new millennium. In D. Heller (Ed.), *The states and public higher education policy: Affordability, access, and accountability* (pp. 155–197). Baltimore, MD: Johns Hopkins University Press.

Zumeta, W., Breneman, D. W., Callan, P. M., & Finney, J. E. (2012). *Financing American higher education in the era of globalization.* Cambridge, MA: Harvard Education Press.

INDEX

Page numbers in italics indicate material in figures or tables.